Learning and Education for a Better World

D1711514

INTERNATIONAL ISSUES IN ADULT EDUCATION

Volume 10

Series Editor:
Peter Mayo, *University of Malta, Msida, Malta*

Editorial Advisory Board:
Stephen Brookfield, University of St Thomas, Minnesota, USA
Waguida El Bakary, American University in Cairo, Egypt
Budd L. Hall, University of Victoria, BC, Canada
Astrid Von Kotze, University of Natal, South Africa
Alberto Melo, University of the Algarve, Portugal
Lidia Puigvert-Mallart, CREA-University of Barcelona, Spain
Daniel Schugurensky, OISE/University of Toronto, Canada
Joyce Stalker, University of Waikato, Hamilton, New Zealand/Aotearoa
Juha Suoranta, University of Tampere, Finland

Scope:
This international book series attempts to do justice to adult education as an ever expanding field. It is intended to be internationally inclusive and attract writers and readers from different parts of the world. It also attempts to cover many of the areas that feature prominently in this amorphous field. It is a series that seeks to underline the global dimensions of adult education, covering a whole range of perspectives. In this regard, the series seeks to fill in an international void by providing a book series that complements the many journals, professional and academic, that exist in the area. The scope would be broad enough to comprise such issues as 'Adult Education in specific regional contexts', 'Adult Education in the Arab world', 'Participatory Action Research and Adult Education', 'Adult Education and Participatory Citizenship', 'Adult Education and the World Social Forum', 'Adult Education and Disability', 'Adult Education and the Elderly', 'Adult Education in Prisons', 'Adult Education, Work and Livelihoods', 'Adult Education and Migration', 'The Education of Older Adults', 'Southern Perspectives on Adult Education', 'Adult Education and Progressive Social Movements', 'Popular Education in Latin America and Beyond', 'Eastern European perspectives on Adult Education', 'An anti-Racist Agenda in Adult Education', 'Postcolonial perspectives on Adult Education', 'Adult Education and Indigenous Movements', 'Adult Education and Small States'. There is also room for single country studies of Adult Education provided that a market for such a study is guaranteed.

Learning and Education for a Better World

The Role of Social Movements

Edited by
Budd L. Hall and Darlene E. Clover
University of Victoria, Canada

Jim Crowther
The University of Edinburgh, Scotland, UK

Eurig Scandrett
Queen Margaret University, Edinburgh, Scotland, UK

SENSE PUBLISHERS
ROTTERDAM/BOSTON/TAIPEI

A C.I.P. record for this book is available from the Library of Congress.

ISBN: 978-94-6091-977-0 (paperback)
ISBN: 978-94-6091-978-7 (hardback)
ISBN: 978-94-6091-979-4 (e-book)

Published by: Sense Publishers,
P.O. Box 21858,
3001 AW Rotterdam,
The Netherlands
https://www.sensepublishers.com/

Printed on acid-free paper

TABLE OF CONTENTS

MARJORIE MAYO

PREFACE

LEARNING AND EDUCATION FOR A BETTER WORLD: THE ROLE OF SOCIAL MOVEMENTS

The publication of 'Learning and education for a better world: the role of social movements' is to be welcomed most warmly. This is such a timely collection of essays, bringing together critical reflections on experiences of social action from across the globe. Previous publications have demonstrated the importance of learning in social movements along with the importance of learning from experiences of participating in social movements (e.g. Eyerman and Jamison, 1991, Foley, 1999 and Kane, 2001). As these writings have demonstrated, these have been two-way processes of learning, acquiring knowledge and skills in order to take action more effectively, and learning through reflecting on the experiences of social action that follow, engaging in movements for social justice and social change. We need to build upon these earlier studies though. Because, as 'Learning and education for a better world: the role of social movements' so clearly demonstrates, the case for this type of learning is becoming more and more urgent in the current economic, social, political, environmental and policy context.

Since the end of the Cold War, neo-liberal perspectives and policy agendas have become ever more predominant. Back in the Reagan / Thatcher years of the 1980s, the case for neo-liberalism was already being promoted, epitomised by the slogan that 'There is no alternative'. This slogan has greater resonance than ever in the contemporary context. Public policy discourses have become increasingly dominated by the argument that priority has to be given to the interests of private profitability, even if this too often entails rising unemployment together with reductions in public services to meet the needs of the most vulnerable. People are being invited to believe that they have to suffer – and preferably to suffer in silence rather than take to the streets – to believe that there is nothing else that can be done.

Even more disturbingly in relation to the concerns of this particular book, neo-liberal perspectives have come to wield increasing influence over the structures of learning and education (as several chapters so clearly demonstrate). Processes of marketisation have been infiltrating the very institutions, including the schools and universities that should have been concerned with preserving the space for the production of critical thinking and challenging debates. The scope for challenging the predominance of neo-liberalism is being potentially undermined, along with the scope for developing alternative approaches, prioritising human needs before the requirements for private profitability. Meanwhile the economic, social, political, environmental and cultural effects are being experienced globally with increasing inequalities within and between nation states. Bankers have been continuing to enjoy their bonuses whilst the poorest and most vulnerable have been experiencing the sharpest reductions in their livelihoods and well-being.

This has, of course, been increasingly challenged. A range of social movements, including the 'Occupy' movement, have been raising fundamental questions about the very nature of capitalism, and the specific impact of the neo-liberal policies that have been producing these growing inequities, in different contexts. As this book so clearly documents, learning has been central to these movements, typified by the seminars that accompanied the 'Occupy' movement outside St Pauls Cathedral in the City of London, for example.

Individuals and communities can and do come to develop critical and more creative understandings of their situations, just as they can and do come to develop critical and creative strategies for change. But praxis doesn't automatically occur spontaneously. Nor do new generations of activists necessarily acquire the theoretical tools that they need in order to make sense of their rapidly changing worlds, providing them with the theoretical basis for developing strategies that effectively demonstrate that another world is possible.

The book is so timely, precisely for this reason. Between them the different chapters bring a series of critical reflections on ways of connecting theory and practice together, linking people's reflections on their learning from their experiences with the authors' reflections on the learning to be gained from more theoretical debates. The potential tensions between different approaches and contexts for learning emerge, together with the implications for promoting learning and education for a better world. There are reflections on the tensions that have been inherent in providing university-based programmes of popular education *with* rather than simply *for* social movement activists. And there are reflections on the key relevance of varying theoretical approaches and practices, if activists are to be equipped to build alternative strategies for progressive social change and environmental justice. **Learning and education for a better world: the role of social movements** offers invaluable tools and understandings for all those who share these goals. This book is to be commended to the widest possible readership.

REFERENCES

Eyerman, R. & Jamison, A. (1991). Social movements: A cognitive approach. Oxford: Polity Press.
Foley, G. (1999). Learning in social action. London: Zed Books (with NIACE: Leicester).
Kane, L. (2001). Popular education and social change in Latin America. London: Latin America Bureau.

BUDD HALL, DARLENE E. CLOVER, JIM CROWTHER
AND EURIG SCANDRETT

INTRODUCTION

To be truly radical is to make hope possible rather than despair convincing.
Raymond Williams

Recently two of this book's Editors participated in an academic conference with other scholars deeply concerned about the issues of our times: injustice, violence against women, the deeply destructive nature of unbridled capitalism, the willingness of most political regimes to sacrifice both human and natural welfare in the interest of economic growth. There were more but you get the idea. It could have been a conference on any of the social science or humanities disciplines in almost any part of Europe or even, North America in the second decade of this 21st century. The mood of the conference mired in the awareness of the impact austerity measures being implemented by the British government and indeed reeling from a series of cuts to community groups, libraries, universities, or the social services where many of these people worked or at least knew of people, who worked in them, was dark. Dark as an Edvard Munch painting, the one with the open mouth, the silent scream pouring out. The session we facilitated was about the arts, learning and social movements. At one end of the debate that erupted was an angry, weary veteran intellectual with a lifetime of rational radical critique, a veteran of leftist and generally progressive intention. At the other end of the spectrum was an angry young woman whose suggestion for a way forward, in England, was violence. She argued for the right of both men and women who wanted to fight with the police to do so. She resented groups like the radical, civilly disobedient yet peaceful Rebel Clown Army who intervene in demonstrations to prevent violence, preferring instead groups such as the Black Block whose tactics De Cauter, De Roo and Vanchaesenbrouck (2011, p. 13) "show uncanny similarities" to terrorist attacks. Still another woman from a former Eastern European country talked of how a right wing movement that had just finished a campaign in her country using the arts and other social learning tools to build support for neo-Nazi action. In the dynamics of the moment, efforts to share ideas about how poetry and other art forms could be used in contexts of social movement learning hit a wall of nihilism, hopelessness and despair.

Why do we mention this in the introduction to a book about social movements, education and action? This story is important for us to reflect and learn from. Firstly, it serves to underscore the deep ruptures and profound grief generated by the crisis neo-liberal politics and policies are creating as they move beyond the poorest and most marginalised persons to encompass the middle class of academics, professionals and social sector workers. These are dark times indeed, for many more than just a few. Secondly, our story draws attention to the fact that social movements in and of themselves are not always progressive or making for a world that many of us may feel would be better. Religious intolerance, misogynist principles, restrictions of human rights, racism and exclusion are the stuff or catalysts of movements such as the Tea Party in the USA, the Neo-Nazi movements in parts of Europe as well as all religious fundamentalist movements world-wide. Thirdly, our story tells us that within movements that work contrary to a better, more just, sustainable and equitable world, the arts and other popular educational activities we use or put into practice are being appropriated.

The theorizing we offer in this collection aims to deepen our understanding of the rich interaction of education, learning, teaching and action; a world of social movement learning that builds on the ideas of all the movements and intellectuals who have gone before us in the pursuit of an engaged and democratic life. This book in fact offers something that the above anecdote could not do as the setting of that story was within the more limited professional academic spaces where scholars share ideas amongst themselves; spaces that are not in and of themselves, social movements. This collection of studies and reflections recognises yet goes beyond a sense of hopelessness and emotional inertia we encountered, to give visibility to rich and varied stories of how ordinary people in literally every part of the world are resisting, organising and learning to overcome a world that we do not like but have no recipe to change.

Our book is about shack dwellers in South Africa, about the struggle for an authentic educational system that has meaning in Austria, about the political ecology of environmental movements in India and Scotland, about Raymond Williams and Antonio Gramsci as resources of hope, about the lessons of 40 years of popular education in Latin America, about the positive yet challenged role of the arts in social movements, about feeding the imagination for a new world in South Africa, about the use of film in building capacity within movements, about social media in the Egyptian revolution and the Occupy Wall Street movements, about privileging knowledge from grass roots movements over professional civil society networks in Asia, and about how learning by one person in one organic farm is connected to a global vision of the relationship of humans to the rest of nature.

We hope that readers will see as we do that one powerful contribution to social movement learning is the rendering visible of the extraordinary scope, diversity, range of actors, breadth of means and methods and indefatigable energy of those who are immersed in the educational work, the teaching and learning, the formal and informal sharing and knowledge-making that is the world of social movement education and learning. We believe that this book, when read through the combined lens of the chapters, offers new insights into the theories of how social movements work, deeper insights into the theory and practice of adult education in context of political struggle, and new resources for hope.

THE CHAPTERS

Equality, Anne Harley argues in the first chapter of this volume, *We are poor, but not stupid*, has to be the basis for educational engagement with social movements if the experience is to be one of liberation. Her argument draws mainly on the visceral experience of social movements of the poor and disposed who have experienced the hardships of a neo-liberal road to (market) freedom in post-apartheid South Africa. Six activists, three from a shack dwellers movement and three from a rural network that connects local struggles for protecting people's rights, produced their own book – *Living Learning* – which was based on their experiences and reflection during a course on participatory development that Harley co-ordinates. The author also uses the view on equality argued by Jacque Ranciere, in his account of *The Ignorant Schoolteacher*. Unless critical education is premised on equality, in the sense of accepting that everyone counts and everyone thinks, it will result in an unintended exercise of domestication. Increasingly, however, demands to increase student numbers and introduce more selective entrance requirements threaten to undermine this work by filtering out the poorly educated who have been the target students for this provision.

Elisabeth Steinklammer's chapter, *Learning to resist: Hegemonic practice, informal learning and social movements,* takes us to Austria where there has been widespread resistance "from below" against the underfunding and re-structuring of education in particular and neo-liberalism in general. Her chapter, presented through the lens of critical theoretical notions of power and hegemony, revolves around the questions of what can be learnt by participating in the protests. Steinklammer argues that in order to sustain hegemonic order, people must internalise and thereby adopt such practices. But critical practices of resistance education, as she illustrates through various examples, have the power to openly encourage struggle and resistance by providing spaces for critical social and self reflection and learning where diverse social movement actors can develop collective, political strategies and new forms of cooperation.

The organic intellectuals of subordinate social groups, such as those Harley's works with are also the focus of Jim Crowther and Emilio Lucio-Villegas' chapter entitled *Reconnecting Intellect and Feeling*, where they develop an account of educational work in communities by drawing from the interrelated analyses of Karl Marx, Antonio Gramsci and Raymond Williams. In the context of a crisis of democracy, where there are no fundamental political alternatives posed to the politics and policies of austerity and where a discourse of the common good has withered, the hope for a better future for all has to be developed with and through communities of endurance and struggle. Only a radical democratic project of cultural renewal from the 'bottom up' will provide the intellectual and practical resources, as well as inspiration for social transformation. The authors argue that radical education has a role to play, not in terms of acting as a substitute for organic intellectuals, but by helping to sustain and deepen the dialectical relationship between activist community leaders and their social base. Too often education acts as a siphoning off process, which weakens resistance rather than enhances it. Their argument is illustrated by drawing on examples of 'participatory budget' projects with local social movements in Seville.

Building on evidence from learning in environmental justice movements in Scotland and India, Eurig Scandrett in his chapter *Social Learning in Environmental Justice* argues that the theoretical approach of political ecology allows us to understand these struggles, not as disparate, restrictive, 'not-in-my-back-yard' local campaigns nor as peripheral forms of environmentalism, but as a distinctive species of social contestation in the conditions of production as well as new forms of accumulation by dispossession and resistance to it. Emergent social movement activity generates dialectical processes between subaltern knowledges and values and their incommensurable dominant and canonical opposites, the latter of which are increasingly commodified. These processes, which ascertain what constitutes 'really useful' knowledge for a project of subaltern emancipation, occur in formal, popular and incidental forms of education in which professional educators may have a limited role.

Forty Years of Popular Education in Latin America is Liam Kane's insightful chapter of lessons from that particularly rich vein of education and social movement experience. Indeed, taking education seriously is a *sine qua non* for learning from Latin America. The idea that 'all education is political' is as relevant in the North, as the South, though it comes with the warning to continually ensure dialogue between 'expert' and 'grassroots' knowledge and enable people to become subjects of change, not followers of leaders. From Freire's approach to teaching literacy to participatory techniques, to Boal's 'theatre of the oppressed', Kane argues that Latin America has produced imaginative ways of putting the principles of popular education into practice. Many have already been adapted for use throughout the world and are an invaluable contribution to the toolkit of would-be activist-educators. Kane also argues that importantly, Latin American academics work with social movements, lending their specialist knowledge as a response to a curriculum dictated by movements.

Like Kane, Astrid von Kotze focuses on the concept of popular education and how it encourages activism. However, she takes a turn towards the imagination. *Composting the imagination in popular education,* and explores how 'popular education schools' in South Africa use creative practices to address issues of inequality, violence and abuse, crime and fear, economic hardship and silence and social marginalisation. The schools, part of a larger popular education programme, provide spaces for creative dialogue and critical reflection. But as von Kotze argues and illustrates, the clearly 'utopian' and most promising vision of radical change comes from tapping into and re-valuing the creative and imaginative faculties of the people of South Africa. She recognises, however, that this work takes courage and a strong sense of determination in order to provide alternative visions of the homeland.

Darlene E. Clover's chapter on *Aesthetics, society and social movement learning* sets the stage for understanding the potential and challenges of the creative learning aspects of social movements. She begins with a discussion of critical standpoints around the place of art in society and in particular, in relation to knowledge and learning, emphasising complex metaphysical and epistemological considerations that have shaped – positively or negatively – contemporary aesthetic discourses, judgements and debates. Using two feminist aspects of cultural political discourse – political art and activist art – she explores two examples of cultural interactions in Canada. Clover's chapter highlights some of the primary education and learning dimensions by women and men who, she argues, work so imaginatively and courageously to create and re-create visions of a more just and sustainable world.

Stephen Brookfield's, *Radical Aesthetics: Ken Loach as social movement educator* argues that the work of filmmaker Ken Loach is an example of an aesthetic that ruptures the dominant consciousness that makes possible the dimension of liberation. Whilst this is intrinsic to Loach's approach to film making and significant throughout his artistic output, Brookfield mines one particular sequence from his 1995 film *Land and Freedom.* The film is set in the Spanish Civil War in the 1930s and the sequence, known as 'the Decision', portrays a debate amongst villagers who have just been liberated from Franco's forces, and members of the international militia who have liberated them. The conflicts over revolutionary ideals, pragmatic compromises and diverse personal aspirations are expounded in a shared spirit of collective emancipation and solidarity that, Brookfield argues, provides fertile material for the work of social movement educators.

Hall in his contribution, *A Giant Human Hashtag: Learning and the #Occupy Movement*, examines the role of social media as an element in the radical pedagogies of #OWS, the Occupy Wall Street movement, and delves more deeply into the pedagogical principles which characterised the movement during its initial physical occupational phase. Hall argues that while democratic knowledge and learning frameworks are extremely helpful in understanding the impact and power of any social movement, the Occupy movement has drawn more attention to the processes of learning, to collective thinking, to active listening and to the creation of new physical, intellectual and political educational spaces, than movements that have preceded it. As with all social movements formal, non-formal and informal learning, structured and experiential education happen both inside and outside of the #OWS movement. Although not without its challenges, key characteristics of the occupy pedagogies include People's Assemblies, the role of space in the occupation, facilitation methods for large-scale groups, the importance of listening, non-ideological discourse, direct action encased within the goal of creating new collective thinking. The #OWS movement has given visibility to the role of movement intellectuals and movement theorists, as well as anarchist scholars, in building the narratives of the movement.

Building Counter-Power From the Ground Up allows Aziz Choudry, an activist scholar with direct involvement in the Indian social movement scene, to reflect upon tensions over learning and knowledge production in international non-governmental organisation (NGO) and social movement networks contesting global free market capitalism, known as the 'global justice movement'. He discusses aspects of NGO/social movement activist networks opposing the Asia-

Pacific Economic Cooperation (APEC) forum during the 1990s, and more recent activism against bilateral free trade and investment agreements, (FTAs) in the Asia-Pacific region. Choudry compares and contrasts the dominant forms of professionalised NGO knowledge/action with knowledge/action emerging from grounded social struggles, and critiques the trend towards the NGOisation/NGO management of social change with particular focus on its knowledge/learning implications. The chapter argues that movements can create counter-power and radical alternatives to the prevailing world order by looking beyond dominant models of transnational NGO-driven campaigns and modes of action towards grounded local struggles against global capitalism.

Catherine Etmanski in her chapter, *Inch by Inch, Row by Row*, draws on her experience of working as a volunteer on organic farms in the Canadian province of British Columbia. The modern organic agriculture movement constitutes a social movement in response to the dominance of the agrochemical industry, and its praxis incorporates experimentation and knowledge generation in crop growing and animal husbandry. These skills, knowledge and culture are passed on through informal educational work to volunteer apprentices and activists such as Etmanski. Analyzing the complexity of learning and knowledge generation inherent in this praxis, she explores its practical, technological, philosophical, political, psychological, gendered and spiritual dimensions and makes a case for the organic movement as a source of education for social justice.

CRITIQUE, RESIST, CREATE

Edmund O'Sullivan, a Canadian radical education theorist whose work on transformative learning shares much in common with the authors in this volume speaks of three educational moments; moments of critique, resistance and creation (1999). In naming these as three identifiable moments, he is not suggesting that they are independent of each other or even separate in time, although that is possible. He is saying that we have a responsibility when theorising or practising educational work within a social movement context to be aware of the responsibility for attending to, rendering visible, or acknowledging these distinct yet inter-weaving functions. These are not to be understood as linear concepts, but rather as existing in the world of social movement life in a combined and mixed discourse that may begin with create, return to resistance, then on to critique and back again in a kind of dance or poetic state.

Each of our pieces begins within a deep sense of urgency and concern for the fates of the majority of people on this planet and in some cases, as with Scandrett, Clover and Etmanski, with the fate of the earth itself. Poverty and exclusion amongst South African shack dwellers and urban poor are highlighted in the Harley and von Kotze chapters. Malone's chapter calls into question the years of undemocratic rule in Egypt whilst Crowther and Lucio-Villegas call forth the contemporarity of Marxist and Gramscian critiques of capital. Hall's chapter gives visibility to the meme of the #OWS movement, the treachery of the 1 per cent in the face of the 99 per cent and particularly, the role of finance capital.

Steinklammer's chapter begins with the impact of neo-liberal private market approaches to shutting down democratic spaces within public education in Austria, a concern that is found in other jurisdictions of course.

Harley's activist intellectuals, and Choudary's subaltern Indian activists are resisting the appropriation of grassroots knowledge creation by intermediate level civil society organisations, let alone academics. Given the savage destruction of the land, which accompanies capitalist resource extraction, resistance to ecological biocide has to be at the heart of environmental movements as Etmanski and Scandrett illustrate through examples from Canada, Scotland and India. Hall and Malone, among other things, show how the social media are being used by contemporary revolutionary and democracy movements to resist manipulation by mainstream media and corporatist domination of the narratives of struggles.

The *create* function maybe the most powerful of the moments that comes from a reflection on our combined work. Our work taken as a whole represents a fresh and unique weaving together of a very rich and diverse variety including fresh interpretations of Gramsci and Williams (Crowther and Lucio-Villegas), voices of political ecology (Scandrett), feminists aesthetics and activist arts (Clover), subaltern and grassroots intellectuals (Choudry, Hall and Harley), Latin American scholars (Kane), the film maker Ken Loach (Brookfield), anarchists (Malone), and organic farmers (Etmanski). The ability to draw from such a broad and diverse base of theoretical perspectives underpins what many believe to be the strongest contribution of social movement learning to the world of political struggle and social movement dynamics: an understanding of radical, democratic and transformative methods and processes which aim to create new spaces for personal, local and global change. Education within and without social movements is a space of pedagogical exuberance and creativity coupled with critique. Each chapter illustrates different aspects of this from the use of theatre and quilting in Clover, the social media in Malone and Hall, to organic farming in Etmanski, to the activists courses by Von Kotze and Harley, to the film for Brookfield, to the act of political action for Scandrett and Choudry and to the creation of new cultural spaces for Crowther and Lucio-Villegas.

Finally the narratives in this volume combine to tell us about the most important role of social movement learning, making hope possible, composting the imagination, building counter-power from the ground up, doing the *hokey cokey* (Kane) with the State when possible, creating new knowledge about the world we want and new pathways to obtain another possible future. Our work calls for the right to a new utopia, a new imaginative vision of a better world, and provides links to many of the rich ways women and men all over the world are doing it right now.

Tweeting History tells the story of how in January and February 2011, Mark Malone used his position as a postgraduate student, radical journalist and activist in Ireland to support those in the front line of the initial stages of the Egyptian revolution. Using social media such as Twitter, Facebook and blogs, with embedded photographs and video, which were being sent from Tahrir Square, Malone demonstrates the important role, which these technologies can play in social movement mobilisation and praxis. However, he rejects the technological determinism of some commentators and draws on Gramsci to analyse social media as a site of struggles over narratives, meanings and political economy with opportunities for emancipatory struggle as much as for authoritarian and corporate repression.

REFERENCES

De Cauter, L. De Roo, R. & Vanhaesebrouck, K. (Eds.) (2011). Art and activism in the age of globalization. Rotterdam: NAi Publishers.
O'Sullivan, Edmund (1999). Transformative Learning: Educational Vision for the 21st Century. London: Zed Books.

SECTION 1

HISTORICISING AND THEORISING, MOVEMENT EDUCATION AND LEARNING

ANNE HARLEY

1. "WE ARE POOR, NOT STUPID"[1]: LEARNING FROM AUTONOMOUS GRASSROOTS SOCIAL MOVEMENTS IN SOUTH AFRICA

INTRODUCTION

Social movements are seen as important for social change. Some argue that the "new social movements" have replaced the working class as the historical agents of revolutionary change (Scott, 1990), and they critique Marxism for failing to account for the rise of social movements, currently "the most visible form of struggle", according to Holst (2002, p. 75). Slater (1985), writing before the advent of leftist governments in Latin America, argued that social movements might play the role that Gramsci had proposed for the working class in the (counter-hegemonic) 'war of position', including the belief that change was possible:

> In countries like Brazil and Argentina with relatively densely-structured civil societies a war of position is indispensable and the radical democratic struggles of the new social movements provide a crucial contribution to just such a 'war'...in the palpable absence of more immediate prospects of radical transformation of state power, new social movements generate new sources of political hope. And optimism of the will can invariably attenuate pessimism of the intellect (Slater, 1985, pp. 18–19).

Others, including Marxists, argue that social movements offer an important alternative to the politics of the state. Allman and Mayo (1997), for example, question the contemporary efficacy of Gramsci's focus on the nation state, in the light of current leverage of international capital over the modern state. Rather, they believe that the 'historic bloc' needs to be larger than the state – some kind of alliance of international movements: "Can progressive social movements...serve as an important vehicle in this regard?" (p. 8).

Adult education (even radical adult education), however, took some time to recognise the significance of social movements for the field. Although by the early 1990s a modest debate had emerged about the implications for adult education of the new social movements (Finger, 1989; Welton, 1993), serious academic engagement with its implications really only emerged after the mid-1990s. Holford (1995), argued that social movement theory provided the basis for "a radically new understanding of the relationship between adult education and the generation of knowledge", but had had very little impact on adult education theory (p. 95).

B. L. Hall, D. E. Clover, J. Crowther and E. Scandrett (Eds.), Learning and Education for a Better World: The Role of Social Movements, 3–22.

Since then there has been increasing interest in social movements by those within the radical tradition of adult education (Kilgore, 1999; Hake, 2000; Kane, 2001; Holst, 2002; Choudry 2009, Choudry and Kapoor, 2010). Much of this work has centred on knowledge and knowledge production – for example, Holford has drawn on Eyerman and Jamison's (1991) arguments about social movements as sites of knowledge production to argue that this is important for adult education "by enabling us to move from the appreciation that social movements are important phenomena in the learning process of the individuals (and even collectively of the groups and organizations) which compose them, to a view that they are central to the production of human knowledge itself" (Holford, 1995, p. 101). Despite this, Choudry (2009) argues that our understanding of the politics and processes of knowledge and theory production within and by social movements is still limited, and that this knowledge and theory itself tends to be undervalued:

> ...even in many supposedly alternative milieus, voices, ideas – and, indeed, theories – produced by those actually engaged in social struggles are often ignored, rendered invisible, or overwritten with accounts by professionalized or academic experts (p. 5).

It is in this context that I wish to explore the thinking and theorising of movement militants in South Africa, and the implications of this for those of us attempting to practice radical adult education within universities.

'LIVING LEARNING'

During the course of 2008, six militants[2] from two South African social movements met every month to reflect on what they were learning through the struggle they were engaged in as social movement actors, and what they were learning as participants in a Certificate-level course at the local university. They called these sessions 'Living learning'. Their reflections were written up after each session, and published in late 2009 as *Living Learning* (Figlan et al., 2009).

'Living learning' was intended partly as a space to reflect on what and how to take back the things that the militants, mandated by their movements to attend the course, had learned in the classrooms of the academy:

> For a living learning, the critical question was always how best to take back to our communities whatever we might gain?; how best can our communities benefit from the few of us who are lucky to have access to the course?; how will we utilise the academic skills we can gain?; how do we take this information back? It has always been the task of a synthesis and a breaking down of the University theory so that we can work out properly what we can learn from it – and so we can understand for ourselves in what way it is different from the daily learning of struggle and life emijondolo [in the shacks] or eplasini [on the farms] (Figlan et al., 2009, p. 7).

But, significantly, 'Living learning' was also about how to combine the university of struggle and the academic university, and indeed 'disrupt' the academic university:

> Living Learning is about what's happening in and outside of the University classroom. So we are trying to combine the two universities – the one of experience and the one of academics (p. 7)...Our task is to plough what we can learn back into the struggles and structures of the movements – and vice versa: to plough the learnings from the struggle back into the University course process (p. 12)...We have work to do at the University too because it is clear that, without us who are from the movements being there, another agenda would be imposed (p. 49).

Publishing their reflections was thus a political act, intended not simply to allow others engaged in struggle to learn from their reflections, but to consciously critique the assumption that knowledge is generated only in the academy:

> Publishing a booklet out of our Living Learning could also be there for those 'smarter' people to learn from the 'fools' (p. 7).

THE MOVEMENTS

Whilst much of the dominant discourse about South Africa involves some kind of 'miracle' in its transition from apartheid to 'Rainbow Nation', South Africa's recent experience has been roughly similar to any other peripheral 'developing' country. Patrick Bond, in his *Elite transition* (2000), showed how the transition from apartheid to democracy included a "...transition from a popular-nationalist anti-apartheid project to official neoliberalism – by which is meant adherence to free market economic principles, bolstered by the narrowest practical definition of democracy (not the radical participatory project many ANC cadres had expected) – over an extremely short period of time" (p. 1). Now, "Freedom is the freedom to pay for food and for housing" (Gibson, 2006, p. 6). Michael Neocosmos (2007, p. 3) similarly argues that "South Africa is...probably the most consistently political neo-liberal of the African countries, at least it is so in the eyes of the Empire, as the latter regularly sets it up as a model for the continent".

Thus, like many other postcolonial countries which adopted the Washington Consensus, South Africa has seen the rich get richer, and the poor poorer, and the gap between the two grow, with increasing unemployment, disconnections from hard-fought-for water and electricity, and evictions (Gibson, 2006, pp. 2–3). The class structure within the country has been de-racialised and thus 'normalised', and the vast economic inequalities have been made to appear natural (Ibid). By the mid-2000s, South Africa was experiencing an "unprecedented process of self-enrichment by the new [black] elite" (Hlatshwayo, 2008, p. 214).

Gramsci (1971) argued there would always be resistance to hegemony; and so there has been in South Africa. Social movements have played an important role in this project. The first wave of post-apartheid social movements[3] was primarily a response to the neo-liberal policies introduced by the ANC government in 1996

(Gibson, 2006). Gibson argues this was particularly because organised labour failed to successfully challenge the new neoliberal policies and their inevitable social results. However, already by 2005 there was a "drastic reduction in social movement visibility [of these movements]", ascribed by leading movement intellectuals to the fact that they had not managed to make concrete links with the popular uprisings beginning to occur at community level all over the country (Hlatshwayo, 2008, p. 219). This failure to connect is largely a reflection on the fact that these 'first wave' movements, to borrow from feminism, were created by middle-class, vanguardist activists of the largely Trotskyite-left.

This 'second wave' of social movements emerged in the mid-2000s, at a time of local rebellions which displayed a 'self-consciousness of the poor' (Gibson, 2006, pp. 8, 10). These revolts, according to Gibson and others, are revolts of 'the obedient' – those who have waited patiently for more than a decade after the end of apartheid for their lives to improve (p. 11). The two social movements who mandated members to attend the course, the Rural Network and *Abahlali baseMjondolo* ('the people of the shacks'), are part of this second wave, but are notably different, in that, although consistently 'local' in the sense of taking up concrete historical struggles of real people in real places, they consciously and consistently avoid any parochial localism.

The Rural Network was founded in 2008 to connect various local struggles against violations of the rights of people living in rural areas. Colonialism and apartheid resulted in less than 20% of land in South Africa belonging to black African people. After 1994, the new constitution guaranteed private property; and the redistribution of land has been minimal (Lahiff, 2008). Thus most black African rural dwellers live either on tribal authority land held by the state (the ex-'homelands' of apartheid), or as insecure workers and tenants on largely white-owned commercial farmland. Struggles include resisting evictions, dealing with assaults and murders (by land owners, private security units as well as the State), and fighting a systematic bias against the poor in the workings of the criminal justice system and other state organs.

Abhlali baseMjondolo is a social movement of shackdwellers who live in what are often called 'informal settlements', places where people have built for themselves houses made of whatever comes to hand – mud, sticks, pieces of plastic, cardboard, corrugated iron. *Abahlali* grew organically out of struggle; it first emerged out of a road blockade by residents of the Kennedy Road shack settlement in the middle-class suburb of Clare Estate in Durban. The Kennedy Road settlement has existed for over 30 years. On Saturday morning, 21st March 2005, 700 people from Kennedy Road blockaded a major thoroughfare for four hours when they discovered that land nearby, which had been promised to them by the local ANC councillor, had been leased to a brick manufacturing company. Police with dogs and teargas ended the protest; 14 people were arrested (Bryant, 2006).

Twelve hundred people from the settlement subsequently marched to the local police station, where the 14 were being held. The crowd insisted that "if they are criminal, we are all criminal", and should thus also be arrested (Bryant, 2006,

p. 54). Two weeks later, 3000 people from Kennedy Road, as well as people from five other shack settlements in the area, marched on the local councillor, and in September, over 5 000 people, now constituted as *Abahlali baseMjondolo* (AbM), again marched on the councillor, telling him that he no longer represented them (Bryant, 2006).

By the end of 2005, 16 settlements had affiliated to the movement (AbM 2005), and by the end of the following year, another 20 had joined (AbM, 2006). The organisation currently has 10,000 members in 64 different shack settlements – 49 in KwaZulu-Natal and 15 in the Western Cape (AbM, 2011). Then in 2008, *Abahlali* and the Rural Network joined with two other South African social movements, the Western Cape Anti-Eviction Campaign and the Landless People's Movement (Gauteng Province), to form the Poor People's Alliance.

At the beginning of 2007, AbM and the Rural Network each sent two elected representatives to attend the Certificate in Education (Participatory Development) (CEPD), offered by the Centre for Adult Education of the University of KwaZulu-Natal (and which I have co-ordinated since 2007). The militants were mandated to attend and bring back what they had learned to the movements.

THE COURSE

The CEPD is a two-year, part-time programme, targeting adults already involved in some kind of community education or development, and in particular those from the poorest and most marginalised of communities in and around the city of Pietermaritzburg and beyond. The students thus bring with them considerable experience and insight to their university learning. The dialogic engagement with these students is thus a learning encounter both for the students and for the university (Harley and Rule, forthcoming).

Certificate students are usually considerably older than most students, and in many cases their secondary formal education was of a poor standard so that they do not have the necessary qualifications to enter a university. For this reason, the CEPD is an access programme, which allows students to enter with less than the usual qualifications required for entry into the University. The programme has the following key objectives:

1. To develop skilled practitioners working in the field of adult education and community development, particularly in marginalised communities;
2. To enable access to students who would not normally be allowed into the University as a result of their prior education level;
3. To enable access to students who would normally find it difficult to access a University education because of: financial difficulty, by providing financial support; distance from the university campus, by running the programme on a part-time basis so students only have to attend once a week.

The programme is strongly influenced by a constructivist understanding of education, as well as by adult education theory and practice, in particular that of David Kolb and Paulo Freire. The programme thus uses a learner-centred,

7

participatory pedagogy in keeping with the principles of experiential learning and critical education. The intensive and interactive nature of this pedagogy means, inter alia, that only a limited number of students can be taken in each year, despite a considerable demand. It is this pedagogy, however, that allows for the kind of dialogic engagement which we think significantly contributes to the success of the programme.

By 2007, when the first movement comrades entered the programme, the CEPD had been running in its current format for six years, although the curriculum continues to develop to ensure its relevance to the learners and the broader social context.

As the current academic co-ordinator of the programme, I would like to believe that it falls within the radical tradition of adult education, in that it consciously aims to tackle issues of injustice and inequality; it makes the political nature of all education overt; it focuses on change at the roots of the system, rather than on the symptoms (Mayo, 1994); it tries to provide useful skills and knowledge; to develop a critical understanding of power and of agency (Foley, 2004); and to connect the local and the global (Crowther, Galloway and Martin, 2005). However, in considering the militants' reflections, it is clear to me that the programme falls short in certain critical respects.

LEARNING FROM THE MILITANTS

Learning About Knowledge and Education

The programme includes in its aims, in its pedagogy, and in its curriculum, a clear bias towards a Freirean understanding of education. Students are specifically taught the basic tenets of Freire, and it is clear from *Living Learning* that the social movement militants found many of Freire's ideas useful because they connect productively with their own thinking and experiences.

Thus the militants start from assumption that education is never innocent. "It is clear now that education is always biased; it has an ideology and a bias. So when we engage with it, our task is to fight to take it back and make it work for us" (Figlan et al., 2009, p. 24). The need to "fight to take it back" arises from the fact that much education is, to use Paulo Freire's (1996) phrase, for domestication. However, the militants use this term themselves, but they also use Figlan et al's (2009) terms 'mind dispossession' and 'mental abuse':

> We see that education is mostly used to control people and keep power for the powerful – but we can disrupt this. This requires us to analyse what kind of education is going on – is it there to make us 'good boys and girls' or is it helping to make us question things and make that part of our struggle to change the world? (Figlan, et al., p. 20).

However, for them a critical aspect of education for control is not simply that it is trying to create "good boys and girls", but that it equates 'education' with 'knowledge'; and then divides people, assuming that those with 'education' are those with 'knowledge', and thus those without education have nothing to say and nothing to teach. "Education can sometimes destroy our struggle – when education makes leaders think of the people that they come from as the 'uneducated' ones, those who 'do not understand'" (p. 9). Universities are greatly complicit in this:

> From what we have seen, there are many at University who think that they are there to learn what to come and 'teach the poor' when they are finished studying. It is clear that they imagine they are our educators. They assume we are empty enough and stupid enough for others to learn what *they* decide, and that they will come and think for those of us who are poor and cannot think (p. 19).

But, even more problematic, the "systems [that] try to keep us silent" (p. 39), in their analysis, include those that are apparently on the side of the struggle – those who claim to speak and act on behalf of the poor and oppressed. Thus the militants expand Freire's conception of education for domestication versus education for liberation:

> We discussed for a bit whether this analysis of people's experiences shows that there are not simply two but maybe three kinds of education? Certainly there is 'education' that is imposed to keep the people suppressed and silent so that the status quo is not threatened. On the other side there is a liberating education that starts with the people's struggles to be fully human. But is there a special kind of 'education' in the middle – usually called 'capacity building' or 'political education' – that civil society organisations specialise in giving when people who are meant to be suppressed start to struggle against their oppression? This kind of education is done in the name of the poor and oppressed and is aiming to teach the language and rules of how to change your struggle so that it can be 'in order', following the protocols, thinking and expectations of the civil society people who want to claim to represent the people's struggles and interests (p. 47).

The movement militants are clear that their task is to question and disrupt this – not simply by analysing education, but by generating new knowledge, and new truth, themselves. This is something argued by Alain Badiou (2005), who says that when there is 'sustained investigation' (reflection) of an 'event' (something that points to the possibility of something different) and its implications, in other words an attempt to sustain the consequences of the event in thought, then there is the construction (not discovery) of truth, which leads to new knowledge:

> A truth punches a 'hole' in knowledges, it is heterogeneous to them, but it is also the sole known source of new knowledges. We shall say that the truth 'forces' knowledges (Badiou, 2005).

Thus Badiou makes a sharp distinction between truth and knowledge (Hallward, 2004, p. 1). He says that "...a truth is nothing other than the process that exposes and represents the void of a situation", the void being that which is not counted in the situation, for example, the proletariat in a capitalist system and the shack dweller in a neoliberal system.

The militants make a similar distinction between knowledge and truth, with the 'truth' of a situation being precisely that which ruptures (extant) knowledge. Badiou argues that truth is both singular) (because it emerges from a particular situation), but also universal (because it is 'the same for all') (Badiou, 2005). The militants argue similarly, that truth is the universal in the thinking of the particular. The act of thinking experience, thinking struggle, is a collective *and universal* one. Indeed, "the thinking together of the oppressed who struggle can unmask [the systems that try to keep us silent] and create learning and alternatives for a better world and for the whole world, everyone" (Figlan et al., 2009, p. 39).

The act of generating new truth and new knowledge is thus itself disruptive, is a powerful political act. In *Living Learning*, they discuss one important space for this within *Abahlali* – the 'night camps'. These monthly meetings start in the evening and will typically run throughout the night. Anyone can participate in these, anyone can speak, anyone can question. "We do it to generate knowledge together – and when we do that, we are also generating power together" (p. 20). But 'Living learning' itself was also such a space for generating new knowledge, of disruption, of 'being out of order':

> The kind of education and knowledge, the searching for truth that we are doing is too dangerous for the powerful. It has no formal 'syllabus' except the life and priorities of the people themselves...This kind of education and knowledge recognises that...'It is better to be out of order', to be outside the prescribed curriculum! We see clearly that the prescribed curriculum has the intention of control built deeply into it and that there are strings attached (p. 27).

In their understanding, then, 'being educated' is very different from the conception of universities and civil society, because education and knowledge are linked not separate or the same, and knowledge is about thinking experience, thinking struggle. "We are all educated. If I need to be educated about development, then the best educator is a real experience of development... [Elites] think we know nothing and must be taught. They think the people don't understand and therefore need education. We start from the opposite assumption" (pp. 46–47).

Learning About Pedagogy

Freire, like Gramsci, argued for a particular kind of pedagogy, a dialectical one where the teacher is also a learner, and the learner is also a teacher, because expertise and experience is shared and reflected on collectively (Freire, 1996; Mayo, 1999). In this pedagogy, what hooks (1994) calls 'engaged pedagogy', both teachers and learners are active participants, and there is an assumption that the teacher does not know it all, and that the students are not blank slates.

The programme uses this kind of pedagogy, a pedagogy that "is a matter of principle and purpose rather than mere technique" (Crowther, Galloway and

Martin, 2005, p. 6); and because it is targeting adult educators, specifically teaches this kind of pedagogy. This clearly resonated with the militants attending the course:

> What is important for real learning is to question and debate it – especially what is presented to you. This is a very different concept from what we were taught in school where 'teacher is always right'! Now we question giving the authority away to a 'teacher' – we can argue and debate. Only in this way can learning provide the possibility of finding different ways of doing things...We discussed how this idea can be connected to the thinking of the living politics of *Abahlali baseMjondolo*. It can stop us becoming arrogant as leaders of a movement because our experience in life and in the movement means that we must always remain open to debate, question, and new learning from and with the people" (Figlan et al., 2009, p. 18).

The militants specifically commented on the ways in which the programme practised what it taught (p. 21), in particular the need to respect the experiences and lives of others. "The right way of working with others respects their local struggles and their sufferings, and in no way undermines the people. This has been exactly how the facilitator of the course has approached us and our movements, struggles, experiences and opinions" (p. 41).

However, simply allowing space to share, respecting other people's experiences and knowledge, is not enough, and the militants directly challenge the notion that the teacher must always know more (Horton and Freire, 1990, p. 98). "So OK, the people need education of a certain kind but really: who must educate whom? The people living in the shacks and in the rural areas know their life, and those on the top must come down to learn from the people...Now to ask and to listen, that would be a liberating education!" (Figlan et al., 2009, p. 46). So 'those who suffer it must lead it'.

For the militants, then, knowledge, and universal truth, is created through the collective process of thinking struggle, led by those who suffer; and at this point of thinking, it is learned if this thinking is immediately acted on, through militant praxis:

> The kind of education we want involves people listening to each other. The learning we talk about is always a learning that is put into practice. At the same moment of learning, we apply it. To share it and apply it is what makes it a living learning. This is not an education to make individuals better in their individual jobs and careers – it is with the people (p. 48).

In this kind of ('out of order') education, there is thus a radical shift in the role of the teacher and the learner – no-one can teach if they are not engaged in the collective thinking of struggle and the praxis of this; no-one can learn if they are not engaged on the collective thinking of struggle and the praxis of this.

Learning About Curriculum

The programme was created in much the same way that all university programmes are created – through debate and discussion amongst academics, who then write down a curriculum 'template' to be reviewed by a variety of university committees before being approved. Depending on the individual academics and the particular configurations of power within the academy, such a procedure can allow space for radical content, but inherently risks varying degrees of dislocation from the spaces and 'curricula' of concrete struggle/s.

By contrast, the kind of education and knowledge that militants created and agitate for in 'Living learning' "has no formal 'syllabus' except the life and priorities of the people themselves...and recognises that...'It is better to be out of order', to be outside the prescribed curriculum" (Figlan et al., 2009, p. 27). Figlan et al go on to argue, as have many before, that a meaningful curriculum must provide 'really useful knowledge', in the sense that it "matches the theory with the reality of the life of the people" (p. 29). Such a curriculum must start with "critical thinking about the life of the people, starting to uncover and name the contradictions this shows against what the powerful want us to believe about our situation" (p. 25). "For the oppressed it becomes necessary that we get an education that allows people to see what is happening in their area, their world. So it must be relevant to our own context of life, and it must expose the reality of their oppression – we must really see the oppressor" (p. 34). Because it must start with the life of the people, with their experience, their struggle, and because this changes, there can never be a set curriculum.

Learning About Praxis

Clearly, a pivotal thrust in the militants' understanding of knowledge, learning and teaching is that of *praxis*, something which is a strong theme within radical education, drawing on Paulo Freire's work (Freire, 1996). For the militants, as for Freire, praxis is necessary for learning; for the militants precisely because truth erupts into a situation through emancipatory praxis. But it is also fundamental to the politics of their movements – you have to *do* what you are fighting *for*. "It is important to look after and put into practice in a disciplined and continuous way within our movements and our struggles exactly the kind of 'politics' and values that we want to achieve in the future we fight for" (Figlan et al., 2009, p. 21). In *Living learning* they talk about what this praxis entails within their movements:

> The first thing is always to ask the views of the members. Only then can we begin to strategise. And when we ask the people's views, this is done with deep respect and to encourage sharing (p. 15)...Debate in our struggles is very important as we are learning how to be democratic (p. 22).

Doing what it is you are fighting for begins to create that thing. AbM runs a campaign each year targeting what is called in South Africa "Freedom Day" – the anniversary of the first democratic elections in the country. They call this day

'Unfreedom Day', and use it to highlight the many ways in which the poor, in particular, are not free. They devoted one of the 'Living learning' sessions to a discussion about Unfreedom Day, and the praxis involved in organising it. As part of the process, *Abahlali* members went to the people in each shack settlement "to listen to their thinking" about freedom and the realities of their lived experience. "We need an open debate about notions of freedom, especially when so much of the people's lives is a contradiction to freedom" (p. 26). This praxis, they insist, not only disrupts the claims of freedom, which is not, but actually begins to create freedom, which is. "It might be a taste of freedom in itself to do this. So this space of discussion and listening is a small but important part of freedom – the freedom that comes from searching for the truth" (p. 26).

LEARNING AND TEACHING OUT OF ORDER

As stated above, I would like to believe that the CEPD is 'radical' in its intent, content and pedagogy. Of course, simply including radical adult education theorists such as Freire in the curriculum is no guarantee of radicalism, as Zacharakis-Jutz (1988) points out. On the whole, the militants appear to find at least some of the theorists that are discussed in the course useful to their struggle; and are fairly complimentary about some aspects of the course, including its pedagogy. Thus in their experience of this programme the academic university is not necessarily entirely useless. In their reflections, the militants discussed two universities – the university of struggle, and the academic university. They argued that although these were often mutually exclusive, this did not have to be the case:

Perhaps we can talk of achieving the 'Universal University' – invading the academic one in order for it to benefit the people (Figlan et al., 2009, p. 59).

Their criticisms of the academy, and those who learn there, tend not to be directed at the course (although there are moments when they are overtly critical of certain lecturers). However, in what the militants have to say, discussed above, it is clear to me that there are a number of (interrelated) fundamental arguments that they make that require reflection:

1. The issue of praxis

As noted above, the relationship between praxis and knowledge and learning is something that is emphasised in radical adult education. Freire (in Horton and Freire, 1990, p. 98), says "Without practice there's no knowledge"; Foley (2001, p. 86) writes "We learn as we act". These hold true as much within the academy as out of it:

...a commitment to praxis must remain at the core of the relationship between popular education and the academy. And praxis in popular education – whatever its difficulties in the context of the academy – must be not only about learning in order to act but also learning from action, even when it fails (Crowther, Galloway and Martin, 2005, p. 7).

A. HARLEY

As we have seen, the social movement militants argue that truth is created out of thinking about the struggle together in militant praxis, although "those who suffer it, must lead it" – it's not enough for someone, no-matter how much they care, or how 'radical' they are, to simply come and talk to the people:

> Paulo Freire emphasised that it is up to the oppressed people to do their own thing to liberate themselves. So even if you are an 'animator' and you want to come and help, you must recognise that the people are the ones who know about their situation. Some people who know more things from academic learning oppress us by saying, more or less, 'you know nothing – so do as I tell you'. This is how education maintains the existing order (Figlan et al., 2009, p. 34).

In the classroom of the CEPD, although there is some space to talk about struggle (but not much to think it – see below), there's really no space to act this thinking. Some of us, as lecturers, are involved in various struggles inside and outside the university; but these remain largely unrelated to what's going on in the class; and we're not involved in the struggles of the students attending the class. At best, we use certain accounts of certain struggles for students to reflect on. And as Hurtado (2007) warns "As soon as I divorce existing knowledge from the act of creating knowledge, I tend to accept existing knowledge as an accomplished fact and to transfer it to those who do not know" (p. 66). However, some of us at least have tried to retain a fidelity to the axiomatic prescriptive character of the praxis demanded by the truth the militants reveal. If the militants and their movements should not speak, but speak, and speak the truth that everyone matters, then that axiom is there to be taken up by everyone everywhere – no less by academics in universities. As an axiomatic truth, it is utterly indifferent to anyone's 'objective' situation and interests – it is simply to be enacted – again, no less in the classrooms of the university than in the face of the police on the streets. Being universal truth it creates the possibility of entirely militant academic praxis.

Part of this praxis is that you have to do what you're fighting for; as I understand it, this means you have to do what you are teaching. So if you are teaching radical education, you have to do it. If you are teaching social change, you have to do it. In their book, *Popular Education: Engaging the Academy* (2005), Crowther, Galloway and Martin argue (and show) how it is possible to radicalise our intellectual work inside universities; but, they concede, this isn't always easy; and praxis is particularly difficult, not least because of the current trends within universities. At one point towards the end of the year (and the end of the programme for some of them), one of the militants pointed to the deep contradiction between the militant praxis of the movements and that of the university: "How can we receive the certificate? Is it in the name of those who sent us? Or is it for me? If it is for me, then that is stealing from the people" (Figlan et al., 2009, p. 60).

2. Knowledge is created through thinking together in struggle: we "listen to their thinking".

It is true that the CEPD curriculum tries to be relevant, and tries to include issues of power and agency and struggle; but the basic framework and architecture of the course is set, and is set by academics. It is true that we acknowledge, even emphasise, that our students come to us with experience and knowledge about that experience, and the pedagogy we use is there to help people share that. It is also true that some us accept the truth that everyone matters, and we try to act that. But "listening to their thinking"?

Gramsci tells us:

A philosophy of praxis cannot but present itself at the outset in a polemical and critical guise, as superseding the existing mode of thinking and existing concrete thought...First of all, therefore, it must be a criticism of 'common sense' basing itself entirely, however, on common sense in order to demonstrate that 'everyone' is a philosopher (Gramsci, 1971, p. 330).

One of the most fundamental tenets of *Abahlalism* (the name used by the *Abahlali baseMjondolo* movement to refer to its ideology and praxis) is, as Gramsci (1971), Fanon (2001) and Freire (1996) asserted, that everyone thinks and everyone is an intellectual. Freire argues that "if the people cannot be trusted, there is no reason for liberation" (cited in Kane, 2001, p. 39), an idea which Liam Kane (2001) says is "something which is completely ignored or forgotten by much of the organised left throughout the world" (p. 39), but which has been an absolutely consistent theme of the movement since its inception. In a documentary made about the Kennedy Road blockade shortly after it happened, an *Abahlali* member, Nonhlanhla Mzobe says, "We think. People must understand that we think". As we have seen, it is thinking that creates universal truth, and new knowledge. Very early on, one of the banners carried by Kennedy Road residents read "University of Kennedy Road"; and by the march of 14 November 2005, "University of *Abahlali baseMjondolo*".

People who can think (i.e. everyone) have something to say, to teach; and are perfectly able to do this for themselves. Thus one of the movement's consistent demands has been that they be allowed to speak for themselves (from fairly early on, *Abahlali* began using the phrase "Talk to us, not for us" (Zikode, 2006c, p. 7)); and one of their consistent criticisms of government and of civil society (and of academics!) has been that they attempt to speak for them.

In his speech to a forum in March 2006, then President of the movement, S'bu Zikode, criticised the role of civil society, and intellectuals in particular:

Our masses are not just bodies without land and housing and bodies marching on the street. We can be poor materially, but we are not poor in mind...Some of the intellectuals understand that we think our own struggle. Others still don't understand this (Zikode, 2006a).

Abahlali have long recognised that it is precisely this assertion that they think, and that they have a right to speak and be listened to, that is most threatening to hegemony; as Zikode wryly remarked in mid-2006, "The state comes for us when we try to say what we think" (Zikode, 2006b),[4] not when the state was needed because of, for example, the emergency of shack fires. This is because "We are the people that are not meant to think" (Zikode, 2008a).[5]

If everyone thinks, then, profoundly, everyone is already equal. "We start from the recognition that we are all equal. We do not struggle to achieve equality. We struggle for the recognition of the equality that already exists" (Zikode, 2008b). "A left politics that starts from the view that everyone matters and that everyone thinks, moves from the assumption of the immediate equality of all people...A left politics that starts from the view that everyone matters but that not everyone is ready to think takes the view that equality is something that will be achieved after a long struggle" (Gibson, Harley and Pithouse, 2009, pp. 77–78). I think our programme has been guilty of the latter – that we have been too ready to teach other thinkers, other theorists, to our students, rather than assume they can do it themselves.

3. The issue of pedagogy

One of the theorists that the militants mention in passing in *Living learning* is Jaques Ranciere, a theorist not discussed in the official Certificate curriculum at all. Ranciere, like Freire, Fanon, Gramsci and *Abahlali*, moves from the assumption that "there is no social actor, no matter how insignificant, who is not at the same time a thinking being" (1991, p. 34). But Ranciere (and *Abahlali*) take this further. He is preoccupied with the consideration of the relationship between knowledge and the masses (Ross, 1991). Much of his work was to document experiences and voices of early-nineteenth century workers who claimed the right to think; and who critiqued the claims of bourgeois observers and intellectuals to know and speak for the worker. Ranciere argues that the basis for the educational theories of such nominally leftist and 'radical' writers such as Bourdieu and Althusser is inequality:

> But what if equality, instead, were to provide the point of departure? What would it mean to make equality a *presupposition* rather than a goal, a *practice* rather than a reward situated firmly in some distant future so as to all the better explain its present infeasibility? (cited in Ross, 1991, p. xix).

His seminal work (so far largely ignored by the field of adult education), *The Ignorant Schoolmaster*, is "an extraordinary philosophical meditation on equality" (Ross, 1991, p. ix), in which Ranciere asserts that "All [people] have equal intelligence" (Ranciere, 1991, p. 18). Ranciere is critical of sociology and much of 'politics' (he has his own understanding of what politics really is) for resting on an assumption of inequality, and argues that "pedagogy has followed politics like a dark shadow" (Barbour, 2010, p. 259). Knowledge, he claims, is not necessary for teaching, nor explication necessary to learning; thus pedagogy is a myth, used to separate those who 'know' from those who are 'ignorant':

> The normal pedagogic logic says that people are ignorant, they don't know how to get out of ignorance to learn, so we have to make some kind of itinerary to move from ignorance to knowledge, starting from the difference between the one who knows and the one who does not know...[the process of

learning must be seen] not as a process from ignorance to knowledge but as a process of going from what is already known or what is already possessed, to further knowledge or new possessions...the idea is that the ignorant always know something, always asks something, and always has the capacity, and the problem is how to make the best of this capacity and start from equality (Ranciere, 2009, interview).

He thus rejects explication in favour of recounting (repeating, retelling that which has been seen, an operation of the intelligence which then allows comparison and identification of causes, i.e. meaning), which is a concrete practice of equality because it presupposes equality of intelligence, rather than inequality of knowledge.

Ranciere (1991) also argues that learning requires two faculties – intelligence and will. Will is what accounts for differences in what is learned:

There is inequality in the *manifestations* of intelligence, according to the greater or lesser energy communicated to the intelligence by the will for discovering and combining new relations; but there is no hierarchy of *intellectual capacity*. Emancipation is becoming conscious of this equality of *nature*. (p. 27).

So emancipation is "that every common person might conceive his human dignity, take the measure of his intellectual capacity, and decide how to use it...Whoever emancipates doesn't have to worry about what the emancipated person learns. He will learn what he wants, nothing maybe" (p. 18). This means that the process of learning can start with anything that 'the ignorant one' knows – it actually doesn't matter what (p. 28). And the method is always: What do you see? What do you think about it? What do you make of it? (p. 23). The method is the same for everyone – there is no specific pedagogy of the oppressed, of the poor.

Thus on several points, Ranciere marks a significant departure from Freire (but is remarkably close to the arguments of *Abahlali*). As Pithouse (2011) has argued, there is a 'slippage' in Freire's work, a tension between his insistence that we must "trust in the oppressed and their ability to reason" (Freire, 1996, p. 48), and his argument that oppression dehumanises, meaning that the oppressed themselves are not able to understand their own condition, and require some kind of humanizing pedagogy to conscientise them, although this is obviously not unique to Freire as the entire concept of false consciousness rests on a similar argument. Pithouse (2011) argues that Freire makes a mistake in casting the oppressed as *actually* dehumanised, rather than as being *misrepresented* as dehumanised;

While oppressed people have to make their lives amidst social relations that are objectifying people are not, even in the most repressive or wretched circumstances, inevitably reduced to those circumstances. On the contrary there are multiple ways in which people defend and tend their humanity (pp. 15–16).

If people are always capable of thinking, and thinking their own oppression (as Ranciere insists), then the need for some kind of particular 'radical teacher', necessary to help them become people (rather than things) so that they can liberate themselves, clearly comes into question:

> Only a politics founded on...equality [of intelligence] deserves the name democratic. And only an education without preordained educators deserves to be called political (Barbour, 2010, p. 262).

CONCLUSIONS

I don't think we're alone in denying the ability of all people to think, everywhere – and in particular for all people to think critically. There is now a vast literature on the ways in which universities act to create and support hegemony; and I think there's a pretty strong thrust even within the tradition of radical education that assumes that some kind of radical teacher *who knows more* (and some kind of radical pedagogy) is absolutely necessary to 'conscientise' or 'transform' those who are not thinking, or not thinking well enough, or not thinking critically enough. The movement intellectuals (and, of course, Ranciere) disrupt this.

It's not particularly surprising that the academy (and even 'radical' intellectuals within the academy) begin from the axiom of inequality, as Ranciere would put it. In a recent paper, Richard Pithouse (2011) shows how the approach of the current (post-colonial) university is, to some extent, a reflection of the emphasis on pedagogy in contemporary neo-colonialism, where "interventions undertaken in the name of development or human rights are often pedagogic, presenting people as ignorant or insufficiently ethical rather than oppressed" (p. 13). Abahlali have made this point very powerfully, in a statement issued during the terrible xenophobic attacks in South Africa in May 2008:

> We hear that the political analysts are saying that the poor must be educated about xenophobia. Always the solution is to 'educate the poor'. When we get cholera we must be educated about washing our hands when in fact we need clean water. When we get burnt we must be educated about fire when in fact we need electricity. This is just one way of blaming the poor for our suffering...we don't want to be educated to be good at surviving poverty on our own (Abahali, 2008).

So the pedagogic bent (i.e. the assumption that some are ignorant, whilst others know) is all around us, precisely because it is the political requirement of hegemony to *prevent* (counter-hegemonic) thinking (i.e. that people are in the state they are in because they are oppressed, not because they are ignorant or insufficiently ethical):

> What had to be prevented above all was letting the poor know that they could educate themselves by their own abilities, that they had abilities...And the best way to do this was to educate them, that is to say, to give them the measure of their inability. Schools were opened everywhere, and nowhere did anyone want to announce the possibility of learning without a master explicator...Social institutions, intellectual corporations, and political parties

now came knocking on families' doors, addressing themselves to all individuals for the purpose of educating them (Ranciere, 1991, pp. 129–130).

And, again (as numerous recent publications have argued), the academy often plays an important role in this, in the way that programmes are chosen, that selection is undertaken, that curricula are set. The course that we offer has always been marginal; it is simply too small, at too low a level. But it has been allowed to continue through the years, probably largely for the same reasons. Recently, however, the course has come under increasing pressure, and increasing threat, often contradictory but with the same ultimate aim. The pressure has been to take in more students, to 'grow' the course (at the risk of the kind of pedagogy we use); and to no longer take in students who do not meet the 'rules' for entry in terms of their education level (at the risk of excluding precisely those we are targeting). The threat has been to shut the programme down, because it is not financially viable, or because it is at a level not appropriate to our institution.[6]

So what does all this mean for those of us in the academy who have "made a permanent commitment" (Badiou, cited in Hazan, 2008, p. 133) to a different world, and see our scholarly activity as part of that? Pithouse (2011) responds:

> In order to take seriously, from within the academy, the fact that people outside of it, including the oppressed, are as capable as thought and ethical action as anyone else it is necessary to be attentive to both what Ranajit Guha calls the "politics of the people" (1997, p. xiv), a subaltern sphere of political thought and action, as well as to Rancière's sustained demonstration that people move between their allocated spaces – that workers are also present in the space that the philosopher kings have allocated to themselves and that moments of mass political insubordination are often characterised by a disregard for allocated places (p. 16).

I'm not yet sure how we put this into action, how we change our praxis and pedagogy, particularly within the constraints of the neoliberal university. But it seems to me that at the most basic level, the task for 'radical' academic intellectuals is to retain some kind of fidelity to the truth that everyone counts, everyone matters; but also, that everyone thinks. This would be, as the militants say, a truly 'out of order' education.

NOTES

[1] This quote is taken from a letter emailed to a South African NGO by Ashraf Casiem, then chair of the Anti-Eviction Campaign, a Cape Town-based social movement. Casiem was protesting against attempts made by some NGOs to control poor people's movements.

[2] I use the term 'militant' for two reasons. Firstly, and most importantly, because this is how the movement members refer to themselves; but secondly, because I wish to indicate what Paulo Freire meant by the term – "something *more* than 'activist'. A militant is a *critical* activist" (Shor and Freire, 1987, p. 50).

3   Most commentators agree that this includes the Landless People's Movement (LPM), the Treatment Action Campaign (TAC), the Anti-Privatisation Forum (APF), the Soweto Electricity Crisis Committee (SECC) etc.

4   In September 2009, a week after *Living learning* was launched, the Kennedy Road settlement was brutally attacked over a period of several hours by an armed mob, leaving many shacks destroyed, hundreds of people displaced, and two of the attackers dead. Two weeks before the attack, the African National Congress (ANC) chair for Durban publicly stated that *Abahlali* was a threat to the ANC, and the day after the attack the ANC Member of the Executive Committee (i.e. of the provincial cabinet) for Safety and Security said that a decision had been taken to disband the movement, and described the attack as a 'liberation' of the settlement. The movement has been adamant that the attacks were politically motivated, and have consistently called for an independent enquiry (AbM, 26/9/2010).
There is little doubt that the Kennedy Road attack profoundly affected the movement; many of the leadership were traumatised, and forced into hiding, so "for some months we had to organise underground" (AbM, 2010); and for quite some time, the movement was unable to have large and open meetings as had been the norm prior to the attacks. However, as the movement says, "It damaged our movement in some ways but it has not destroyed our movement" (Ibid.). The attack has served to re-emphasise the claims by the Poor People's Alliance that no-one in South Africa is yet free.

5   Abahlali are not alone in this insight: A housing activist in Scotland says "It became obvious to us that they [the Labour Party] were terrified of people like us – not because we had any political power, but because uneducated people like us had become experts in understanding what we were talking about" (Martin & McCormack, 1999, p. 261).

6   In late 2011, the University's Senate agreed to reject any future applications for new Certificate or Diploma programmes, and to review all existing Certificate and Diploma programmes with a view to shutting them down.

REFERENCES

Abahlali baseMjondolo. (2005). March on mayor Obed Mlaba on 14 November 2005. Pamphlet.
Abahlali baseMjondolo. (2006). Sydenham police launch savage attack on democracy. Press release, 12/9/2006.
Abahlali baseMjondolo. (2008). Abahlali baseMjondolo statement on the xenophobic attacks in Johannesburg. Press statement, 21/5/2008.
Abahlali baseMjondolo. (2010). Statement on the anniversary of the attack on Abahlali baseMjondolo in the Kennedy Road Settlement. Press statement, 26/9/2010.
Abahlali baseMjondolo. (2011). We are all S'bu Zikode. Press statement, 18/10/2011.
Allman, P. & Mayo, P. (1997). Freire, Gramsci and globalisation. *27TH Annual SCUTREA conference proceedings*, 6–9.
Badiou, A. (2005). *Being and event*. London: Continuum.
Badiou, A. (2008). Roads to renegacy: Interview by Eric Hazan. *New Left Review*, 53, 125–133.
Barbour, C.A. (2010). Militants of truth, communities of equality: Badiou and the ignorant schoolmaster. *Educational philosophy and theory*, v. 42, no. 2, pp. 251–263.
Bond, P. (2000). *Elite transition: from apartheid to neoliberalism in South Africa*. London: Pluto Press.
Bryant, J. (2006). Towards delivery and dignity: community struggle from Kennedy Road. In Alexander, A. & Pithouse, R. (Eds.). *Yonk'indawo umzabalazo uyasivumela: new work from Durban*. (pp. 49–80). Durban: Centre for Civil Society.
Choudry, A. (2009). Learning in social action: Knowledge production in social movements. *McGill Journal of Education, 44(*1), 5–10.
Choudry, A. & Kapoor, D. (Eds.) (2010). *Learning from the ground up: Global perspectives on social movements and knowledge production*. New York: Palgrave Macmillan.

Crowther, J., Galloway, V. & Martin, I. (2005). *Popular education: Engaging the academy. International perspectives.* Leicester: NIACE.

Eyerman, R. & Jamison, A. (1991). *Social movements: A cognitive approach.* Cambridge: Polity Press.

Fanon, F. (2001) *The wretched of the earth.* London: Penguin.

Figlan, L., Mavuso, M, Ngema, B., Nsibande, Z., Sibisi, S. & Zikode, S. (2009). *Living learning.* Pietermaritzburg: Church Land Programme.

Finger, M. (1989). New social movements and their implications for adult education. *Adult Education Quarterly, 40,* 15–22.

Foley, G. (2001). Radical adult education and learning. *International Journal for Lifelong Education, 20*(1/2), 71–88.

Foley, G. (2004). *Learning in social action: A contribution to understanding informal education.* Leicester: NIACE.

Freire, P. (1996). *Pedagogy of the oppressed.* London: Penguin.

Gibson, N.C. (2006.) Introduction. In Gibson, N.C. (Ed.). *Challenging hegemony: social movements and the quests for a new humanism in post-apartheid South Africa.* Trenton, N.J.: Africa World Press.

Gibson, N., Harley, A. & Pithouse, R. (2009). Out of order: A living learning for a living politics. In Figlan et al. *Living learning.* Pietermaritzburg: Church Land Programme.

Gouin, R. (2009). An antiracist feminist analysis for the study of learning in social struggle. *Adult Education Quarterly, 59*(2), 158–175.

Gramsci, A. (1971). *Selections from the prison notebooks of Antonio Gramsci.* (Edited and translated by Q.Hoare & G.N.Smith). London: Lawrence & Wishart.

Hake, B. (2000). Social movements and adult education in a cross cultural perspective. In Cooke, A. & MacSween, A. (Eds.). *The rise and fall of adult education institutions and social movements: the proceedings of the Seventh International Conference on the History of Adult Education.* Frankfurt: Peter Lang.

Hallward, P. (2004). Introduction: consequences of abstraction. In Hallward, P. (Ed.). *Think again: Alain Badiou and the future of philosophy.* London: Continuum.

Harley,A. & Rule, P.N. (Forthcoming). Access, redress, success: Exploring an alternative access programme in education and development. In Dhunpath, R. and Vithal, R. (Eds.). *Access to Higher Education in South Africa: Reflective of under-prepared students or under-prepared institutions?* Cambridge: Pearson.

Hlatshwayo, M. (2008). The state of the movements and our tasks for the rebuilding process (an address at the fifth annual national meeting of the SMI). Lehulere, O. (Ed.). *Political and theoretical perspectives from the South African social movements 2002–2007. Vol.1: the state of social movements in South Africa 2007.* Johannesburg: Khanya College.

Holford, J. (1995). Why social movements matter: adult education theory, cognitive praxis, and the creation of knowledge. *Adult Education Quarterly, 45*(2), 95–111.

Holst, J.D. (2002). *Social movements, civil society and radical adult education.* Westport, CT: Bergin & Garvey.

hooks, b. (1994). *Teaching to transgress: Education as the practice of freedom.* New York: Routledge.

Horton, M. & Freire, P. (1990). *We make the road by walking: conversations on education and social change.* Philadelphia: Temple University Press.

Hurtado, C.N. (2007). The continuing relevance of Paulo Freire's ideas. *Adult Education and Development, 69,* 51–78.

Kane, L. (2001). *Popular education and social change in Latin America.* London: Latin America Bureau.

Kilgore, D.W. (1999). Understanding learning in social movements: a theory of collective learning. *International Journal of Lifelong Education, 18*(3), 191–202.

Lahiff, E. (2008). *Land Reform in South Africa: A status report 2008.* PLAAS Research report 38. Cape Town: PLAAS.

Martin, H. & McCormack, C. (1999). Making connections: learning through struggle. In Crowther, J., Martin, I. & Shaw, M. (Eds.). *Popular education and social movements in Scotland today*. Leicester: NIACE.

Mayo, P. (1994). Synthesising Gramsci and Freire: possibilities for a theory of radical adult education. *International Journal of Lifelong Education, 13*(2), 125–148.

Mayo, P. (1999). *Gramsci, Freire and Adult Education: possibilities for transformative action*. London: Zed.

Neocosmos, M. (2007). Civil society, citizenship and the politics of the (im)possible: rethinking militancy in Africa today. Unpublished paper.

Pithouse, R. (2006). 'Our struggle is thought, on the ground, running': the University of Abahlali baseMjondolo. In Alexander, A. & Pithouse, R. (Eds.). *Yonk'indawo umzabalazo uyasivumela: new work from Durban*. Durban: Centre for Civil Society.

Pithouse, R. (2011). The academy, the occult zone and the universal. Paper presented at the *Conference on the Humanities and Popular Struggles*, Rhodes University, Grahamstown, 11 & 12 September 2011.

Ranciére, J. (1991). *The ignorant schoolmaster: Five lessons in intellectual emancipation*. Stanford, Ca.: Stanford University Press.

Ranciere, J. (2009). Interviewed by Lawrence Liang, 5 February 2009, Lodi Gardens, Delhi. http://kafila.org/2009/02/12/interview-with-jacques-ranciere/. Accessed 25 January 2010.

Ross, K. (1991). Translator's introduction. In Ranciere, R. *The ignorant schoolmaster: Five lessons in intellectual emancipation*. Stanford, Ca.: Stanford University Press.

Scott, A. (1990). *Ideology and the new social movements*. London: Unwin Hyman.

Shor, I. & Freire, P. (1987). *A pedagogy for liberation*. Massachusetts: Bergin & Garvey.

Slater, D. (1985). Social movements and the recasting of the political. In Slater, D. (Ed.). *New Social Movements and the State in Latin America*. (pp. 1–25). Amsterdam: CEDLA.

Welton, M. (1993). Social revolutionary learning: the new social movements as learning sites. *Adult Education Quarterly, 43*(3), 152–64.

Zacharrakis-Jutz, J. (1988). Post-Freirian adult education: a question of empowerment and power. *Adult Education Quarterly, 39*(1), 1–47.

Zikode, S. (2006a). Transcribed speech at the Centre for Civil Society and Rosa Luxemburg Foundation Colloquium, 4 March 2006, UKZN, Durban.

Zikode, S. (2006b). The greatest threat to future stability in our country. Harold Wolpe memorial lecture, Durban, July 2006.

Zikode, S. (2006c). Presidential message (to the 1st AGM of Abahlali baseMjondolo). Izwi Labampofu, December 2006, v.1, issue 1.

Zikode, S. (2008a). Land and housing. Speech at Diakonia Council of Churches Economic Justice Forum, Durban, 28 August 2008.

Zikode, S. (2008b). Post Annual General Meeting speech, Durban, 14 December 2008.

AFFILIATION

Anne Harley
Centre for Adult Education
University of KwaZulu-Natal

ELISABETH STEINKLAMMER

2. LEARNING TO RESIST[1]

Hegemonic Practice, Informal Learning and Social Movements

RESISTANCE!

In the fall of 2009, widespread resistance "from below" emerged at Austrian universities and kindergartens. Resistance was against, to name but a few areas addressed by the protesters, the underfunding of education, the re-structuring of educational institutions according to market mechanisms and their orientation towards the preparation of students for business life (Steinklammer, 2007). Beginning with the kindergarten sector ('Collective Kindergarten Rebellion', http://www.kindergartenaufstand.at), the first protests were staged in the spring of 2009 (Steinklammer, Botka, Fleischmann and Tinhofer, 2010). In the autumn students and teachers from universities (#unibrennt, http://www.unibrennt.at), addressed not only the unacceptable general conditions and chronic underfunding of Austrian educational institutions, but also raised the issue of how learning took place and what was being learned in those institutions. The resistance movement in the field of education shaped the year 2009 in Austria. It made more Austrians pay attention to and reflect upon the topic of education. But what effect did this resistance have on the people involved? What kind of learning processes took place in the course of this resistance?

Figure 1. Banner of the collective kindergarten rebellion
© collective kindergarten rebellion.

B. L. Hall, D. E. Clover, J. Crowther and E. Scandrett (Eds.), Learning and Education for a Better World: The Role of Social Movements, 23–40.

In this chapter I examine the question of what can be/was learned by participating in the protests through the lens of critical education and what conclusions can be drawn for this critical learning through social conflicts. I begin this chapter with a brief overview on two central analytical categories of critical education theory: power relations and hegemony. I argue that to sustain a certain hegemonic order not only is the adaptation of a certain ideology necessary but also those of hegemonic practices. I continue with a discussion of subjective hegemonic instances of stability and informal learning-in-practice in order to open a discussion of learning processes that illustrates the internalisation and adoption of practices that sustain hegemony. I then apply these theoretical constructs to some examples of the education protests in order to discuss and outline several tasks and areas of work relating to critical education theory.

CRITICAL EDUCATION, POWER AND SOCIETY

Central to critical approaches to education is the analyses of the human being and his/her learning in social contexts. In the 1970's and 80's, in particular the critical theory of the Frankfurt School but also the works of Paulo Freire and Antonio Gramsci constituted an important point of reference for critical education theorists in Western Europe. In recent years a number of critiques and refinements have made reference to feminist theories, theories of international political economy, postcolonial and anti-racist approaches, cultural studies, psychological theories and many more (Lösch and Thimmel, 2010).

At the same time critical education doesn't remain simply a theory but claims that education should have an empowering, emancipatory effect and should help to overcome oppression within society. Moreover,

> Critical learning extends the learner, moves her beyond her current understanding. [...] Emancipatory learning involves learning generating emancipatory action (Foley, 2004, p. 105).

These emancipatory claims are based on analyses of power and leadership relations, in both society and education. Yet power is not something that humans or social groups simply possess. Power rather represents a relation between ruling classes or factions and those subjected to domination (Demirovic in Bescherer and Schierhorn, 2009). That is to say, power originates from the relations between individuals or between groups and the different ways these groups are integrated into one and the same society (Becksteiner, Steinklammer and Reiter, 2010). Therefore, different factors of integration have to be taken into account such as the questions of division of labour, of gender relations, everyday culture, family structures, migration and much more. Every model of society presupposes a specific way of shaping and producing ways of life, ways of thinking, and cultural coexistence, which correspond to the requirements of the material productive forces (Merkens, 2007a). Therefore in critical debates on education one recurring theme is that socially organised education processes can be understood as attempts of the ruling group(s) not to leave learning processes to chance, but that capitalist societies are characterised by providing significant resources to educate young people so that "the social division of labour can be reproduced, renewed and dynamically changed" (Demirovic, 2010, p. 70*[2]). In our example one can argue that by linking the controversies about general conditions in educational institutions with the questioning of dominant concepts of education in society and their correspondence with supposed requirements of the material productive forces, the education protests countered existing power relations. By putting the reduction of education to economic utility up for debate the current neo-liberal forms of social integration were attacked by the movement, by opposing the idea of the human as homo economicus which reduces and psycho-physically adjusts human beings to their economic utility and applicability and by holding wide-ranging discussions about concepts of education and definitions, the current neo-liberal forms of social integration were attacked by the movement. Thereby it is essential to recognise that power and relations of domination do not have to be established and maintained by force. Power can also be established and stabilised if social groups succeed in defining and enforcing their own interests and the social formations that go along with them as common social interests (Brand and Scherer, 2003). This type of domination is generally referred to as hegemony. The debates and actions within the education movement in Austria can therefore be (partly) understood as forms of counter hegemony, as I will elaborate later on.

Hegemony and its Subjective Instances of Stability

Hegemony as an analytical concept of critical education theories refers to a type of domination that is not based on direct force but on the leadership and consensus of a large part of the population. The latter adopts and supports the ideology of the dominant social group as their own meaningful and action-guiding interpretation of the world, as guiding principle, without the exertion of direct force being necessary.

> Hegemony describes how a dominant group can project its particular way of seeing social reality so successfully that it's view is accepted as common sense, as part of the natural order, even by those who are in fact disempowered by it (Borg and Mayo, 2008, p. 30).

In order to implement a hegemonic project, the interests of the (future) leading group have to be generalised so that they acquire a progressive function for the entire society. This includes that the needs and interests of the subaltern have to be rearticulated and redefined so that they are represented in the hegemonic order (Candeias, 2007). Consequently Gramsci's concept of hegemony essentially includes two aspects: political hegemony (political leadership and organisation of different political groups) and cultural hegemony (establishing consensus; reaching a leading position in the creation and maintaining of consensual cultural, moral and intellectual mentalities of a society) (Bernhard, 2005). By squatting and protesting the education protest movement questioned certain aspects of the current cultural hegemony in Austria for the first time in years. This was a new experience to many as in most cases people are not aware of the effectiveness of political and cultural leadership. The dominant worldview seems like the natural order, and is taken for granted. Its historical and social context is obscured. The emancipatory approaches of critical education concepts (for example the work of Paulo Freire in 1970) therefore imply that the educational goal of consciousness raising to counter our unconsciousness of these power relations as the basis of overcoming oppression.

A characteristic of this type of domination is that people adopt and reproduce the conception of a specific hegemonic social order, even if they occupy a subaltern position within it and even if this order is opposed to their own interests. The education protests for example challenged the current conception of gender relations especially in the kindergarten sector. One goal of the 'Collective Kindergarten Rebellion' was and is, to change, as women, the image of this profession in society and to challenge the image of the female kindergarten teacher (99% of all employees are women), who is always friendly and puts up with everything; even tough working conditions that are harmful to their health and in obvious violation of current labour legislation. Articles and pictures of fighting pedagogues were published. For the first time many women experienced what it means to stand up, fight for better working conditions and social appreciation. Conversations with activists revealed that the self-images of many pedagogues were changed through the struggles they were involved in (Steinklammer et al., 2010).

But theoretically speaking one has to consider that adopting or opposing a certain ideology alone is not enough to hegemonically secure and reproduce or challenge a specific social order. In addition, practices that support or oppose hegemony need to be created and adopted. Practices represent meaningful socially acceptable and standardised modes of acting by means of which subjects are able to integrate themselves into the hegemonic constellation in their respective personal surroundings. Lipietz (1988) writes that social relations are

> Embodied in individuals…in the form of acquired habits and routines, like the accepted rules of a game, even if everyone seeks to improve his game. The capacity of a dominant group to impose a game that benefits it will be called hegemony (p. 13).

This quotation draws attention to several aspects central in the production and maintenance of hegemony and therefore, important to critical or emancipatory education. The "rules of the game" can be understood as socially accepted and approved behaviour corresponding to the respective situation, behaviour to which acting subjects adapt themselves and which ensures that the 'game' remains stable over a relatively long period of time, even though the process of establishing and maintaining hegemony includes counteractions by individuals as well as contradictions that arise from within. Hegemonic 'rules of the game', however, are characterised by the fact that they determine how these contradictions are to be dealt with, and they ensure that the resistance of individuals does not threaten the social order. This makes it hard to predict if and when contradictions erupt and suddenly 'challenge the expectations of routine social behaviour' (Kurzman 2005,

p. 5). In Austria, for example, most of the existing critical political groups and organisations were altogether overtaken by the beginning of the protests and played a minor role within.

Habits, on the other hand, are long-term continuous practices we repeat on a regular basis, almost like a ritual that becomes ingrained. Most of the time we no longer perform these actions consciously, but rather in a taken-for-granted, almost automatic way because they belong to us, they have become part of us, have been embodied in us.

Therefore, when looking at social practices and their hegemonic meaning it becomes apparent that order and existing relations of domination are not maintained from the outside alone, but deeply inscribed into us – even into the body – and as a result are reproduced and stabilised in our practices. Thus, processes must take place that result in cultural hegemony being deeply embedded in the acting subjects. According to Gramsci (1971) 'every relationship of hegemony is necessarily an educational relationship' (p. 350) existing between individuals and social groups, in so far as the production, challenge, reproduction and transformation of consciousness and practice or consent primarily take place through teaching and learning processes. Some of these are formally organised but a large part are informal learning processes. This has to be taken in account by emancipatory education approaches and developed further.

A SOMEWHAT DIFFERENT VIEW OF INFORMAL LEARNING PROCESSES

For this reason I will continue to examine the question of what role informal learning-in-practice, that takes place apart from the organised processes in educational institutions, could play for the question of empowerment from the perspective of critical education.

Learning by Participating in the Social World

As a first step to approaching this issue, it is necessary to take an even closer look at specific learning processes and to further elaborate on thoughts of how hegemonic practices are acquired.

Human beings are social beings, who are made to live together and who only adopt social behaviour with and through participation in the social world. Actions/practices (as distinguished from instincts and reflexes) are not something predestined, innate, or fixed, but are socially developed and learned in interaction with others. It is learning that takes place in practice, while we participate in the social world that surrounds us. Markard (2008, p. 154*) argues that

social conditions/meanings [...] are integrated into the experiences of individuals made in concrete situations.

The individual appropriates the world by learning, takes his/her place in society, and participates in its formation. Thus the individual is shaped by his/her experiences with the surrounding world and his/her acquired knowledge about the world. At what point experience becomes learning and how this process works, has, to this day, not been resolved (Foley 2004). It is a case of informal learning, however, that occurs while participating in the social world that surrounds us.

The social world constitutes a reference point for our actions, a socially and culturally pre-structured framework that we adopt by participating in it and by interacting with others and to which we attribute meaning. This attribution of meaning itself happens in the process of our practice, as

> it is doing in a historical and social context that gives structure and meaning
> to what we do. In this sense, practice is always social practice (Wenger 2008,
> p. 47).

Thus participation in the social world is the basis for the production of meaning and for the structuring of our actions. It not only shapes how we appropriate the world, how we understand, attribute meaning to and act within it, but also how we see ourselves, our taste, our relationships to our own bodies and how we interpret our own actions as well as the actions of others and so forth.

> Experience of meaning [...] is what practice is about. [...] Meaning arises out
> of a process of negotiation that combines both participation and reification
> (Wenger 2008, p. 135).

One has to consider that the meanings of facts of the world represent possibilities for action or restrictions of action to which we can but do not have to relate (Holzkamp, 1995; Allespach, 2008). This does not determine our actions, but the meaning we attribute to things and how important they are to us has a bearing on if and how we relate to them. In this respect, practices and the enforcement of practices sustaining hegemony cannot be seen in isolation from the internalisation of an ideology and the adoption of a specific worldview whose establishment and reproduction is again always based on practices. As Lave and Wenger (2008) summarize it:

> Learning, thinking, and knowing are relations among people in activity in,
> with and arising from the socially and culturally structured world. This world
> is socially constituted (p. 51).

Hence the considerations here go beyond the socialisation processes of our childhood since these learning processes continue to take place through our participation in the social world. On the one hand, we repeatedly enter new communities of practices (e.g. at work, at university, in political groups, etc.) in the course of our lifes and have to integrate ourselves into their collective practices and on the other hand, as Lave and Wenger (2008) indicate, social practice in itself is contradictory and these contradictions have to be worked out and negotiated anew each time, no matter if the aim is to change them or to maintain what already exists. Maintaining and reproducing the status quo needs as much experience, explanation and learning as changing it would need.

We learn in and by experiences, how we can, should and are allowed to behave according to the respective situation. In the course of these informal learning processes we internalise the existing social conditions and develop a practical sense – what Bourdieu calls habitus – "for what is to be done in a given situation" (Bourdieu, 1998, p. 25). In this learning process the social order is adopted as a way of seeing the social and is internalized as part of our practical sense (Bremer, 2010). We develop an intuitive knowledge of the world, its contexts and conventions. The practical sense can be understood as the unconscious dimension of actions and practice, as a direct, intuitive understanding of the world that is related to what is expected of the world and of the actions of other agents. The acquired explicit rules, the lived regularities and habits provide agents with orientation and stability. Their practical sense stabilises the inner balance by enabling them to adequately react to interpellations of the social environment. As a consequence, it does not only contribute to the maintenance of the social order, but also tends to contribute to the maintenance of existing power relations (McDonough, 2006), – by drawing on their practical sense, that they have built over a long period of time, human beings permanently rebuild structures of domination in their daily actions.

The example of the kindergarten protests shows this rather clearly. The working conditions have been bad for quite some time (at least 10 – 15 years) and kindergarten teachers were complaining about it a lot on an individual basis. At the same time many of them realized that their position within society gives kindergarten teachers rather effective power resources- there are not enough pedagogues and therefore it should be easy to get concessions from the employers. Furthermore, if they would go on strike many other production areas would be affected and the pressure would be high. Nonetheless, nothing happened and employers were able to shift the effects of staff shortage on to the employees. What we see here is that since our practical sense influences our conception of the social world and of our position in it, it also influences the perception of our possibilities for action – that is, how we can act in a certain situation – but also the perception of the position that can be and is taken in the struggle for change or maintenance (Schroer, 2006). As mentioned above, the facts of the world do not determine our actions. Mostly we have different options, if and how we relate to them. Nevertheless we are shaped by social structures, by our incorporation into the social context, and by the existing relations of power. We all know situations in which we have different possibilities for action. Sometimes those are clear to us and we consciously choose one or the other, but often this decision is made unconsciously, in the course of action, without giving it much thought. Sometimes we are not even aware that we have different options and just do what we see as our only option. Experiences made within specific social positions as well as informal learning processes that have taken place – the developed practical sense – promote the fact that, human beings are more susceptible to some options for action than to others. Their preferences have adapted themselves to their respective surroundings and the demands perceived within them. They have developed adaptive preferences for specific options for action and the practical sense blocks the perception or (in the case of the Austrian kindergarten teachers) activation of alternative options, as this acquired collection of schemes of perception and appreciation directs the individual's focus of action entirely towards their integration into the hegemonic constellation. How dominant these schemes are became clear after the first protests and demonstrations were staged successfully with more than 4.000 kindergarten teachers in Vienna. Existing hegemonic negotiation structures between trade unions and employers were activated by the establishment and these managed to channel and hush dissident moments by offering small improvements of working conditions, a ridiculous low pay raise (in some cases only € 0.40.- cent) and the promise of reforms that employees are still waiting for. Yet, protests have calmed down and it has become more and more difficult to mobilise the employees.

PRACTICE, INFORMAL LEARNING PROCESSES AND CRITICAL EDUCATION

What conclusions can we draw from the above considerations for critical education and its claim that education should have an empowering effect? To begin, I would argue that when looking at the informal learning of (hegemonic) practices it becomes clear that cultural hegemony permeates all aspects of our subjectivity, not only our consciousness or worldview. The acquired practical sense as unconscious principle of production of practices is structured by practice and at the same time has a structuring effect. Hence, reflection and consciousness-raising are important aspects of empowering education processes. They alone, however, are not sufficient, as the practices of the subjects are of essential importance for the internalisation and reproduction of relations of power and domination. These practices again are deeply embedded in us and in our practical sense. In order to fight against the effectiveness of cultural hegemony, it is necessary to work on the elements of domination, on the practical sense within us as well.

> In his/her subjectivity, consciousness, corporality the human being is rooted in cultural hegemony, from which s/he can only be released by radically fighting its influence within him/herself. Therefore, each critical concept of education today is necessarily connected with the perspective of resistance. Education itself is to be understood as an attitude of resistance against one's own habitus that is functional with regard to existing relations of power and domination. By attacking this habitus, education creates the condition for the possibility of releasing resistant actions against destructive projects of dominant social groups (Bernhard, 2010, p. 94).

Thus it is necessary to connect the claims that education should have an empowering effect with the perspective of resistance.

RESISTANT LEARNING AND LEARNING HOW TO PUT UP RESISTANCE

By doing so several tasks and areas of work present themselves for critical education. In the following I will discuss them in the context of the education protests.

Resistant Learning

A central conclusion drawn from the considerations set out above is that resistance is necessary in order to work on and change one's own practical sense. Thus, resistant learning directed at challenging and changing one's own practical sense is needed. This includes two essential aspects.

Figure 2. Squatting teachers' flyer
© Squatting teachers Vienna.

On the one hand, there are calls for critical education processes which create space for learning subjects to distance themselves from their own practice, to contextualise it, and to connect it with an analysis of social conditions (Becksteiner et al., 2010). Their own practical sense has to become the object of consciousness-raising processes and reflection in order to remove it from the unconscious and to challenge it. This is a precondition for recognising adaptive preferences and directing one's attention to alternative ways of acting or developing new options for action. Bernhard 2010 comes to similar conclusions when he argues that

> Insofar as a human being recognizes that his/her habitus is not an imposed fate, but [that] it represents a social form of altering human nature, s/he will basically be put in a position to offset it (p. 98).

He further argues that this consciousness-raising and reflection are tasks for critical education, because education constitutes an anti-habitual attitude, in which the human being critically decides again and again on his/her consciousness and relation to the world rather than letting it become affirmative. Education is not a habitus, but a force that objects to every kind of habitualisation of habits that chains the human being to what already exists (p. 98).

On the other hand, this cannot be done in isolation from practice, since the practical sense is structured by practice and at the same time has a structuring effect. Therefore, practical experiences and action learning are necessary for a new practice to be developed and for the practical sense to be worked in interaction with the social world. Within the education protests, numerous efforts to develop such alternative practice can be identified: for example the emancipatory orientation of the protesters and their aiming for a decentralised, grass-roots democratic organisation within the movement. These attempts encountered several limitations and challenges the protesters had to take on and deal with, which was an important learning experience itself. Thereby they adapted and developed their practice further and had to constantly reflect on it. Another example of action learning in the protest movements were the so-called 'Volxküchen' (derived from the German word "Volksküchen", which literally means "people's kitchens") that were established rather fast and maintained by volunteers cooking donated food and provided meals for free in return for a voluntary donation. For certain people involved in the protest this was a new experience of handling food and enabled them to experience other forms of supplying goods beyond capitalism. The establishment of the 'Collective Kindergarten Rebellion' can be interpreted as an attempt to develop a distinct practice of networking and of defending one's interests as a base, since they aimed at providing themselves with the opportunity of exchange, reflection, articulation of concerns, discussion and of political decision-making processes that went beyond those of the usual, hierarchical interest groups and trade union structures (Collective Kindergarten Rebellion 2011, p. 7).

Figure 3. Daily plenum, in the main auditorium of the University of Vienna
© #unibrennt.

My thesis is that in the examples mentioned above, as well as in many other examples, an unconscious reworking of the practical sense took place, or, since alternative forms of practice could be experienced, the practical sense was changed little by little. At the same time, we have to bear in mind that our practical sense is in itself relatively stable and cannot be changed abruptly overnight. After all, the dispositions, schemes of perception and appreciation, and structuring principles of a human being have developed over a long period of time and the purpose of this unconscious collection is to give stability to us and our actions so that we can find our way in the world. That is why the reworking and change of the practical sense can only be achieved in the long term and always requires new experiences that then can be reflected upon and adapted. Bremer (2010) states that for a long lasting transformation of one's habitus,

It is important that social subjects are also able to have new experiences. These experiences are to be understood as bodily performed actions [...] and the reflection upon them (p. 189).

The examples mentioned above already show, however, that it is difficult to organise such learning experiences in planned educational processes. In social conflicts such informal learning processes are much more likely to take place. However, there is the danger that these learning experiences remain covert and unconscious and, without conscious educational processes in which those resistant and empowering experiences of practice can be taken up or used as point of departure, they cannot fulfil their full empowering potential (Foley, 2004). Thus a task of critical education is to provide the space to bring those informal learning processes to consciousness, to reflect on them and to develop further strategies for action in exchange with others. By doing this, their own resource of experiences should become clearer so that it can be resorted to in other situations. As Foley (2004) stated very clearly, it also needs "the special powers of theory" (p. 50) as basis for critical reflection. He argues that

This is the creative paradox of consciousness-raising work: personal experience is its necessary point of departure, but for critical consciousness to emerge people must gain theoretical distance from their subjective experience (pp. 50–51).

In this respect he quotes Hart (1990a) who states that theory

Does not follow the contours of immediate experience. It 'sets a distance' which enables people 'to fathom aspects of the world hidden from the eyes of its own authors and actors' and to make transparent the relations that obtain among isolated and fragmented incidents of personal experience (pp. 66–67).

When looking at informal, resistance learning, the necessity of linking theory and practice, or processes of consciousness-raising and experiences of practice, becomes apparent. Practically speaking, this means that critical education has to relate consciousness-raising to social struggles. It is a question of learning in practice and of combining theory and practice.

"How to Put Up Resistance" has to be Learned as Well

Another essential conclusion regarding learning to resist can be drawn on another level. After all, opposing one's own habitus means to question and challenge social conditions, that is, to offer resistance. In the education protests, this challenge of a dominant worldview and social order has clearly taken place, even if it was not always explicit and not intended by everyone. Putting up resistance and questioning hegemonic social conditions cannot be taken for granted, however, and does not necessarily represent an adaptive preference for most of us. Otherwise it would not be considered a hegemonic relation of domination if it were not consensually accepted. From this, two conclusions can be drawn for critical education.

Developing a Practice of Resistance

If resistance does not represent an adaptive preference for most of us, this means that there are few experiences that we can draw or build on in this context. Thus also a practice of resistance first has to be developed and learned. In the example of the education protest movement, such learning occurred in the experimentation with alternative forms of resistance like flash mobs and other forms of political activism. It also became clear, however, that protesters have to constantly make traditional forms of protest like demonstrations their own again. The experience of claiming the public space in the course of demonstrations, of taking to the streets, taking this space and articulating their political intent, was something new and unfamiliar to many in the kindergarten sector, something they had to learn to deal with. After experiencing the first demonstration how hard it was for many of the participants to voice their discontent and demands and to make noise, the next demonstration was an experiment to start with something closer to their previous practical experiences and to adapt elements that have an empowering effect; for example, by setting new, political lyrics to tunes of popular children's songs and singing them together during the demonstration, which turned out to work much better than shouting demands. Another example of developing a practice of resistance is the establishment and use of autonomous communication and organization structures in the Web 2.0 or the use of new information technologies for the self-organisation of the students' protest movements. This organization in Web 2.0 represents a significant resource of knowledge, since by using these structures as communication platforms, information is stored for a long time, and that way campaigns and discussions are documented within the movement (Note the enormous amount of photos: http://www.flickr.com/groups/unibrennt), to which people can return at a later time or in another context and from which they can learn.

Figure 4. Flash mob of kindergarten teachers in Vienna 2009
© collective kindergarten rebellion.

From the conclusion that a practice of resistance first has to be developed and learned emerge several tasks for critical education- like fighting for, providing and maintaining autonomous space for reflection and learning in which the parties involved can work out how they want to politically work together and in which new forms of cooperation can be developed. An example of such an attempt is the 'Critical and Solitary University of Vienna' (http://krisu.noblogs.org) that was founded on the initiative of students, teachers and staff from different institutes and universities.

Since resistance does not represent an adaptive preference, it can be concluded for critical education that a learning process conceived for the long run is needed, one that takes place in several learning loops. Practically speaking, this means that periods of learning in practice have to alternate with periods of reflection and development of alternative options for action and then with periods of implementation in order to try to strategically implement a different practice step by step. In another learning loop these attempts again have to be reflected upon and the process starts all over again. Thus the long-term conception would make it possible for the learning process to contain theory and practice, yet it also assumes that critical education takes place in social conflicts or is related to them (Becksteiner et al., 2010).

Taking Up and Communitarising Dissident Elements

At least one other conclusion can be drawn from the fact that resistance is not necessarily an adaptive preference for many of us. Just because this might be the case in principle, it does not have to mean that, in the creation and maintenance of hegemony contradictions do not arise. Dealing with them successfully does not always have to be possible within the existing order. Thus, time and again dissident elements express themselves within us. They often remain hidden, below the surface, however, and are therefore elusive and difficult to grasp. Since these elements of dissent, as well as the attitudes and acts of resistance that might go along with them, remain sporadic and hidden, their impact is limited. From the perspective of critical education it is necessary to take up these elements, to seize and communitarize them. It is not only a question of processes of consciousness, but also of the informal learning that takes place while participating in the protests, in the resistance. Similar to the demonstrations in the kindergarten sector, amongst the people who put up resistance in the university protests were not only those who wanted to make a stand against economic utility, but also those who felt deprived of the possibility to prepare themselves for neoliberal competition (Kratzwald 2009). Because the growing experiences of contradiction in the existing system could no longer be successfully dealt with within, groups joined the resistance not questioning the hegemonic ideology itself but its corresponding with experienced possibilities to integrate themselves into it. Paulo Freire already stated 1988 that

> Conscientization is not exactly the starting point of commitment. Conscientization is more of a product of commitment. I do not have to be already conscious in order to struggle. (Freire 1988 in McLaren, Fischman and Serra 2002, p. 172).

Figure 5. "No comment" protests of students in Vienna 2009
© *#unibrennt.*

This implies that experience/ informal learning is one important basis for conscientization and not the other way round. However, as Foley points out, this learning in action is often not recognised as such and therefore might remain only potential. (Foley 2004) What seems important is that through being part of the movement (for which reason so ever) all groups could gain alternative experiences of practice/resistance and that informal learning processes took place to which they can return to at a later point. Once people were involved in the protest movement, they challenged the existing hegemonic order together and had to experience firsthand, if leadership by consensus starts to crumble, the element of hegemonic force would become more apparent. In the course of the education protests, learning through participation in the social world (as basis for the production of meaning and for the structuring of our actions) meant, in concrete terms, the people involved, who all had different motives, could make many concrete learning experiences about their own involvement in social conditions, power structures and their own subalternity. These practical experiences are a necessary (also bodily and sensual) precondition for being able to locate oneself in the ensemble of social conditions and for developing something like class consciousness. In the educational processes it is essential to seize and reflect upon these experiences of subalternity, but also of community, solidarity, and the experienced differing interests. From this follows the task of constant awareness-raising in the context of practice that changes society.

LEARNING TO RESIST – A CHALLENGE FOR CRITICAL EDUCATION

When looking at practices that sustain hegemony, at informal learning, and at social conditions internalised as practical sense, it becomes apparent that critical education has to make the learners' practical sense the object of processes of consciousness-raising, and that a process of reflection is necessary that encompasses the acting human being in his/her historical and social entirety. This should serve as a basis for developing alternative options for action. As a point of departure for working on one's own practical sense, however, informal learning processes and practical experiences of resistance are needed as well. In addition, action learning is called for in which a new practice can be developed in practice, just as education loops are necessary, in which those can be reflected upon and adapted. The basis for this is a combination of theory and practice as well as of consciousness-raising and struggles in society.

However, this orientation towards learning to resist in all facets presents us with several challenges. Not only is there the task of creating and maintaining autonomous space for learning and reflection, but the question also is how to organize such partly informal learning processes. Learning and education processes within institutions clearly are the centre of attention of all parties involved. Even if learning in institutions does not always happen voluntarily, and even if the question of which parts of the planned curriculum and which other aspects (also of the hidden curriculum) are in fact learned remains unanswered, the reason for being there as well as the orientation and aim of the process are clear to all parties involved. In social conflicts instead, the orientation and goals are others than that participants should learn within them. Learning rather takes place incidentally, often it is not intended, and it mostly occurs unconsciously (Foley 2004).

At that point a shift in the pedagogical approach to learning is called for. There has to be more emphasis on the importance of voluntary and spontaneous learning processes directly tied to the collective political practice and experiences of social movements. This has to be taken as a starting point for planned education processes (Merkens 2007a). Thus it is necessary to pursue pedagogy from the viewpoint of the learners and to act accordingly. This can mean that self-initiated learning processes are supported, taken up and further developed together. Therefore one can try to allocate space in existing institutions and to grant it to the learners or to create new learning space together with the learners. Pedagogy from the viewpoint of the learners can also mean, however, to start from the experiences of the conflicts and to plan and shape educational processes together with the learners.

The shift in the pedagogical approach to learning also involves the necessity of a changed (self-) image of teachers and those accompanying the educational process. They have to assume the role of organic intellectuals and see themselves as such. Gramsci describes organic intellectuals as being culturally involved in social movements and being part of the process themselves (Merkens, 2007b). To Gramsci the task of organic intellectuals is – as counter-concept to the traditional notion of intellectuals as thinkers in the ivory tower–the "active participation in practical life" (Gramsci 1971, p. 10).

This means their practice has to aim at setting out a systematic critique of the common sense, in which the social struggles of today are reflected (Merkens 2006, pp. 18–19*).

In conclusion, it is important to stress that more research and reflection is needed on how human beings learn and what they learn in empowering struggles.

According to the view developed here, this research process would have to be devised as critical self-research, and as a combination of theory and practice it would have to relate the research to social conflicts and to allow for exchange between them.

NOTES

[1] A longer and slightly different version, in German, of this article has been published in: Sandoval, Marisol/ Sevignani, Sebastian/ Rehbogen, Alexander/ Allmer, Thomas/ Hager, Matthias/ Kreilinger, Verena (Ed.) (2011). University burns! Education, Power, Society, Verlag Westfälisches Dampfboot, Münster

[2] All quotations marked with a * are translated by the author.

REFERENCES

Allespach, Martin (2008). Bedeutsamkeit als Grundkategorie einer partizipativen Bildungsplanung und als Voraussetzung für expansives Lernen in der betrieblichen Weiterbildung, In: Faulstich, Peter/Ludwig, Joachim (Ed.) (2008). Expansives Lernen. Grundlagen der Berufs- und Erwachsenenbildung, Band 39, Schneider Verlag Hohengehren GmbH, Baltmannsweiler, pp. 220–231.

Becksteiner, Mario/ Steinklammer, Elisabeth/ Reiter, Florian (2010). Betriebsratsrealitäten – Betriebliche Durchsetzungsfähigkeit von Gewerkschaften und Betriebsräten im Kontext der Globalisierung, ÖGB Verlag, Wien.

Bernhard, Armin (2005). Antonio Gramscis Politische Pädagogik. Grundriss eines praxisphilosophischen Erziehungs- und Bildungsmodells. Argument Verlag, Hamburg.

Bernhard, Armin (2010). Elemente eines kritischen Begriffs der Bildung, In: Lösch, Bettina/Thimmel, Andreas (Ed.) (2010). Kritische politische Bildung. Ein Handbuch, Wochenschau Verlag, Schwalbach, pp. 89–100.

Bescherer Peter/ Schierhorn Karen (Ed.) (2009). Hello Marx. Zwischen »Arbeiterfrage« und sozialer Bewegung heute. VSA Verlag, Hamburg.

Borg, Carmel/Mayo, Peter (2008). Curriculum as Political Text, Power Point Presentation for the workshop "Gramsci, Freire and Political Education", on 5/6 December 2008 in Vienna.

Bourdieu, Pierre (1998). Practical Reason: On the Theory of Action, Stanford University Press, Stanford.

Brand, Ulrich/ Scherrer, Christoph (2003). Contested Global Governance: Konkurrierende Formen und Inhalte globaler Regulierung. Renner Institut, Akademie für internationale Politik, http://www .renner-institut.at/download/texte/brand_scherrer.pdf [22 Dec. 2010].

Bremer, Helmut (2010). Symbolische Macht und politisches Feld. Der Beitrag der Theorie Pierre Bourdieus für die politische Bildung, In: Lösch, Bettina/Thimmel, Andreas (Ed.) (2010). Kritische politische Bildung. Ein Handbuch, Wochenschau Verlag, Schwalbach, pp. 181–192.

Candeias, Mario (2007). Gramscianische Konstellationen. Hegemonie und die Durchsetzung neuer Produktions- und Lebensweisen. In: Merkens, Andreas/Regio Diaz, Victor (Ed.) (2007). Mit Gramsci arbeiten. Texte zur politisch-praktischen Aneignung Antonio Gramscis, Argument Verlag, Hamburg, pp. 15–32.

Collective Kindergarten Rebellion (2011). Kollektiv Kindergartenaufstand ist mehr als Arbeitskampf, In: Malmö (2011/ Nr. 57): Occupy Christkindlgarten 2012, p. 7 (or online: http://www.malmoe.org/ artikel/widersprechen/2346 [06.01.2012])

Demirovic, Alex (2010). Bildung und Gesellschaftskritik. Zur Produktion kritischen Wissens, In: Lösch, Bettina/ Thimmel, Andreas (Ed.) (2010). Kritische politische Bildung. Ein Handbuch, Wochenschau Verlag, Schwalbach, pp. 65–76.

Foley, Griff (2004). Learning in social action. A contribution to understanding informal education, Zed Books.

Freire, Paulo (2000/1970). Pedagogy of the Oppressed, Continuum, London, New York.

Gramsci, Antonio 1996. Gefängnishefte. Kritische Gesamtausgabe, Band 7, Herausgegeben von Bochmann, Klaus/Haug, Wolfgang Fritz/Jehle, Peter unter Mitwirkung von Graf, Ruedi/Kuck, Gerhard. Hamburg/Berlin (Argument-Verlag).

Hart, M. (1990a). Liberation through conscoiusness-raising. In: Mezirow, J. (Ed.) (1990). Fostering Critical Reflection in Adulthood, Jossey-Bass, San Francisco.

Holzkamp, Klaus (1995). Lernen. Subjektwissenschaftliche Grundlegung. Campus Verlag, Frankfurt/ New York.

Kratzwald, Brigitte (2009). Für eine solidarische Universität in einer solidarischen Gesellschaft, In: Plattform MASSENUNI (Ed.) (2009). Jenseits von Humboldt. Von der Kritik der Universität zur globalen Solidarischen Ökonomie des Wissens, MHFdlv: Plattform Massenuni, Wien, pp. 15–17.

Kurzman, Charles: The unthinkable revolution in Iran, First Harvard University Press, 2005.

Lave, Jean/Wenger, Etienne (2008). Situated learning. Legitimate peripheral participation, Cambridge University Press, New York.

Lipietz, Alain (1988). "Accumulation, crises and ways out: some methodological reflections on the concept of regulation", In: International Journal of Political Economy, Summer 1988, pp. 10–43.

Lösch, Bettina/Thimmel, Andreas (Ed.) (2010). Kritische politische Bildung. Ein Handbuch, Wochenschau Verlag, Schwalbach.

Markard, Morus (2008). Lehren/Lernen als methodisch organisierte (Selbst-) Kritik ideologischer Standpunkte der Subjekte, In: Faulstich, Peter/Ludwig, Joachim (Ed.) (2008). Expansives Lernen., Grundlagen der Berufs- und Erwachsenenbildung, Band 39, Schneider Verlag Hohengehren GmbH, Baltmannsweiler, pp. 150–160.

McDonough, Peggy (2006). Habitus and the practice of public service. In: British Sociological Association (Ed.) (2006; 20). Work Employment Society, pp. 629–647, SAGE Publications http://wes.sagepub.com/cgi/content/abstract/20/4/629 [22 Dec. 2010].

McLaren, Peter/Fischman, Gustavo/Serra, Silvia (2002). The Specter of Gramsci: Revolutionary Praxis and the Committed Intellectual, In: Borg, Carmel/Buttigieg, Joseph/Mayo, Peter (2002). Gramsci and Education, Rowan & Littlefield Publishers, Plymouth, pp. 147–178.

Merkens, Andreas (2006). Hegemonie und Gegen- Hegemonie als pädagogisches Verhältnis. Antonio Gramscis politische Pädagogik, Hamburger Skripte 15, Rosa-Luxemburg- Bildungswerk Hamburg, Hamburg.

Merkens, Andreas (2007a). Die Regierten von den Regierenden intellektuell unabhängig machen. Gegenhegemonie, politische Bildung und Pädagogik bei Antonio Gramsci, In: Merkens, Andreas/Regio Diaz, Victor (Ed.) (2007). Mit Gramsci arbeiten. Texte zur politisch-praktischen Aneignung Antionio Gramscis, Argument Verlag, Hamburg, pp. 157–174.

Merkens, Andreas (2007b). Antonio Gramscis politische Pädagogik, Power Point Presentation for the Gramsci Symposium on 15 December 2007 in Vienna.

Schroer, Markus (2006). Räume, Orte, Grenzen. Auf dem Weg zu einer Soziologie des Raums, Suhrkamp, Frankfurt am Main.

Steinklammer, Elisabeth (2007). Wer will denn schon, dass alle Menschen mündig sind? – Die pädagogischen Konzepte von Antonio Gramsci und Paulo Freire im Vergleich. Möglichkeiten die sich daraus für eine Politische Bildung heute ergeben, University of Vienna, Vienna.

Steinklammer, Elisabeth/ Botka, Kristina/ Fleischmann, Gloria/ Tinhofer, Barbara (2010). Aufstand ist (k)ein Kinderspiel, In: Perspektiven Nr. 10, pp. 36–43, Wien, http://www.perspektiven-online.at/2010/08/26/aufstand-ist-kein-kinderspiel [22 Dec. 2010].

Wenger, Etienne (2008). Communities of Practice. Learning, Meaning and Identity, Cambridge University Press, New York.

EURIG SCANDRETT

3. SOCIAL LEARNING IN ENVIRONMENTAL JUSTICE STRUGGLES: A POLITICAL ECOLOGY OF KNOWLEDGE

This chapter builds on theoretical discussions of learning in environmental justice movements based on empirical research in Scotland and India (see Scandrett et al., 2010), and develops these insights into social movement learning, using the theoretical resources of political ecology. I will argue that political ecology allows us to understand environmental justice struggles, not as disparate NIMBY localisms or peripheral forms of environmentalism, but as a distinctive species of social contestation in response to the current stage of capitalism. There is no uniform agreement amongst scholars working in political ecology on how to interpret the role of social movements in resistance to capitalism, but the terrain of analysis is fruitful for understanding where learning may be generated through dialogue between knowledges in struggles against capitalism.

Although much has been written over the past twenty years on political ecology (Blaikie, 1999; Robbins, 2004), the political economy of adult education (Foley, 1999; Holst, 2001) and ecological education (Sterling, 2001; Scott and Gough, 2003; Walter, 2009), there has been little explicit attempt to address the connections between these, nor the lessons each might have for the others. Elsewhere I have argued that popular education can be employed to generate a discourse on environmental justice which is accountable to communities directly affected by pollution (Scandrett, 2007) and that environmental justice struggles provide insights into the relationship between material interests and learning in social movements (Scandrett et al., 2010). Here I seek to develop this analysis, and propose that a political ecology analysis leads to a distinctive approach to social movement learning.

Before introducing political ecology, it is valuable to summarise aspects of social movement theory and adult education theory that can help us to think about learning in movements. There are at least three categories of theoretical question which can be employed when seeking to interpret social movement learning: What theories of *social movements* help us to understand learning in social movements?; What theories of *adult education* help us to understand learning in social movements?; What theories of *society* help us to understand learning in social movements? This third question is important because theoretical understandings of society affect how we understand social movements and their roles in contributing to social change, as well as the generation and interpretation of knowledge, which

B. L. Hall, D. E. Clover, J. Crowther and E. Scandrett (Eds.), Learning and Education
for a Better World: The Role of Social Movements, 41–56.
© 2012 Sense Publishers. All rights reserved.

constitutes key aspects of learning. Many of us involved in social movement learning research share with the social movements we study, a commitment to particular visions and forms of social change, and so our role as researchers and educators is offered as a contribution to social movement activity for a better world.

SOCIAL MOVEMENT THEORIES

Theories of social movements have been extensively outlined elsewhere (see, for example, McAdam, McCarthy and Zald, 1988, Eyerman and Jamison, 1991 chapter 1, della Porta and Diani, 2006, Ruggiero and Montagna, 2008, Goodwin and Jasper, 2009, Annetts et al., 2009) and it is not proposed to repeat here the standard, if contested accounts of the development of theorising about social movements with which sociologists have been involved, primarily since the 1960s. These can be crudely summarised in terms of theories which focus primarily on activists, those focusing on movement organisation and those interested in social change.

Theories which primarily address the actors and activists in social movements tend to be interested in motivation, experience, communication, networks, identity and frame development, and are often inspired by symbolic interactionist traditions in sociology (eg Mellucci, 1996, Snow and Benford, 1988, della Porta et al., 2006). Those whose primary unit of analysis is the organisations and organisation of social movements have often drawn on functionalist or Weberian sociology, and include such diverse approaches as social strain theory, resource mobilisation theory and political process theory (eg Tilly, 1978, McAdam, 1982). Both interactionist and functionalist approaches primarily developed in the USA although with a number of followers in Europe. European traditions of social movement theory have tended to draw on Marxist sociology and focus attention on the relationship between social movements and socio-economic structures, and include new social movement theory, cognitive praxis, structural and systems theories as well as more mainstream Marxist theory (eg Touraine, 1981; Habermas, 1989; Eyerman & Jamison, 1991; Cox & Nilsen, 2007; Annetts et al., 2009).

Whilst the sociology of social movements has certainly produced committed advocates of one or another theoretical approach – including the more militant paradigm warriors (Tarrow, 2004) – there have been attempts to bridge the divisions and to draw on the breadth of theoretical approaches in seeking to explain the development and fortunes of social movements. One significant division which remains, however, is that between the, largely North American traditions of understanding social movements as phenomena of collective action *within* society, and the approach originating in Europe, and critically embraced by scholars from the global South, of interpreting social movements in terms of their potential for and role in social *change*. This has resulted in contestation and some confusion in even defining what social movements are, the North American scholars tending to include a wide range of phenomena involving collective action, from NGOs to religious cults, fashions to street riots, to the point where generalisation has at times been problematic. Sociologists in the European/Southern tradition have tended to include as social movements, only those phenomena which are engaged in a politics of contestation in which demands are made on powerful groups, social elites or political structures, with the objective of obtaining concessions or else revolutionary transformation. At times this approach has been criticised (eg della Porta and Diani, 2006) for dismissing from analysis such collective action whose objectives are not 'progressive', or else of interpreting social movement activity as nothing more than another form of class struggle.

Notwithstanding these criticisms, the approach taken here can be located within this 'social change' tradition. The purpose of understanding social movements, and generating theory about them and the learning which occurs within them, is to contribute to the dynamic changes in society of which social movements are part, and selectively to identify social movements – and forms of learning – which are emancipatory, and distinguish from those which are reactionary. In this context, it is argued that political ecology provides an analysis which is both theoretically robust and normatively progressive.

Moreover, recent developments in social movement theory have emphasised not only the contribution of theoretical work to social movements themselves, and the importance of theorists to be accountable to the social movements which they study, but also the significant amount of theory which is generated within social movements. Bevington and Dixon's (2005) movement-relevant theory does not categorically reject earlier theoretical perspectives, but instead seeks to glean what is most useful *for movements* from these earlier works. Likewise, this emergent direction entails a dynamic engagement with the research and theorizing already being done *by movement participants* (p. 185).

For those working in the field of adult education, this approach resonates with conceptions of really useful knowledge and popular education in which scholarly knowledge is interrogated by movements of the oppressed for its value in interpreting and promoting their own material interests. Such material interests embedded within knowledge are exposed through dialogical methods such as popular education and lifelong education (Freire, 1972; Gelpi, 1979; Griffin, 1983; Kane, 2001; Crowther, Martin and Shaw, 1999; Scandrett at al, 2010).

This then takes us to the interface between, on the one hand, the structured educational processes which are sometimes employed within social movements based on a range of methods derived from Freire, Illich, Boal, Rogers and community organising and consensus decision making techniques; and on the other hand the informal and incidental learning and knowledge generation within social movements through political practice, repertoires of contestation (Tilly, 2004) and collective reflection (Foley, 1999; Field, 2005): in short, between what may be called *popular education* and *incidental learning*. Incidental learning in social movements has been noted by a number of social movement theorists. Krinsky and Barker (2009), working with an urban movement defending public services in the USA, analysed the role of strategising as a learning process, which served to radicalise the group's demands. Nilsen (2006, 2010), working in the movement against the damming of the Narmada River in central India, identified movement processes in which resistance to everyday tyranny at a local level was learned through 'discovery, confrontation and transmission', subsequently became more coherent as a 'militant particularlism', which developed into a generalised campaign, drawing on 'conflictual learning' and 'counter-expertise'. The final phase of movement learning in Nilsen's analysis is where activists must engage in the complex labour of joining the dots between their struggles in order to build a capacity for hegemony that can challenge the totality in which these struggles are embedded. (Nilsen 2010, p. 201)

Of course not all incidental – or indeed all structured – learning, even in social movements, is dialogical, but the structured methods are designed to encourage that dialogical interrogation between the concrete and the abstract, or the experiential and the canonical etc. However, incidental learning does, at times, have the character of dialogical interrogation of knowledge which leads to the process of critical analysis which Freire calls conscientisation. This form of incidental learning in social movements, which has the dialectical character of popular education but without its structure, (or the 'methodology' as distinct from the 'method' of popular education, Scandrett, Crowther and McGregor (In Press)) remains under-researched.

ENVIRONMENTAL JUSTICE STRUGGLES

Elsewhere, empirical research into environmental justice struggles in Scotland and India has been described (Dunion and Scandrett, 2003; Scandrett, O'Leary and Martinez, 2005; Scandrett, 2010b; Mukherjee and Scandrett, 2010; Crowther et al., 2009; Scandrett et al., 2010; Hemmi, Crowther and Scandrett, 2011). In Scotland, activists from a number of communities involved in environmental justice struggles participated in structured popular education programmes facilitated by the environmental NGO Friends of the Earth Scotland (FoES) and Queen Margaret University. Two of these communities were subsequently the focus of empirical research into social movement learning: Scoraig, a small, rural community in the North-West of Scotland campaigned against the locating of salmon farms in adjacent sea-lochs. Through exposure to FoES' environmental justice campaign, their initial narrative, based on aesthetics and romanticisation of wild nature, developed a political dimension which challenged control of the littoral zone and sea bed by a public body – the Crown Estates – behaving as a private, profit maximising business. In Greenock, women employed in a National Semiconductor factory experienced cancers and gynaecological problems through exposure to chemicals in the workplace. Their self-help group recognised the political nature of their illness, built connections with both trades union and environmental campaigners, and mobilised to challenge the company and collusion by health services. In both cases, the structured popular education programme was not the cause of mobilisation or politicisation, nor even the primary source of learning, but rather contributed analytical tools through which knowledge obtained elsewhere (from experience, the internet, sympathetic academics, trade union officials, environmental activists, allies within environmental regulatory and health agencies etc) could be assessed, selected, critiqued and made 'really useful' to their struggles (e.g. Scandrett, 2010a).

Indian case studies include several campaign groups of survivors of the Bhopal gas disaster (Mukherjee et al., 2011; Scandrett and Mukherjee, 2011) and community resistance to pollution in SIPCOT, Cuddalore, Tamil Nadu (SACEM and CEM 2010; Shweta Narayan, personal communication). In Bhopal, the majority of activists are not literate and have little or no experience of formal or structured education of any kind. In this case, it has been argued, incidental learning has occurred informally, through political praxis and engaging with others in struggle ('joining hands to join the dots' Alf Nilsen, personal communication), but also, significantly, through 'discursive encounters' (Baviskar, 2005) with other social movements. It is suggested that a dialogical process occurs between the militant particularism of the local movement and the abstraction offered by contact with wider social movements, which allows for a framing of experience and learning to occur within such frames (Scandrett et al., 2010; Scandrett and Mukherjee, 2011). The discursive encounter is not the process of learning but rather provides a structured framework for such dialogue to occur, much as popular education is able to, usually more effectively. Such a dialogical process may be said to be similar to structured popular education in the selection and construction of 'really useful knowledge' through dialogue between knowledge borne of collective experience and practice, and abstract, analytical and canonical knowledge.

This can lead to divergent results however. Scandrett and Mukherjee (2011) suggest that rival groups within the Bhopal survivors' movement have utilised differing abstractions for explaining their militant particularism. The International Campaign for Justice in Bhopal (ICJB), a coalition of small survivor and solidarity groups, interpret their struggle in terms of environmental justice, build alliances with large environmental NGOs such as Greenpeace and anti-toxics groups (largely made up of cosmopolitan Indian and international professional middle class activists) and other pollution impacted communities, and their learning occurs within a frame which privileges the analysis of environmentalism. An alternative group, the *Bhopal Gas Peedit Mahila Udyog Sangathan* (BGPMUS, Bhopal Gas Affected Women Workers' Union), has built alliances with adivasi, dalit, peasant, workers' and poor peoples' movements, frames their struggle in terms of class, and learning is driven by class analyses.

In the case of SACEM, activists from villages affected by the development of chemical factories and other polluting industries have been trained in observing and monitoring for pollution incidence, including sampling for chemical analysis, and volunteers regularly mobilise their communities to challenge the industries. Contrary to allegations of Flowers and Swan (2011) about the food movement, activists in SACEM, ICJB, Scoraig and Greenock have all engaged dialogically with scientific knowledge, neither demonising nor reifying science and recognising conflicting interests in the production of scientific knowledge. Expert science is interrogated for its 'really useful knowledge' content, its material interests and class bias exposed and alternative forms of scientific production offered. Where there is little evidence of this is in BGPMUS which privileges a class analysis and whilst utilising specialist technical expertise from sympathetic academics who share a class analysis, demonstrates little interest in the interrogation of the scientific knowledge produced.

In summary therefore, I have argued for a theoretical approach to social movement learning derived from the 'social change' tradition in social movement theory which is more or less rooted in Marxist sociology – but without neglecting the insights of other social movement theories for interpreting the agency of social movement organisation and activists – and insights from the 'dialectical' tradition in adult education in which learning occurs through both structured events and movement praxis. This takes us to the political economy analyses of adult education (Foley, 1999; Holst, 2001) in which education and learning is understood in terms of its dialectical relation to socio-economic conditions of production, both reproducing and challenging the logic of capitalist development. However, weaknesses in the political economy analysis have been identified, particularly in relation to its inadequate explanation of the relations between socio-economic dynamics and the ecological resources and conditions on which it depends and within which it is located. It is to this question that political ecology is primarily addressed, and which environmental justice movements provide a pivotal case.

POLITICAL ECOLOGY

Political ecology is a contested approach to the study of social relations (see Peet and Watts, 1996) occupying analytical space encompassing ecology (environmentalism or ecologism *sensu* Dobson, 2000) and (Marxist) political economy. The relative degree of emphasis on these two poles defines whether political ecology is regarded primarily a development of ecological analysis or of political economy. Robbins (2004), by contrasting political ecology with 'apolitical ecology', regards the former as a variant of ecological analysis, which nonetheless highlights political and social processes, especially inequalities of power (Bryant and Bailey, 1997), which shape and are shaped by ecological systems.

By contrast, Blaikie and his co-workers (Blaikie and Brookfield. 1987; Blaikie, 1999; Springate-Baginski and Blaikie, 2007, see also Guha and Martinez-Alier, 1998) locate political ecology as essentially a political economy of ecological processes, environmental science and environmental policy. For example, Springate-Baginski and Blaikie (2007, pp. 9–11) outline the "four main strands of political ecology" which comprise:

- "the contested ways in which biophysical ecology is interpreted and negotiated ... [the] politics of science ... [and] other knowledge ...
- "structural explanations of the ways in which different groups gain access to [ecological resources] ...
- "the dialectical relationship between ecology and society [which are understood in a] strong historical sense ...

- "[a] critical understanding of how environmental policy is made, the exercise of power, practices on the ground and the discourses that shape them at different levels."

Haywood (1994) has proposed that political ecology constitutes a threefold critical development of Marxist political economy through ecological theory: First, the insights of ecological Marxism (eg. Benton, 1996; O'Connor, 1998; Harvey, 1996; Capital and Class, 2000; Bellamy Foster, 2000; Magdoff and Bellamy Foster 2010), which regard ecological resources either as potential means of production to be dispossessed by capital for the purposes of accumulation (Harvey's (2005) 'accumulation by dispossession') or else as a component of the conditions of production which are in dialectical conflict with both the forces and relations of production (O'Connor's (1996) 'second contradiction of capitalism'). Second, following the analysis of feminist Marxists, production must be differentiated from reproduction, and capitalist production must then be understood within the context of (ecological) reproduction; and Third, ecological analysis brings the recognition that ecology transcends conditions of production or reproduction: i.e the ecological analysis is not reducible to Marx's political economy.

From an economic perspective, Martinez-Alier (2002) locates political ecology as the incorporation of political economy within ecological economics. Where economic systems are understood as flows of resources and energy governed by forms of valuation, social conflicts over the distribution of ecological resources reflect competing languages of valuation. In particular the 'environmentalism of the poor' emerges from social movements of people whose environmental resources are threatened with valuation by chronocistic cost-benefit analysis. By presenting alternative, incommensurable values through social struggle, such movements challenge neoclassical market economics and its response to environmental problems as 'externalities' to be 'internalised' to a market system.

> one can see externalities not as market failures but as cost-shifting successes which nevertheless might give rise to environmental movements. Such movements will legitimately employ a variety of vocabularies and strategies of resistance, and they cannot be gagged by cost-benefit analysis or by environmental impact assessments (Martinez-Alier, 2002 p. 257).

Although Martinez-Alier does not highlight the fact, the processes of developing and articulating alternative narratives and languages of valuation of environments is essentially a learning process. Martin O'Connor (2000) analyses the interactions between knowledge and valuation in the context of attempts to manage competition over scarce resources, so that social learning occurs through a process of negotiating different knowledge sources about resources and articulating their valuation. In the more contested context of social movements, this is likely to be more acute since the power differentials between conflicting parties will be more explicit.

Political ecology therefore is concerned with what is known about the ecological, physical and social environment in which human societies are situated, how actors with differential access to power know about it, what values are attached to it, especially by social movements of the dispossessed, and how this dynamic relationship might evolve in the direction of social and ecological justice. This emphasis on knowledge, value and justice makes political ecology a crucial insight into education and learning in the context of ecological destruction. In other words, a political ecology of learning in social movements seeks to build on adult education theory which is grounded in Marxist political economy (see, for example, Foley, 1999) whilst recognising the developments in the latter from the perspective of ecology (Benton, 1996).

CONTRASTING POLITICAL ECOLOGIES OF SOCIAL MOVEMENTS

In order to move from political economy to political ecology, the relations of production need to be interpreted in their ecological context. From ecological economics, the economy must be understood as a through-flow of materials and energy in constant interaction with ecological resources (mineral, biological, geophysical) and systems (carbon and water cycles, climatic systems etc): Thus, not only are social relations properly understood in relation to economic forces, but also these economic forces can only be understood in relation to the environment in which they are situated, from which they derive materials and energy and into which they deliver these same materials and energy in a less useful form as waste. The laws of thermodynamics determine that materials are never created or destroyed; the economy can only ever reconstitute and convert these into a useful form through the input of energy. In the absence of energy input, these materials tend towards increasing entropy, or disorder. In natural systems, physical and ecological cycles reconstitute materials into forms used within the ecosystem through the input of energy primarily from photosynthesis. So long as economic activity extracts materials and generates waste at a rate within the capacity of the ecological cycles to absorb, then permanent damage is largely avoided. However, as Marx noted in the exploitation of soil (Marx, 1990 p. 637), and as many ecologists have increasingly highlighted since the middle of the 20th Century, the capacity of the ecological systems to regenerate resources is not unlimited, and in a number of contexts, limitations are being reached or breached. The social implications of this in terms of social movement learning can be analysed by the contrasting analyses of James O'Connor and David Harvey.

James O'Connor usefully contrasts Marx's primary contradiction of capitalism, between the *relations* and *forces* of production, manifest in the conflicting interests of labour and capital, with the 'second contradiction' of capitalism, between the relations and forces of production and the *conditions* of production. This second contradiction is manifest between the interests of capital accumulation and that of the environment (both ecological and social) in which production takes place. In practical terms, this conflict is seen in the exhaustion of natural resources, the accumulation of pollution, the despoliation of natural and built environments, the deterioration in public and workers' health, the distribution of investment and neglect of urban environments, conflicts over distribution of consumption (eg food and fuel poverty), the gendered conflicts over reproduction and domestic divisions of labour, and disruption to the living conditions of workers and livelihoods in non-capitalist forms of production.

O'Connor further suggests that the second contradiction of capitalism leads to a distinctively different form of social movement conflict than that between capital and labour. Conflicts over the conditions of production emerge in the form of environmental movements, especially of those most directly affected by pollution and environmental degradation – the environmental justice movements. Such contradictions also emerge as contestations over land, fisheries, forests and other natural resources, urban space, workers' health and safety, housing, feminist movements, tribal and indigenous people's movements, anti-displacement and movements of displaced people and migrants. In studies of enterprise zones in Mexico, where trades unions are banned and employment conditions and environmental protection regulations relaxed, Sklair (2001) identified low levels of industrial conflict involving workers, but highly contested land dispossession.

An alternative political ecology account of the emergence of environmental justice movements comes from David Harvey's thesis of 'accumulation by dispossession'. Rather than a new, 'second contradiction' of capitalism, Harvey describes many of the same phenomena as a re-emergence of primitive accumulation during the neoliberal phase of capitalist expansion, essentially bringing into capitalist relations previously uncommodified resources. This includes

> The commodification and privatisation of land and the forceful expulsion of peasant populations ...; conversion of various forms of property rights (common, collective, state etc) into exclusive private property rights; suppression of rights to the commons; commodification of labour power and the suppression of alternative (indigenous) forms of production and consumption; colonial, neo-colonial and imperial processes of appropriation of assets (including natural resources); monetisation of exchange and taxation, particularly of land; the slave trade (which continues particularly in the sex industry); and usury, the national debt and, most devastating of all, the use of the credit system as radical means of primitive accumulation. (Harvey, 2006 p. 43)

Under such conditions, social movements emerge which are fragmented and particular, their common source obscured. Solidarity therefore is often expressed, not in material terms but universals, such as discourses on human rights, thereby seeking a different form of accommodation with capital than labour movements have in material terms through social democratic welfarism.

In an address to the World Social Forum in 2010, Harvey located the various emergent movements in dialectical relations to each other, and the socio-economic and cultural milieu (Harvey, 2010). These inter-relationships may be regarded as 'moments' of social process (Harvey, 1996) comprising the political economy (class conflict); externalities (pollution and environmental destruction); accumulation by dispossession (expropriation of land and other resources); the conditions of production (socio-ecological environment required for capitalist production); reproduction ('free' services, largely from ecological cycles and women's labour); and nature (as yet uncommodified).

In summary, Harvey, O'Connor and Martinez-Alier all offer analyses of social movements based on political ecology which may be drawn on in understanding their emergence as resistance to current conditions of capitalism, and therefore with opportunities for interpreting learning in support of such resistance. Where Harvey's and O'Connor's scope overlap there is a disagreement, which we need not address here, although their analyses offer useful interpretations of differing phenomena. Harvey's interpretation of accumulation by dispossession applies particularly to the forcible incorporation of non-capitalist processes into capitalist relations, whereas O'Connor's can be attributed to points where capitalist accumulation reaches limits as a result of resource constraints or the socio-environmental damage caused by its own operation. In the former case, once brought into capitalist relations, fragile resources might rapidly reach limits, whereas in the latter case, at its limits, capitalism is forced to innovate, including identifying new rounds of accumulation by dispossession. Both processes involve attempts to apply capitalist cost-benefit analysis to non-market resources, including the natural environment and human health, which is resisted by movements of the dispossessed through alternative valuations. Such valuations emerge from forms of knowledge, which reject the logic of capital accumulation, through a process of learning and interrogation of knowledges with the potential of becoming really useful.

Scoraig might be regarded as accumulation by dispossession as fish farm development is an attempt to commodify the littoral zone of Lochs Broom, without reference to the environmental costs. These costs are resisted through narratives, which posit aesthetic, naturalistic and ultimately democratic values against the language of economic benefit. Bhopal on the other hand is better understood as a conflict in the conditions of production, in which the logic of capital expansion is limited by the moral unacceptability of large-scale slaughter of the poor in an industrial disaster. Such a tension has been played out in political struggle in India, between 'business as usual' (typified by the 1989 'settlement' between Union Carbide and Government of India and in the post 1991 neo-liberalisation of the Indian economy) and alternative valuations from the survivors' movements which prioritise health and environmental quality.

IN CONTRAST: SUSTAINABLE DEVELOPMENT LEARNING

Adopting a political ecology analysis contrasts with a dominant approach to understanding learning in the context of the interaction between social, economic and ecological processes, illustrated in the work of Scott and Gough (2003). Scott and Gough argue that social, economic and ecological interrelationships lead to situations of such complexity and with inherent uncertainty that it is not possible to discern relations of oppression, or to identify a direction of social change which achieves greater social justice. On the contrary, they argue, complex problems can only be addressed through expansive and open ended social learning processes, tackling problems simultaneously from several different viewpoints. They therefore argue for *meta-learning*, a collective social process which is able to harness diverse learning situations working with multiple epistemologies. Insights from diverse formal and informal processes of learning in concrete situations are systematically distilled at a higher organisational level. Thereby, whole societies are able to learn what is necessary for sustainable development to occur.

This approach gives the appearance of undermining power structures and challenging interests

> The question of understanding sustainable development and related learning revolves not around *how* to sustain things, but about *whose* things it is proposed to sustain, *what* is to be developed in *whose* interests, and *who* is to be encouraged to learn *what*. (Scott and Gough, 2003 p. 26, original emphasis)

However, these interests are interpreted ideally. Scott and Gough's understanding of social change denies the dynamics of material interests and their role in sustaining oppressive social relations. Their analysis ignores the role of social movements, or indeed structural conflictual relations. Complexity is used to obfuscate dialectical social processes: meta-learning reifies complexity and collapses structural contradictions into incommensurable epistemologies.

This leads Scott and Gough to a pluralist interpretation of learning in the context of interactions between social, economic and ecological processes. Learning, for them, is directionless and pragmatic, without ambition to contribute to emancipatory social change. They are dismissive of popular education and the radical adult education tradition on the mistaken grounds that it attempts to impose an analysis and a solution and therefore to exclude others. Such learning

> Tends to be associated with a particular egalitarian project in which superior social knowledge – which dismisses contrary opinion as either selfishness or false consciousness – coupled with socialist managerial ingenuity, will create a collectivist utopia. (ibid, p. 49)

On the contrary, it is the dialectical nature of learning in social movements, whether popular education or incidental learning, which ensures that really useful knowledge is neither reified nor relativised, but tested against emancipatory struggle through praxis. Whilst epistemologies may be multiple, they are not infinitely so but are rather constrained or made possible by material conditions. A political ecology approach to knowledge recognises this dialectic in the context of material social, economic and ecological relations.

CONCLUSIONS

Political ecology analysis explains the emergence of a diversity of social movements including, centrally, environmental justice movements. These may be interpreted as a re-emergence, during neoliberal capitalist expansion, of new forms of primitive accumulation, described as accumulation by dispossession (Harvey, 2005), or else as conflicts between the relations of production and the productive conditions in which it they are situated (O'Connor, 1998. Such movements redefine contestations through confronting capitalist expansion with alternative, incommensurable valuations based on diverse knowledges. Within this context learning may take place as a dialectical interrogation of knowledge from the perspective of struggle, and may occur through structured popular education or incidental learning, and in a complex relationship between the two as values and knowledge interact. Incidental learning occurs prior to and as a result of structured popular education, but is affected by such experience through dialogue with knowledge to discern what is 'really useful'. At the same time, incidental learning, even in the absence of structured popular (or indeed didactic) education, can take place through alternative processes, such as in discursive encounters with other movements, in which the methodology, if not the method of popular education occurs.

Moreover, with the increasing commodification of canonical knowledge, the professional class, which has been central to the production and consumption of knowledge, achieved significant influence in the 20th century and forms the principal support base of mainstream environmentalism, is likely to decline. Learning in environmental justice struggles therefore is likely to play an important role in engendering social change in resistance to capitalism.

If we are to understand social movement learning, it is important to recognise social processes which generate social movement activity at any particular stage of development of capitalism, to interpret how such social movement activity facilitates learning and to discern where such learning involves a dialectical interrogation of knowledge for the production of 'really useful knowledge'. Within that context it may be possible for adult educators and researchers, with commitment to struggle, contribute and subject their own contribution to radical critical interrogation to expose its own interests. Political ecology provides such an analysis, where disparate movements responding to accumulation by dispossession and conflicts in the conditions of production, both through their praxis and through structured education, are able to obtain, critique and use instrumental, analytical and normative in support of their struggles and the possibilities of socially just relations beyond struggle.

REFERENCES

Annetts, J., Law, A., McNeish, W. & Mooney, G. (2009). *Understanding social welfare movements* Bristol: Policy Press.
Baviskar, A. (2005). 'Red in Tooth and Claw? Looking for Class in Struggles over Nature'. In Ray, R. and Fainsod Katzenstein, M. (Eds.), *Social Movements in India.* New Delhi: Oxford.
Bellamy Foster, J. (2000). *Marx's Ecology: materialism and nature* New York: Monthly Review Press
Benton, T. (1996). *The Greening of Marxism* Guilford Press.
Bevington, D. & Dixon, C (2005). 'Movement-relevant Theory: Rethinking Social Movement Scholarship and Activism'. *Social Movement Studies, 4*(3), 185–208.
Blaikie P. M. & Brookfield, (1987). *Land Degradation and Society.*
Blaikie, P. M. (1999). 'A review of political ecology' *Zeitschrift fur Wirtschaftsgeographie. 43,* 131–147.
Bryant, R. L. & Bailey, S. (1997). *Third World Political Ecology* London: Routledge.
Capital and Class, (2000). *Environmental Politics: Analyses and Alternatives* Special Issue: Capital and Class *72.*

Cox, L & Nilsen, A. G. (2007). 'Social Movements Research and the 'Movement of Movements': Studying Resistance to Neoliberal Globalisation'. *Sociology Compass*, *1*(2), 424–442.

Crowther, J. Martin, I. & Shaw, M. *Popular Education and Social Movements in Scotland Today* Leicester: NIACE.

Crowther, J., Hemmi, A., Martin, I. & Scandrett, E. (2009). 'Real and virtual margins of resistance: the struggle for environmental knowledge and the contribution of information and communication technologies to campaigning.' In Evans, R. *Local development, community and adult learning – learning landscapes between the mainstream and the margins*. Magdeburg: Nisaba Verlag.

della Porta, D., Andretta, M., Mosca, L. & Reiter, H. (2006). *Globalization from Below: Transnational Activists and Protest Networks*. Social Movements, Protest and Contention Volume 26 London: University of Minnesota Press.

della Porta, D. & Diani, M (2006). *Social Movements: an introduction*. Oxford: Blackwell.

Dobson, A. 2000 *Green Political Thought* London: Routledge.

Dunion K. & Scandrett E. (2003). 'The campaign for Environmental Justice in Scotland as a response to poverty in a Northern nation.' J Agyeman, R Bullard & B Evans (Eds.), In *Just Sustainabilities: Development in an unequal world*.

Eyerman, R. & Jamison, A. (1991). *Social Movements: a Cognitive Approach*. Cambridge: Polity Field, J. 2005 *Social Capital and Lifelong Learning*, Bristol: Policy Press.

Flowers, R. & Swan, E. (2011) Eating at us: food knowledge and learning in food social movements. *Studies in the Education of Adults*. *43*(2), 234–250.

Foley, G. (1999). *Learning in Social Action: A Contribution to Understanding Informal Education* London: Zed Books.

Freire, P. (1972). *Pedagogy of the Oppressed* London: Penguin.

Gelpi, E. (1979). *The Future of Lifelong Education* Manchester: University of Manchester Press.

Gelpi, E. (1985). *Lifelong Education and International Relations* London: Croom Helm.

Goodwin, J. & Jasper, J. (2009). *The Social Movements Reader* Chichester: Wiley-Blackwell.

Griffin, C. (1983). *Curriculum theory in adult and lifelong education* New York: Nichols.

Guha, R. & Martinez Alier, J (1998). 'From Political Economy to Political Ecology' in *Varieties of Environmentalism: Essays North and South* ed by Ramachandra Guha and Joan Martinez Alier. London: Earthscan.

Habermas, J. (1989). *The Structural Transformation of the Public Sphere* Cambridge MA: MIT press.

Harvey, D. (1996). *Justice, Nature and the Geography of Difference* Oxford: Blackwell.

Harvey, D. (2005). *A Brief History of Neoliberalism* Oxford: Oxford University Press.

Harvey, D. (2006). *Spaces of Global Capitalism: Towards a Theory of Uneven Geographical Development* Oxford: Oxford University Press.

Harvey, D. (2010). 'Organizing for the anti-capitalist transition' *Interface: a journal for and about social movements*, *2*(1), 243–261.

Haywood, T. (1994). 'The Meaning of Political Ecology' *Radical Philosophy*, *66*, 11–19.

Hemmi, A., Crowther, J. & Scandrett, E. (2011). 'Environmental activism and "virtual social capital": help or hindrance?' in Fragoso, A., Kurantowicz, E. and Lucio-Villegas, E. (Eds.), *Between Global and Local: Adult Learning and Development* Frankfurt: Peter Lang Internationaler Verlag der Wissenschaften.

Holst, J. D. (2001). *Social Movements, Civil Society, and Radical Adult Education*. London: Bergin & Garvey.

Kane, L. (2001). *Popular Education and Social Change in Latin America*. London: Latin America Bureau.

Krinsky, J. & Barker, C. (2009). 'Movement Strategizing as Developmental Learning: Perspectives from Cultural-Historical Activity Theory'. In *Culture, Social movements and Protest*. H. Johnston (Ed.), Farnham: Ashgate. pp. 209–226.

McAdam, D. (1982). *Political Process and the Development of Black Insurgency: 1930–1970* Chicago: University of Chicago Press.

McAdam, D., McCarthy, J. D. & Zald, M. N. (1988). *Comparative Perspectives on Social Movements: Political Opportunities, Mobilising Structures, and Cultural Framings.* Cambridge: Cambridge University Press.

Magdoff, F. & Bellamy Foster, J. (2010). 'What every environmentalist needs to know about capitalism'. *Monthly Review, 61*(10), 1–30.

Martinez-Alier (2002). *Environmentalism of the Poor: a study of ecological conflicts and valuation.* Cheltenham: Edward Elgar.

Marx, K (1990). [1867]. *Capital, Volume 1.* Trans. Ben Fowkes. London: Penguin Books.

Melucci, A. (1996). *Challenging Codes: Collective Action in the Information Age.* Cambridge: Cambridge University Press.

Mukherjee, S., Scandrett, E., Sen, T. & Shah, D. (2011). 'Generating Theory in the Bhopal Survivors' Movement' in Motta, S.C. and Nilsen, A.G. (Eds.), *Social Movements in the Global South: Dispossession, Development and Resistance* Basingstoke: Palgrave Macmillan.

Nilsen, A. G. (2006). "I release you, fear": building subaltern power in the context of everyday tyranny. In Barker, C. and Tyldesley (Eds.), *Alternative Futures and Polular Protest – Conference Papers* Manchester Metropolitan University.

Nilsen, A. G. (2010). *Dispossession and Resistance in India: The river and the rage.* London: Routledge.

O'Connor, J. (1998). *Natural Causes: Essays in Ecological Marxism.* London: Guilford Press.

O'Connor, M. (2000). "Pathways for Environmental Evaluation: A Walk in the (Hanging) Gardens of Babylon", Special Issue on Social Processes for Environmental Valuation. *Ecological Economics, 34*, 175–193.

Peet, R. & Watts, M. (1996). *Liberation Ecologies: Environment, Development, Social Movements* New York: Routledge.

Ruggiero, V. & Montagna, N. (2008). *Social Movements: A Reader* London: Routledge.

Robbins, P. 2004 *Political Ecology* London: Routledge.

SACEM & CEM (2010). *Activity Report of SIPCOT Area Community Environmental Monitors (SACEM) December 2003 to December 2009* Chennai: SIPCOT Area Community Environmental Monitors and Community Environmental Monitors. www.sipcotcuddalore.com. accessed August 2011.

Scandrett, E (2007). 'Environmental justice in Scotland: policy, pedagogy and praxis' Environ. Res. Lett. 2 045002 (7pp) http://stacks.iop.org/ERL/2/045002

Scandrett, E. (2010a). 'Popular Education in the University'. In Amsler, S. Canaan, J. E., Cowden, S. Motta, S. and Singh, G. (Ed.), *Why critical pedagogy and popular education matter today.* Birmingham; C-SAP.

Scandrett, E. (2010b). 'Environmental justice in Scotland: Incorporation and Conflict'. In Davidson, N., McCafferty, P. and Miller, D. (Ed.), *NeoLiberal Scotland: Class and Society in a Stateless Nation.* Cambridge: Cambridge Scholars Publishing.

Scandrett, E., Crowther, J., Hemmi, A., Mukherjee, S., Shah, D. and Sen, T. (2010). 'Theorising education and learning in social movements: environmental justice campaigns in Scotland and India'. *Studies in the Education of Adults, 42*(2).

Scandrett, E. Crowther, J. and McGregor, C. (In Press). 'Poverty, protest and popular education in discourses of climate change' in Carvalho, A and Peterson, T. R. (Eds.), *Climate Change Communication and the Transformation of Politics,* London: Cambria.

Scandrett, E. & Mukherjee, S. (2011). 'Globalisation and abstraction in the Bhopal survivors' movement' *Interface: a journal for and about social movements, 3*(1), 195–209.

Scandrett E., O'Leary T. and Martinez T. (2005). 'Learning environmental justice through dialogue' in *Proceedings of PASCAL conference: Making Knowledge Work.* Leicester: NIACE.

Scott, W. & Gough, S. (2003). *Sustainable Development and Learning: Framing the Issues.* London: RoutledgeFalmer.

Sklair, L. (2001). *The transnational capitalist class.* Blackwell, Oxford.

Springate-Baginski & Blaikie (2007). *Forests, people and power: the political ecology of reform in South Asia* London: Earthscan.

Snow, D. A. & Benford. R. D. (1988). 'Ideology, Frame Resonance and Participant Mobilization,' *International Social Movement Research, 1*, 197–219.

Sterling, S. (2001). *Sustainable Education: Re-Visioning Learning and Change* Totness: Green Books.

Tarrow, S. (2004). 'Paradigm Warriors: Regress and Progress in the Study of Contentious Politics' in Jeff Goodwin and James Jasper (Eds.), *Rethinking Social Movements: Structure, Meaning and Emotion* Lanham, MD: Rowman and Littlefield Publishers.

Tilly, C. (1978). *From Mobilization to Revolution* Reading MA: Addison-Wesley.

Tilly, C. (2004). *Social Movements 1768–2004*. Boulder, VO: Paradigm.

Touraine, A. (1981). *The Voice and the Eye: an Analysis of Social Movements* Cambridge: Cambridge University Press.

Walter, P. (2009). Philosophies of adult environmental education. *Adult Education Quarterly, 60*(1), 3–25.

JIM CROWTHER AND EMILIO LUCIO-VILLEGAS

4. RECONNECTING INTELLECT AND FEELING: MARX, GRAMSCI, WILLIAMS AND THE EDUCATOR'S ROLE

INTRODUCTION: PESSIMISM OF THE INTELLECT

Remarkable events are often those that go by unremarked. One of these is the lack of public debate about the democratic impact of the economic crisis of 2011–12. In Greece, a new government was formed without a popular mandate led by a so-called 'technocratic' leader (in reality a former European banker) vouching an austerity programme to appease the markets; a similar process happened shortly afterwards in Italy, although the reputation of its feckless and self-serving leader Berlusconi resulted in few regrets at his removal. He was nonetheless legitimately elected and deposed primarily, it would seem, as a result of US credit rating agencies giving the Italian economy the 'thumbs down'. Suddenly, these previously obscure credit agencies with dubious records of financial assessments (e.g. on Standard and Poor's record see the *New York Times* Feb. 6th 2012, p. 4) appear to have greater political muscle than democratically elected governments.

Moreover, the Euro crisis resulted in the European Union (EU), led by governments in France and Germany, agreeing to reformulate the Union's constitution to centralise power and control member countries' public expenditure. Whilst these discussions were going on, US credit rating agencies threatened all EU governments with a potential down grading of their credit status, presumably to galvanise attention on the need for public sector spending cuts. The only voice of opposition came from the UK's Conservative led coalition government, whose leader was primarily concerned with appeasing a powerful group of isolationist politicians on the far right of his own party and protecting the City of London's financial sector from regulation – although lack of financial regulation was a key factor in the global economic collapse. Despite serious economic problems in the UK economy, the political fortunes of the coalition are riding high with no sign that welfare cuts are reversing the government's popularity. Moreover, an annual survey of attitudes in the UK shows for the first time that a majority of people blame the poor for their own poverty (*The Guardian*, December 2011, p. 8). Deep cutting austerity measures have public credibility as a response to economic crises.

In other parts of Europe, with the exception of France, when democratic elections took place in Spain and Portugal, the popular vote moved sharply to the ideological right in support of austerity politics aimed at a reduction in social welfare and public expenditure. Traditional 'left wing' political parties appear to

B. L. Hall, D. E. Clover, J. Crowther and E. Scandrett (Eds.), *Learning and Education for a Better World: The Role of Social Movements*, 57–68.

have no answer to the crisis and pose no genuine alternatives. In Spain, the former socialist government initiated severe reductions in social welfare, which paved the way for a historic victory of the political right. In the UK, the Labour Party in opposition seeks electoral support for less severe austerity programmes and espouses a commitment to 'responsible capitalism' i.e. the rich should show personal restraint in wealth accumulation at a time of cutbacks rather than the need for governments to intervene to redistribute resources.

The above trends all looks very unfavourable for the educator committed to a democratic project for social justice and equality. The aims of this type of educational engagement is to build a social and political order that is willing to subordinate economic activity to democratic mandates, a goal which many progressive social movements also aim to achieve.

A case in point are the democratic revolutions sweeping across Arab states, which have led to the creation of popular public spheres in situations where until quite recently the prospects for democracy seem to have been unthinkable. In Burma, the military regime has had to free the popular leader of the National League for Democracy, Aung Sang Suu Kyi and other dissidents. The student movement in Chile is determinedly rejecting the commodification of higher education with remarkable levels of public support. In many western capitalist economies the labour movement has been galvanised to protect their members' interests, particularly in relation to pension 'reform' and have mobilised massive demonstrations of trade unions and public support for their aims. Moreover, the emergence and proliferation of grassroots movements to 'Occupy' across the globe have called into question the activity of the political and economic elites and their visibility poses a moral challenge, at least, to the political hegemony that there is no alternative to the poor shouldering the brunt of economic crises (see Hall this volume).

However, as Harvey (2010 p. 250) argues in his address to the World Social Forum on its tenth anniversary, social movements have so far failed to produce a coherent alternative to galvanise a mass base of support for the radical transformation of capitalism: 'The central problem is that in aggregate there is no resolute and sufficiently unified anti-capitalist movement that can adequately challenge the reproduction of the capitalist class and the perpetuation of its power on the world stage'. We concur with the problem – it is not a new one. Part of the solution however, as Harvey points out, is 'to develop new mental conceptions of the world' (2010, p, 250), which social movements aim to foster. Hall, Clover, Crowther and Scandrett (2011) demonstrate that learning 'in and from' social movements can entail a critical process of awareness raising, organisation building, supporting new social relations, constructing knowledge and developing skills. But unless disparate movements build alliances for sustained and systemic transformation of capitalism their potential is constrained. It is our view that educators have something to assist the process of producing 'new mental conceptions of the world' and building alliances by seeking to align work in communities with the aim of developing resourceful social movements. We address this issue from our own context, not as social movement participants or activists, but as university adult educators involved in the preparation of students who will work as educators with communities of endurance and struggle. Our focus, therefore, is on the educator's capacity to contribute towards the struggle of grassroots communities in order to maximise their potential for creating progressive change.

We argue that what is required is a radical democratic project of cultural renewal from the 'bottom up'. Unless radical democratic values, genuine freedom (not the market kind) and social justice are to galvanise people and sustain their struggles the prospects for transforming the current or future crises of capitalism are slim. But how can educators make a difference? Partly the problem is one of scale. The global nature of social, economic and environmental problems can lead to feelings of being immobilised by the sheer size of the task; alternatively, shrinking the scale of the problem to community size solutions is to embrace parochialism. Educators working in neighbourhoods have to connect an analysis of social change and awareness of the wider context, but at the same time begin with people in communities 'where they are'. The latter is, of course, the starting point not the end goal of educational engagement. Our argument involves returning to some inspirational thinkers of the ideological left to revitalise our politics as educators whilst at the same time keeping in mind that education for social change often begins at a local level. We draw on the analyses of Karl Marx and his critical disciples, Antonio Gramsci and Raymond Williams, because of their interrelated concern with capitalist exploitation, cultural politics and education in communities.

MARX ON CAPITALISM

Marx (1983) is essential for understanding the dynamics of capitalism, even today, long after his death. Whilst the events of 2008, which led to the current economic crisis caught mainstream economists unawares, the tendencies of capitalism to produce deep-seated crises are fundamental to a Marxist understanding of the nature of wealth production.

For Marx, capitalist exploitation is disguised by the so-called fair exchange between buyers and sellers of labour, a claim which his analysis exposes as false. Capitalists exploit labour as a commodity by extracting an unpaid surplus from its activity, which then becomes their profit. Control over time is critical to this process of exploitation; time can be stretched to lengthen the working day although this has natural limits as well as social, cultural and political ones relative to the readiness of labour movements to protect their gains. Capitalists can use other means to reduce their labour costs so that the surplus can be expanded (e.g. weaken trade unions and pressurise workers into accepting less pay by expansion of 'reserve armies of labour); expand worker productivity through technological means or payment systems (e.g. automation of work process, payments-by-results etc); organise the labour process to enhance profitability (e.g. introduce economies of scale, increasingly operate an international division of labour to profit from cheap labour supplies across the globe). Exploitation is both relentless and expansive in capitalism's drive to enable one value to dominate all others – value for money.

Transforming all manner of goods and services into commodities ensures that capitalist principles of accumulation spread over all aspects of life in society. The drive towards commodification goes hand-in-hand with the diminution of democratic life, as market mechanisms and processes take over the distribution of public services and political spaces; the economic trumps democracy.

The other primary form of accumulation, according to Marx, comes historically through dispossession so that, by various legal and illegal means, wealth is concentrated into fewer hands. Whilst Marx saw this as appropriate to an early stage of capitalism, subsequent writers such as Harvey (2010), argue it is still a primary and significant process today. Some examples of this can be seen in terms of poor people being deprived of their land rights, repossession of homes and goods, the reduction of the value of pensions and so on.

The global nature of the economic crisis is brought about by the penetration of capital into all parts of the world; no corner is left untouched and therefore resistance to it must eventually be global in scope. During this process vast wealth is produced; wealth, that is, which is unevenly distributed by social class within countries and between advanced capitalist economies and subordinate ones. The result is that poverty and riches are relational, in that they are two sides of the same coin rather than being minted in different places. But this trend can lead to the over production of surpluses, that is, commodities which cannot be absorbed because there is insufficient purchasing power, which in turn leads to a crisis of accumulation as enterprises are unable to realise their surplus as profit. Credit funding is an option to expand the demand for surplus goods. But over indebted populations, which cannot earn sufficient to pay off the credit loaned to them, fuel another crisis of overproduction as debts go toxic, enterprises lay off workers, and capital assets subsequently decline in value. The intrinsic nature of the system is anarchic and crisis ridden.

One of Marx's major intellectual achievements in *Capital* is that he combines a dialectical analysis of the tensions and contradictions of capital accumulation with an historical analysis of the changing relationship between social and economic life. The nature of exploitation and commodification spans across the entire life of people: health, family life, education, holidays, friendships and so on become influenced by the economic logic of capitalism. Alternatively, in a socially just society, the production of commodities to serve use values (not merely exchange value) has to be created through the socialisation of the means of production to serve the community. In other words, enterprises should be democratically controlled to produce goods and services, which serve individual as well as collective wants and needs.

Marx's political economy leads to the need for a radical expansion and deepening of democratic life as a solution to the crises of capitalism. Social movements on the other hand allow for precisely this possibility because they create spaces to share and collectively think about alternatives and 'will recreate their social relations and thus themselves as a necessary and fundamental requirement for building a new social order' (Allman 2001 p. 163). New personal sensibilities and non-exploitative social relations need to be created and sustained on a social, cultural, moral and psychological level. The exploration of this problem and what could be done about it inspired the work of Gramsci.

THE REVOLUTION AGAINST CAPITAL: ANTONIO GRAMSCI

The subtitle 'A revolution against Capital' refers to an essay Gramsci wrote in *Avanti* after the Russian revolution (1917). It is not a rejection of Marx's analysis but a criticism of economistic readings of *Capital* which emphasise transformations occurring in a mechanical series of stages; a perspective that suggests the contradictions of capitalism inevitably produce socialism, so it is simply a matter of waiting for the revolution to occur. Gramsci was also critical of reformist versions of Marxism, which implied a stepping stone approach to socialism achieved through piecemeal reform of capitalism. In contrast the revolution was, for him, a matter of determined effort that had to be consciously created as ideas became a material force in the sense of informing different social practices to those which merely legitimised capitalism. The revolution against capital was not a dismissal of the importance of material inequalities and struggle at the point of production, but an argument to widen struggles for transformation through cultural politics.

Gramsci's reframing of the dynamics of social transformation addressed the relationship between political society (the institutions of the state) and civil society (outside the economy in the more or less private sphere and communal associations free from state control). Of course in reality the boundaries between the two are permeable and the relationship a dialectical one of shaping and influencing each other. In Gramsci's view 'the state equals political society + civil society, in other words, hegemony protected by the armour of coercion' (1971 p. 263). What he means by this is that the state is not simply a monolith of repressive institutions and structures but also provides services and resources which people need and this reinforces its legitimacy. It also fosters social relations to protect the legitimacy of state power and wider capitalist social relations by endowing them with common sense, moral authority and political credibility (e.g. business knows best, public services need to be run like businesses, having businessmen in the public sector is a good thing, competition is always beneficial, etc). The authority of the state is, in turn, buttressed through a wide range of social practices in civil society that directly or indirectly reinforce the view that capitalism is the natural, fairest and most efficient mode of organisation possible. In effect, therefore, Gramsci argues that the struggle for transformation must occur within civil society in a cultural struggle for hegemony, prior to challenging the authority and power of the capitalist state.

Articulating, inspiring and organising alternatives to the 'common sense' of the dominant order are tasks for 'organic intellectuals' of the subordinate social groups. Importantly, the intellectual from Gramsci's perspective is defined by the function served rather than being merely an individual attribute of people. He defines an organic intellectual as:

> The one who emerges in response to demands of a necessary function in the field of economic production. Therefore, for example, the capitalist entrepreneur creates alongside himself the industrial technician, the specialist in political economy, the organisers of a new culture, of a new legal system etc. (1971, p. 5).

The problem Gramsci seeks to resolve is how to produce this intellectual role from subordinate groups with little previous experience of generating their own leaders, who are able to articulate grievances in terms which connect the problems experienced by subordinate social groups with an analysis that goes to the root of the problem in terms of the virus of capitalist social relations. The challenge is a significant one:

> If our aim is to produce a new stratum of intellectuals including those capable of the highest degree of specialisation, from a social group which has not traditionally developed the appropriate attitudes, then we have unprecedented difficulties to overcome. (1971, p. 43)

But the necessity of this task cannot be avoided if a genuine democracy is to be developed from the grassroots upwards: dissent, grievances, misery, exploitation and oppression experienced 'from below' are the ingredients required for social change. Gramsci goes onto say that:

> The popular element "feels" but does not always know or understand; the intellectual element "knows" but does not always understand and in particular does not always feel. (1971, p. 418)

Knowledge, feeling and understanding come out of a process of sustained educational engagement. The relationship between the popular and the intellectual is a critical one for the emergence of a persuasive hegemony sufficiently robust to challenge common sense. Social movements do precisely this but the problem, as Harvey (1971, p. 418) highlights, is that single-issue movements fail to cohere into a joined up alternative which can mobilise mass support. Interestingly, in Eyerman and Jamison's account of social movements as 'cognitive praxis' (i.e., knowledge creating spaces for social learning) they draw on Gramsci's analysis but use the term 'movement intellectuals' (1991). The function of this group is to articulate the values, aspirations and arguments informing distinctive movement goals. They perform a critical intellectual role similar to that proposed by Gramsci's organic intellectuals of the working class and subaltern groups. Typically, however, movement intellectuals in Western liberal democracies appear to have been recruited from a professionally educated middle class. Whilst they can be a positive resource for change, for example in relation to the environment, the original problem which Gramsci identified is still the same: 'the unprecedented struggle' necessary to educate a subordinate social group to produce its own organic intellectuals who think, feel and understand.

Adult educators can align themselves with this 'unprecedented struggle' by supporting the emergence of subaltern organic intellectuals. We believe this task is fundamental to building a democratic culture as a basis for a genuine political democracy with the determination to rectify economic and social injustices. An important process for educating organic intellectuals of subordinate social groups is through active participation in movements for change *and* by scaling up their resources for change by building alliances between them.

Strategically, Gramsci identified the need to build alliances between progressive social forces that would act as a counterweight to the dominant hegemony. For Marx the emphasis was very much on the class struggle whereas for Gramsci a variety of progressive social forces in civil society widen the possibilities for movement in the direction of socialism. Gramsci uses the metaphor of the 'war of position', something akin to 'trench warfare', to explain a process that links the fight for cultural dominance with the efforts of people to build new social relationships (Mayo 1999). When Gramsci was making his analysis, in the 1920s and 1930s, the communist party was to play a key educative role in this process of leading change, however, the subsequent experience of the reality of socialism in authoritarian and repressive states in the former Soviet Union, Eastern Europe, Asia and parts of Africa make it highly unlikely that political parties of the same mould could ever again have widespread credibility. The result is that a vision for social change is caught between radical political parties which lack credibility and mainstream socialist parties which seek to merely manage capitalism; between this 'rock and a hard place' the only social force able to release sufficient critical creativity and galvanise significant political support has to come from the grassroots. It is the voice of the exploited and oppressed (see Holst 2011) based on experiences at the sharp end of capitalism, and the development of organic intellectuals from this social base, which offers hope for a new social order. The rootedness of organic intellectuals is, however, a critical factor where we believe educators in communities have something to offer struggles 'from below'. For Gramsci, there has to be a dialectic between the organic intellectual and their constituency which, if undone, separates 'intellectuals' from the 'popular'. Movements cease to move *without* the dynamic relationship between the two. In our view, the significance of community and culture as emphasised by Raymond Williams addresses this problem of linking learning, education and relationships for fostering social change.

BUILDING A CRITICAL SOCIALIST AND COLLECTIVE CULTURE: RAYMOND WILLIAMS

Raymond Williams was a Welsh intellectual and a co-founder of the first New Left in the UK (Steele 1997). Some of his early work on literature and culture was written whilst working in the field of adult education in the immediate post-World War II period. Two recurring themes in Williams' work are the importance of community and culture.

Community, as Williams knew, is a dangerous word because of its capacity to be deployed for a range of ideological purposes whilst seeming to be unquestionably good.

Community can be a warmly persuasive word to describe an existing set of relationships, or the warmly persuasive word to describe an alternative set of relationships. What is most important, perhaps, is that unlike all other terms of social organisation (state, nation, society etc) it never seems to be used unfavourably, and never to be given any positive or distinguishing term. (1983, p. 76)

The association of community with place, in a geographic sense, is both a strength and a weakness. We all live in places and frequently generate attachments to them. As Richard Sennett (1998) argues, community as place is where we are more likely to interact with people on an on-going basis over a longer time scale than is now likely or possible in the flexible workplace. Of course, the danger is that place can be parochial and act as a blinker to the outside world beyond it. The ambivalence of community is that it can lead to experiences of exclusion as well as inclusion, a source of stability and social order, as well as being a resource for constructing and developing resistance. If the latter is to be achieved the significance of community as place is that it can be a site where movements are generated as well as being the setting where their grievances connect and link people across places. Social movements which initially emerge from localised issues can extend their reach and scope to act on a national and international level. In addition, real places can be connected virtually. Digital spaces are no less real than physical places and potentially can enhance them, as witnessed during the Arab Spring, where social media were used to accelerate and magnify the occupation of public spaces (see Malone this volume).

The identification of threats and social problems at the grassroots has to be built through committed relationships seeking change, which are often developed through on-going contact in local places and lead to the emergence of organic intellectuals. Education is a resource to sustain and nurture the performance of this function and to ensure that the dialectical relationship between 'thought' and 'feeling' is strengthened in communities. To achieve this, educators need to attend to culture as well as community.

Williams (1954) identified the danger posed by the commercialisation of culture which undermined and trivialised everyday life. Cole (2008) argues that one of the most important lessons that we – as educators – can draw from Williams' concept of culture is his emphasis on considering it as an element in the social system and, at the same time, as one of the most powerful means for changing it. This is possible because of the double role of culture. On the one hand, culture is political in the sense that it has influence on the everyday life of people in communities. But, on the other hand, politics is always cultural because it is necessary to elaborate new forms of culture for producing political changes that expand the possibility of alternative forms of hegemony. We would want to add to this the increasing need to address the individualisation of culture, which writers such as

Beck and Beck-Gernsheim (2001) have identified and which clearly undermine a collective way of life. Educational work on popular culture is a critical task. As Gramsci notes,

> To create a new culture is not only doing 'original' individual discoveries, it means also – and specially – to disseminate critically [between people] the knowledge already known (Gramsci, 1976 p. 14).

So, we need – and Gramsci and Williams agree on this point – a space to disseminate, create and recreate a popular culture in resistance to the dominant one.

An example of this type of work occurred during the time of the experiment in creating a participatory budget in the city of Seville, Spain (2003–2007), where one of the authors conducted a research and educational action project focusing on 'Participatory Budget and Adult Education'. A key part of the educational project was a 'Participatory and Citizenship School', which recruited people involved in social movements across different parts of the city. The idea for developing this school was based on two different references: firstly, the fact that a lot of people involved in the process of the 'participatory budget' were people who took part in social movements. Secondly, this recruitment of participants was linked with the idea of enriching democracy inside the social movements so as to deepen and extend their social base and power resources. The programme involved the design and organisation of 14 courses of 24 hours, working on developing participation, conflict resolution, mediation skills, community analysis, and finally the development of a community project. The intervention has also produced teaching materials to both support the courses and encourage people within social movements to develop internal democratic processes inside their own organisations. The aim of this work is not for adult educators to advocate for social movements or to become substitute leaders for them. It is to support the generation of movement leaders and the democratic structure and processes that ensure a close relationship between participants and their organisations. The social base of a movement is always its main resource as a lever for change.

We want to stress two different outcomes derived from this work. The first is related to the heterogeneity of people attending courses; these were taught in community centres situated in the city's districts, and people attended from a variety of associations such as flamenco groups, motorbike clubs, women's associations, and so on. This diversity brought together a range of interests and actors who could begin to develop new networks in the districts and therefore strengthen their sharing of experiences, problems and understandings.

The second outcome is connected to the skills, which were developed by the intervention. Sometimes, ordinary people will deprecate their own ability and consider that they are not able to be active subjects shaping their future. They think that they do not possess the knowledge and skills needed for engaging in educational and political tasks. Because of this fear to act, individuals undermine their capacity for autonomy in favour of appointing technicians, professionals and/or leaders in associations to carry things through. The aim of the courses was to work with these people to achieve the knowledge, skills and confidence to develop a project by themselves and therefore to become more active, critical and challenging. One of the main learning outcomes of participatory budget processes is to create in individuals a new feeling of political efficacy and self-esteem, in the sense that Lerner and Schugurensky (2007) define it.

Adult educational work at the level of communities does not, of course, transform global capitalism and the kind of movement it generates may not easily scale up to become such a threat. But it does begin to turn people into critical and active agents who are less easily managed or manipulated and it provides an opportunity to make visible alternative values and visions which animate people. It also develops networks and relationships based on shared interests rather than commodified relations. This activity echoes the claim made by the historian E.P. Thompson (1963), in relation to the historically formative period in the making of the English working class, where he draws attention to its contribution to the development of collective institutions and a culture which promoted the common good, both of which have been systematically undermined by the hegemony of capitalist production and are in need of re-making.

CONCLUSION: OPTIMISM OF THE WILL

Speaking of the common good today seems almost an anachronism because it is seldom heard in public discourse in advanced capitalist economies. As Tony Judt (2010 p. 120) reminds us '...the symptoms of collective impoverishment are all around us...[but]...are so endemic that we no longer know how to talk about what is wrong, much less set about repairing it.'

The role of social movements is of course to open or re-open a public discourse of the common good – where it is missing or inadequate – on a range of concerns or in relation to identities which are misrecognised (see Honneth 2007). The only way of sustaining such a discourse is for the public to participate and be part of shaping its content and its articulation with their everyday lives. Motivation for such participation springs from a sense of connectedness that, primarily, is felt through experiencing problems in everyday living in communities. Participation in collective processes of debate and decision-making, built around immediate issues, which influence people's lives, is essential for nurturing and sustaining the connection between 'thought and feelings'.

Building communities of resistance and struggle from the 'bottom up' is the task of socially committed educators prepared to address the generative themes (in Freire's 1973 terms) that provide opportunities to mobilise support. What has to be avoided, however, is the co-option of such communities into state sponsored initiatives of localism, which merely deliver people to meeting top-down policy objectives, rather than addressing the claims and concerns that derive 'from below' (Crowther et al., 2007). Connecting communities of endurance and resistance is critical for scaling up opportunities for action to challenge hegemonic power. But in doing this, the central problem of the dialectic between organic intellectuals and their social base has to be supported. Critical intellects without a social base are useful but with a social base they are 'really useful' in the sense of linking learning and action with social interests (Johnson 1988). It is by making this action a key task adult and community educators can offer a distinctive contribution to the role of social movements in efforts for social change. Returning to Harvey, he too points to the important role organic intellectuals make in offering new conceptions of the world:

> To listen to peasant leaders of the MST in Brazil or the leaders of the anti-corporate land grab movement in India is a privileged education. In this instance the task of the educated alienated and discontented is to magnify the subaltern voice so that attention can be paid to the circumstances of exploitation and repression and the answers that can be shaped into an anti-capitalist program (2010, p. 259)

We want to re-emphasise the need to maintain the organic nature of the intellectual function. As Gramsci insists, 'the process of development is tied to a dialectic between the intellectuals and the masses' (1971 p. 334). Too often education is constructed as a ladder out of communities for individuals to climb rather than a collective resource for change. Only through a democratic and sustained dialogue between leaders and supporters can the necessary momentum for collective action be achieved. Educators in communities are not substitute organic intellectuals, they cannot replace the leadership that needs to emerge within communities, but they can facilitate the democratic process of engagement that is necessary to cement 'thought' and 'feeling'. In reference to this dialectic Gramsci used what seems now to be a quaint and old-fashioned metaphor: 'the whalebone in the corset' (1971 p. 340). But the task is not quaint or unnecessary. Adult and community educators can be a resource for making this shaping and firming process, between communities and their leaders, actually work.

Finally, the global crisis of capitalism is generating an unprecedented crisis of democracy as economic choices are reduced to 'technical' solutions of selecting the right level of austerity measures. These measures inevitably create experiences which connect with the reality of people's lives at a local level. This is often the place where community educators begin from because it is where people meet and experience common grievances. However, technical solutions about the appropriate level of austerity measures hollow out politics from the real business of developing arguments, values and priorities which can make a positive difference to people's lives. Making a contribution to this public sphere is a political imperative and an educational task.

REFERENCES

Allman, P. (2001). *Critical education against global capitalism. Karl Marx and Revolutionary Critical Education.* Wesport, CO: Bergin & Garvey.
Beck, U. & Beck-Gernsheim, E. (2001). *Individualization,* London: SAGE.
Cole, J. (2008). 'Raymond Williams and education – a slow reach again for control', *The Encyclopaedia of Informal Education.* [www.infed.org/thinkers/raymond_williams.htm]

Crowther, J., Martin, I. & Shaw, M (2007). 'Rescuing community education in Scotland from the smothering embrace of partnership', in Mark, R., Jay, R., McCabe, B. & Moreland, R (Eds.), *Researching Adult Learning: Communities and Partnerships in the Local and Global Context*, SCUTREA 37th Annual Conference, 3–5 July, Belfast: QUB, 109–116.

Eyerman, R. & Jamison, A. (1991). *Social Movements as Cognitive Praxis*, Bristol: Polity Press.

Freire, P. (1973). *Pedagogy of the Oppressed*, London: Penguin.

Gramsci, A. (1971). *Prison Notebooks*, London: Lawrence and Wishart.

Gramsci, A. (1976). *Introducción a la filosofía de la praxis*. Barcelona: Península

Gramsci, A. (1917). 'The revolution against Capital', *Avanti*, 24th December.

Hall, B., Clover, D., Crowther, J. & Scandrett, E. (2011). (Eds.), 'Social movements: A contemporary re-examination, *Studies in the Education of Adults*, vol

Harvey, D. (2010). 'Organizing for the anti-capitalist transition', [reprinted] in *Interface*, 2(1), 243–261.

Holst, J.D. (2011). Frameworks for understanding the politics of Social Movements. *Studies in the Education of the Adults, 43(2)*, pp. 117–127.

Honneth, A. (2007). *Disrespect: The Normative Foundations of Critical Theory*, Cambridge: Polity Press.

Johnson, R. (1988). "Really useful knowledge" 1790–1850: Memories for education in the 1980s', in Lovett, T. (Ed.), Radical Adult Education, London: Routledge.

Judt, T. (2010). *Ill Fares the Land*, London: Allen Lane.

Lerner, J. & Schugurensky, D. (2007). Who learns what in Participatory Democracy? In R. van der Venn, D. Wildemeersch, J. Youngblood & V. Marsick (Eds.), *Democratic Practices as Learning Opportunities* (pp. 85–100). Rotterdam: Sense Publishers.

Marx, K. (1983). *Capital*, London: Lawrence and Wishart.

Mayo, P. (1999). *Gramsci, Freire and adult education. Possibilities for transformative action*. London: Zed Books.

Sennett, R. (1998). *The Corrosion of Character: the Personal Consequences of work in the New Capitalism*, New York: W.W. Norton & Company.

Steel, T. (1997). *The Emergence of Cultural Studies 1945–65*, London: Lawrence & Wishart.

Thompson, E. P. (1963). *The Making of the English Working Class*, London: Penguin.

Williams, R. (1953). The idea of culture. In J. McIroy & S. Westwood (Eds.), *Border County. Raymond Williams and adult education*, (pp. 57–77). Leicester: NIACE.

Williams, R. (1983) *Keywords*. London: Fontana.

LIAM KANE

5. FORTY YEARS OF POPULAR EDUCATION IN LATIN AMERICA: LESSONS FOR SOCIAL MOVEMENTS TODAY

In attempting to understand the contribution of social movements to education for social change, recent experiences in Latin American offer rich pickings for research. The region contains a wide variety of social movements that explicitly address the question of how education can and should contribute to their struggles. Education for change – more commonly known as 'popular education' – is not only a philosophy-cum-practice in Latin America but has come to constitute a social movement in its own right

> I would particularly emphasise these two elements of the phenomenon: on the one hand it is a broad and open movement, with a degree of articulation and organisation (such as CEAAL, ALFORJA and other regional networks), while, on the other, it is a particular brand of critical thinking (with its conceptual formulations, its systematisation of experiences, its dialogue with the social sciences, its publications and so on). (Zarco, 2001, p. 30)

Based on documentary analysis and personal interviews with educators and learners all over the region, this chapter examines what is meant by popular education in Latin America, charts its development over the last forty years, analyses its relationship to social movements and considers what lessons it might hold for social movements elsewhere.

POPULAR EDUCATION IN LATIN AMERICA: PRINCIPLES AND PRACTICE

There are many definitions of 'popular education' (Arnold & Burke, 1983; Crowther et al., 1999; Núñez, 1992; Schugurensky, 2010), none definitive or absolute; the differences are often subtle, simply emphasising some characteristics more than others, and occasionally serious, though this usually reflects attempts by conservative educationists to co-opt popular education for their own ends (Carr, 1990; Gibson, 1994).

In Spanish and Portuguese, the lingua francas of Latin America, the adjective 'popular' normally has different connotations from the English equivalent. 'Popular' suggests belonging to 'the people', understood as the vast majority of a nation's citizens who, in the context of Latin America, are normally poor. Though

B. L. Hall, D. E. Clover, J. Crowther and E. Scandrett (Eds.), Learning and Education for a Better World: The Role of Social Movements, 69–84.

not very precise, the term carries clear connotations of social class and could often be translated simply as 'poor' or 'working class'.

'Educación popular' (Spanish) or 'educação popular' (Portuguese), then, means an education, which serves and belongs to 'the people' rather than the elite. By extension, a movement like the Landless Rural Workers Movement in Brazil is often characterised as a *popular* social movement, to emphasise the class-based nature of its concerns. More recently, as people organised around issues not explicitly linked to class – gender, human rights, interculturalism and so on – the meaning of 'popular' has been stretched to include these initiatives as well. But, since their protagonists mainly come from lower economic sectors anyway, the class-based nuances generally still apply.

Strongly influenced by the work of Paulo Freire (1972, 1974, 1993), 'popular education' refers to a generic educational practice relating to a wide variety of social actors – from peasants to factory workers, women to Indigenous people's groups and so on. In most definitions there are a number of common, principal characteristics. For teaching purposes I have summarised these in the (slightly non-sensical) mnemonic sentence:

'The aim of popular education is to promote: Political Knowledge, Dialogue and Critical Subjects whose Method of Collective Action Humanises the Educator' an *aide-memoire* for:

Political: popular education has a political commitment in favour of the 'oppressed', 'poor', 'marginalised' or 'excluded'. All education is considered inherently political, either working to support or change the prevailing unjust social order, and popular education addresses this openly.

Knowledge: epistemologically, it recognises that all people have important knowledge derived from the particular experiences in which they find themselves: useful knowledge is not the exclusive preserve of academics, technicians or experts.

Dialogue: education should consist of dialogue between different 'knowledges', not simply the depositing of an expert's knowledge into the mind of those perceived to be ignorant, what Freire (1972) calls 'banking education'.

Critical: it should develop critical thinking among learners, so that people can recognise and understand the mechanisms which keep them oppressed; increasingly, it encourages creative thinking and the ability to make concrete proposals for change.

Subjects: the aim is not to manipulate thoughts or create dependency on charismatic leaders but to enable people to become authentic agents or 'subjects' of change themselves.

Method: accordingly, the methodology of popular education should promote a 'dialogue of knowledges' (Ghiso, 1993) and encourage people to think and act for themselves. To this end popular education has developed an impressive range of 'participative techniques' (Bustillos & Vargas, 1993).

Collective: the concern is to help enable people progress collectively, not to single out individuals for special treatment. This does not mean, however, that individual needs are ignored.

Action: echoing Marx, the point is not just to theorise but to try and bring about social change. As such, popular education is linked to *action* for change, particularly in the different *popular* social movements all over Latin America, where 'the movement is the school' (Freire, 1991).

Humanises: some argue that the *raison d'être* of popular education is 'above all an ethical commitment in favour of humanisation' (Zarco, 2001:30).

Educator: the role of the educator is not to provide answers but to ask questions and stimulate dialogue, debate and analysis. But popular educators also contribute to the dialogue and are not merely 'facilitators': in the end, though it should never be manipulative, popular education is undeniably interventionist.

These are the basic principles of popular education, albeit in real life they take shape in different ways. Partly, this is down to ideological interpretation. A range of ideas – Marxism, liberation theology, feminism, nationalism, and combinations of these or others, inspires popular educators. Inevitably, this affects their understanding of what constitutes 'critical consciousness' and influences both the type of questions they ask and the contributions they make to the dialogue. Partly, how principles translate into practice depends on the social context in which popular educators try to intervene. This context varies both between and within countries and also over time.

A BRIEF HISTORY OF POPULAR EDUCATION IN LATIN AMERICA

It is possible to trace popular education back to Europe and the French revolution (Núñez, 1992; Puiggrós 1994; Soethe, 1994) but in its contemporary manifestation I theorise Latin American popular education as having five broad periods of development. The divisions are debatable and not clear-cut but they offer a starting point for understanding popular education in Latin America today.

Period 1. The Development of New Ideas: the Late 1950s and the 1960s

The first stage began in Brazil in the late 1950s and early 60s, with attempts by the radical wing of the Catholic Church to bring basic education to the rural and urban poor. It was also a period of radicalisation throughout Latin America, spurred on in particular by the Cuban revolution of 1959. Liberation theology (Boff, 1985) grew in importance and the influential Catholic Church adopted a preferential 'option for the poor'. Against this background, the ideas of Paulo Freire on education were developed and refined, culminating in the publication of his seminal 'Pedagogy of the Oppressed' in 1970. These ideas would serve as the ideological backbone of the popular education movement about to grow up.

Period 2. The Rise of Movements: the 1970s till the Mid 1980s

The second period covers a time of uneven capitalist development, rapid urbanisation and increasing economic hardship, often accompanied by repression and dictatorship. A lack of formal democracy provoked a flourishing of movements that attempted to bring about change through extra parliamentary activities. Aware of the need for 'really useful learning' to support their efforts, the ideas of Freire landed on fertile soil (CEAAL, 1994).

While the previous period saw the development of educational ideas that it was hoped, would lead to action for change, now the relationship was reversed. Having first taken action, movements looked round for alternative ideas in education to support them. This was the boom period in popular education: Freire's ideas were radicalised further, new educational resources were produced and networks like CEAAL and ALFORJA were developed. Popular education methodology became famous, publicised internationally by progressive NGOs with links to Latin America. Popular education belonged to the movements and State education was seen as conserving the status quo. The exception was in revolutionary Nicaragua, where the Sandinista government attempted to implement popular education on a large scale. Many of Latin America's major figures in popular education spent time there in the early 1980s (Barndt, 1991).

Period 3. Crisis and Rethinking the Basics: the Late 1980s till the Late 1990s

Popular education in Latin America experienced a minor crisis during this period. Externally, with the fall of the Berlin wall in 1989 and the defeat of the Nicaraguan revolution in 1990, a 'crisis of paradigms' affected many activists in Latin America (Mejia, 1995). The utopia of large-scale social change was damaged and many popular educators were disorientated. Simultaneously, there was a demise in dictatorial government and more spaces opened up for the participation of civil society. From a previous clarity of purpose – against the State, on the side of the oppressed, located within movements and part of the struggle for radical, if not revolutionary social change – the picture was now more complex.

And there were critiques from within the movement too: that the category of 'oppressed' should relate to issues such as gender and ethnicity as well as class; that popular education had privileged action over actual learning processes (Cendales et al., 1996; Gutierrez & Castillo, 1994; Ponce, 1999); that with the opening up of democratic spaces popular education should now engage the State sector as opposed to remaining oppositional and external. Gadotti argued that popular education had failed 'to adequately explore the contradictions within the State, sometimes mechanistically opposing it and at other times isolating itself and thus losing strength' (Gadotti & Torres, 1992: 65).

Educators reacted in different ways to the confusion. In 1994 CEAAL set up a process of 'rethinking the basics' – some saw it 'giving new meaning' to popular education rather than re-inventing it (Jara, 2004, p. 113) – to try and address systematically the challenges facing the popular education movement (Dimension Educativa, 1996; CEAAL, 1996; Mendoza, 1997).

Period 4: Settling Down. the Late 1990s and Early 2000s

These issues continue to be debated, though with less urgency than before. I identified three broad tendencies in the popular education movement as it tackled the crisis. One seemed to abandon class struggle as an old-fashioned concept and concentrated instead on the issues of democracy and citizenship, with new social actors and spaces; another remained concerned about class and structural change but tried to develop its practice by opening up to new issues and 'subjects', as well as learning from past mistakes; another chose the practical route of just continuing to work with oppressed groups in the belief that appropriate 'paradigms' would emerge in the process (Kane, 2001).

Popular education now broadened its scope to a variety of settings, formal and informal, from autonomous movements to within State education. And it addressed newer themes, like citizenship, democracy, human rights, local power, intercultural/peace education and so on. But the multiplicity of practices also presented difficulties in interpreting whether 'authentic' or sanitised versions of popular education were taking place, with the possibility of co-option always a danger (Betuto Fernández, 1998:76). When CEAAL (2004) published 40 articles on popular education for the new century, engagement with the State was widely supported (CEAAL stands for the 'Latin American Council for Adult Education', the region-wide network bringing popular educators together). Some warned, however, that in reality, State education policies were often dictated by the World Bank, that the pendulum should not be allowed to swing too far back and that social movements should not be abandoned (de Souza, 2004, p. 48).

Finally, even movements themselves were having variable relationships with governments and in some cases were able to procure State funding and recognition for their own autonomous programmes.

Period 5: A New Radicalism: the Mid 2000s Onwards.

By the mid 2000s, there had been a so-called 'turn to the left' in Latin American politics, a complete discrediting of neoliberalism and a flourishing of inter-governmental attempts to promote Latin American solidarity – all accompanied by the rhetoric, if not necessarily the delivery, of increasing participatory democracy from below.

The most notable changes are in Bolivia, under president Evo Morales, where social movements have been fundamental in pushing and supporting the government to bring about change (Dangl, 2010) and in Venezuela where president Hugo Chavez has declared popular education one of the five 'motors' of the Bolivarian revolution (Wilpert, 2007). While both these and other countries face enormous difficulties and contradictions in putting theory into practice, the effect has been to put radical structural change on the agenda again and create spaces of possibility for engaging in popular education on a large scale.

SOCIAL MOVEMENTS, POPULAR EDUCATION, THE STATE
AND THE 'HOKEY COKEY'

Social Movements and Popular Education

Popular education in Latin America blossomed with the rise of social movements and though attention shifted towards other sites of practice from the late 1980s onwards, movements were not 'a temporary outgrowth of the suppression of conventional politics by bureaucratic-authoritarian regimes, a trend that would fade again with the return of electoral democracy' (Stahler-Sholk et al., 2007, p. 5). In fact the role of social movements grew. They seemed to be 'not only a continuation of historical resistance and mobilization of the masses but a specific response to the advance of neoliberal globalization within the process of normal democratization' (p. 5). Today prominent movements in Latin America include 'the Indigenous mobilizations led by the Confederation of Indigenous Nationalities of Ecuador (CONAIE), mobilisations against water privatizations and gas pipeline investments in Bolivia, the Zapatista movement in Mexico, the Landless Rural Workers' Movement in Brazil, Afro-Colombians resisting displacement in a region coveted by investors, eruptions of workers and the urban poor in the wake of Argentina's financial crisis, and the incipient cross-border and migrant movements and mobilizations against "free-trade" agreements' (see also Álvarez et al., 1998; Thomas, 2011 and Olcese, 2011). Most movement activity, though not all, continues to be of a popular, class-based nature.

In terms of popular education, some movements now have their own independent, systematic approaches to maximising the educational potential of every part of the movement's activity. The Landless Rural Workers' Movement (MST) in Brazil, for example (Caldart, 1998), spent years building its own education centre, produces excellent education materials, runs courses for its activists and has around 1800 schools for 200,000 children, with 4000 teachers (Zibechi, 2008, p. 4). Most impressive is its teacher-education course: when landless groups successfully acquire land, the 'settlement' elects someone to become its teacher. S/he then attends the MST residential course, in which students conduct participatory research in their communities, find out what education is required, negotiate the curriculum with co-ordinators and, as a group, organise the logistics – who will cook, clean, earn money and so on. Pedagogically, since the MST aims to work the land co-operatively, the course promotes co-operative learning (Kane, 2001). Discussing the MST, Zibechi (2008:4) concludes 'that the social movement itself becomes an educational "subject", and that as a result all its spaces, actions and reflections have a 'pedagogical intentionality', seems to me to be a revolutionary change with respect to our understanding of education, and also of the way in which we should understand social movements'.

Other movements have developed similar, highly organised educational provision. Since April 2003 the 'Popular University of the Mothers of May Square' has run courses for tens of thousands of movement activists from Argentina and all over Latin America, creating space for 'resistance and struggle' in the production of 'really useful knowledge' (p. 1). In the war-torn province of Caqueta in Colombia, *campesinos* from over twenty communities set up the Universidad Campesina (Peasants University) in 2004, to exchange experiences among communities trying to prevent the spread of war. The Confederation of Indigenous Nationalities of Ecuador (CONAIE) runs 2.800 schools, but 'a different type of school, which totally depends on the participation of the community, a pedagogy which our ancestors practised' (Macas y Lozano, 2000). CONAIE also developed the Intercultural University for Indigenous Nationalities and Peoples and in the various 'autonomous spaces' which they have won in the state of Chiapas, Mexico, the Zapatistas now have their own schools and teachers in what they call the Rebellious and Autonomous Zapatista Education System for National Liberation (EZLN, 2008).

Social Movements and the State

So popular education within social movements continues to be important. The shape it takes, however, may depend on the association movements have with the State. Burgos et al (2008) schematise State-movement relationships into four categories. The first is of radically autonomous movements that 'develop their educational experiences through a political-pedagogical project seeking to consolidate social practices opposite to those promoted by the State and with resources managed completely by the movement itself' (p. 2). This describes the Zapatistas, who have forged zones of total autonomy and generally view State action as an attempt to co-opt them.

The second is movements that campaign to receive State resources but manage them themselves. These try to 'force the State to act "as if" it really were working for the collective social good. That means they consciously force apart the intrinsic contradictions within the state, provoking it to act in favour of the weakest...without losing sight of the danger of being co-opted, adapted or subsumed" (in Thwaites Rey, 2004, p. 11). This describes the MST, which maintains its autonomy but also campaigns, often successfully, for the State to accredit MST courses, pay teachers' salaries and provide resources for the building of schools in the settlements. Recognising that only the State has the wherewithal to organise mass education, the MST is also active in broader campaigns for universal 'popular' public education.

The third is movements that are themselves embedded within State structures. These can be closely allied to a political party, which will have a strong influence over its direction, or simply be supportive of the government. Here there is a significant gap between the grassroots and the leaders and some authors consider these movements 'clientelist' and populist.

The final category covers movements that are autonomous from the State but work strategically with other social actors, including businesses, in pursuit of their aims. These are mainly rooted in communities, concerned with promoting direct democracy, such as some re-occupied factories in Argentina. Critical of *asistencialismo* – aid, with strings attached, deflecting attention away from real, political problems and issues – they decide not to make financial demands of the State. In economic and educational projects, they work with a variety of funders, including private companies. In recent times, however, some of these movements appear to be moving towards some dealings with the state.

The Hokey Cokey Approach to Popular Education

Like me begin with an explanation. The Hokey Cokey is a game in the UK where children – or adults! – form a circle and, acting out the movements, sing 'you put your left foot in, your left foot out, your left foot in and you shake it all about, you do the Hokey Cokey and you turn around, that's what it's all about, see! Oh Hokey Cokey Cokey…'.

Currently in Latin America, then, there continues to exist a plethora of (popular) social movements that independently of the democratic credentials of particular States play, an important role in challenging and combating the negative effects of neoliberalism. Many have taken earlier practices in popular education to a much higher level and developed well-organised, systematic approaches to creating alternative learning organisations: their articulation with State structures is variable. There continues to be debate about the extent to which the loosely-defined popular education movement should have a relationship with the State or concentrate on working with movements, though where movements do engage with the State, both can be done at the same time. This reflects the broader picture in Latin America where arguably, the relationship between social movements and the State is the driving force of most social change. Dangl (2010) characterises this as governments 'dancing with dynamite', an allusion to the raging hunger in the bellies of the oppressed.

As an outsider first drawn to popular education in Latin America precisely because of its independence and alternative nature, I was initially disappointed by its rapprochement with the State, fearing it would end in co-optation, as happened, arguably, in the UK (Fieldhouse, 2000). However, I now support what I think of as the 'Hokey Cokey' approach to popular education, coincidentally extending Dangl's metaphor of a dance between movements and the State. To me it encapsulates Gadotti's argument that the popular movement and popular education should have one foot inside the state apparatus

> But it has to be only one foot, inside. The other foot should be outside. Tactically inside, strategically outside…Maintaining this dialectical relationship between being outside and being inside is important for the movement's own survival. The negotiating strength of the movement within the State depends on its own capacity for mobilisation outside it' (Gadotti, 1992, p. 71).

And for good measure the Hokey Cokey wants the foot inside to stir things up and 'shake it all about'!

LESSONS FOR SOCIAL MOVEMENTS TODAY

Outside focused comparative studies, drawing broad, generalised lessons from Latin America is a speculative activity. What is good for one movement, in one context, may be inappropriate for another elsewhere. Does the Brazilian MST's approach to training teachers, for example, have any relevance for a small social movement in a Northern country with full State education? In the end, I believe social movement activists can learn from three different areas of Latin American popular education: theory or conceptual understandings, pedagogical practice and general organisation.

This analysis centres on movements in the North, for whom lessons are likely to be less apparent than for movements in the South. I also have in mind progressive movements working for social justice: the aims of conservative social movements have nothing in common with those of popular education.

Theoretical/conceptual Understandings

Perhaps the first lesson to take from Latin America is that social movements ought to address explicitly the educational dimension of their activity and not simply leave it to chance. For a movement's members, and the public it targets, learning takes place in many forms: readings designed to inform or persuade, planned educational 'workshops', incidental learning acquired in action (Schugurensky, 2000), the hidden curriculum of a movement's organisation. Acknowledging this reality and taking education seriously are a *sine qua non* for learning from Latin America.

Then movements have to consider how the educational dimension should be approached. Here the principles outlined earlier offer solid foundations. The idea that 'all education is political' is as relevant in the North as the South, though it comes with the warning not to engage in banking education but to start from people's own experiences, ensure dialogue between 'expert' and 'grassroots' knowledge and enable people to become subjects of change, not followers of leaders. These ideas will clash with some movements' practice. In particular, campaigns for specific objectives may privilege key activists at the expense of wider participation ('campaigning' and 'education' imperatives sometimes collide). But the principles emanating from Latin America potentially offer guidance on how movements can conceptualise their educational work.

Another insight, a critique from within the Latin American movement itself (in Period 2 of the historical outline), is that sometimes, given its commitment to action, popular education simply makes assumptions about what learning takes place. Some argued that more serious attention should be paid to exactly what was being learned, how and by whom. The critique provoked a renewed interest in how individuals learn and in the ideas of more mainstream educationalists like Piaget and Vygotsky. In turn, there was a counter-critique against an exaggeratedly 'pedagogist' orientation, an attempt to seek refuge from difficult political choices by narrowly focusing on pedagogy, in the abstract, at the expense of education linked to action (Núñez, 1993; Ponce, 1999). But the outcome was an increased awareness of the need to examine what learning actually takes place, taking nothing for granted, and to consider how this relates to both individuals and the movement as a whole.

Then there is the concept of 'the educator'. Latin Americans argue that 'the most important popular educator should be the leader of an organization' (IMDEC, 1994:60). Key activists are the people best placed to promote practices encouraging the movement's participants to become either autonomous 'subjects' of change or merely a supporting cast. Even the best of campaigners could take this lesson to heart and appreciate that within a movement their actions have educational consequences, intended or not.

Pedagogical Practice

Popular education in Latin American is probably best known for its methodology. From Freire's approach to teaching literacy (Taylor, 1993), to 'participatory techniques', to Augusto Boal's (1979) 'theatre of the oppresed', Latin America has produced imaginative ways of putting the principles of popular education into practice. Many have already been adapted for use throughout the world (Arnold & Burke, 1983; Arnold et al., 1994) and are an invaluable contribution to the toolkit of would-be activist-educators. However, in Latin America employers and even the CIA have attempted to use the same techniques for very different ends (Ponce, 1999). By itself, their use does not mean popular education is taking place. As Bustillos & Vargas' (1993) warn, the relationship between principles and methodology is far from mechanical.

Another useful practice is referred to as the 'systematisation' of experiences. Popular educators 'confront situations which are fluid, unstable, changing and uncertain; everything seems messy and confused, a collection of interacting problems' (Barnechea et al., 1994): 'systematisation', taking the form of written documents, books, video/dvds, photographic expositions or theatrical productions (Alforja, 2011) is the attempt to bring order to, reflect on, interpret, and make sense of practices which intervene in this constantly changing reality. This enables organisations and educators to learn from each other's experiences, successes, problems and failures; it helps educators analyse and evaluate their own work; it is part of the educative process itself, in which encouraging people to interpret developments helps them reach new levels of understanding. Importantly, systematisation is not about dispassionate, 'neutral' reporting: those who collectively engage in systematisation are also the focus of enquiry, both 'subjects' and 'objects' at the same time. Jara stresses that systematisation is not simply about narrating events but should pay attention to 'the interpretation which "subjects" give to these events so that a space is created in which these interpretations are discussed, shared and challenged' (Jara, 1994, p. 24. See also Palma, 1992 and Magendzo, 1994). So, making a systematic attempt to document and reflect on whatever learning might be taking place could be a useful practice for social movements to adopt if they are serious about addressing the educational dimension of their activities.

Organisation

Latin America also offers examples of the way in which popular education might be organised. The region has centres engaged in many types of work, enmeshed in different social movements, but with popular education as a prime concern and *modus operandi*: see IMDEC (the Mexican Institute for Community Development), CANTERA (Centre for Popular Education and Communication) in Nicaragua and Rede Mulher de Educação (Women's Educational Network) in Brazil. Being organised into national, international and region-wide networks facilitates mutual support and development. The networks have grown organically, though as non-profit organisations they will often struggle with issues of finance and staffing. But as social movements elsewhere develop an interest in educational work, they offer future models to consider.

How these centres relate to grassroots activity is also insightful. IMDEC runs an annual 'School of Methodology', for example, split into four one-week residential workshops (Kane, 2001). This is targeted at key activists who, in collaboration with the co-ordinating team of trainers, work to embed the principles of popular education into the fabric of their movements. As activists come from a variety of movements all over Mexico, the training also fosters inter-movement solidarity.

We have seen that Latin American movements can have complete independence from or various degrees of engagement with the State. The particular example of the popular education movement could be instructive to Northern movements considering whether, and if so how, to relate to State-funded education. This would require analysis of different case-studies to examine the pros, cons and details of different approaches. For me, two particular strategies stand out. One is the 'hokey cokey' approach, that from the bottom up, without losing control, the popular education movement can put demands on the State to support it, as with the case of the MST in Brazil or ENFODEP in Venezuela (Kane, 2010). A second is that movements can elicit – rather than demand – the support of sympathetic knowledge specialists and engage them in dialogue. Many Latin American academics work willingly and voluntarily with movements, lending their specialist knowledge by responding to a 'problem-posing' curriculum dictated to them by movements, rather than delivering lectures.

Another inspirational example comes from Brazil, in particular, the godparent of educational 'Forums'. The first World Social Forum took place in Porto Alegre, in 2001, and stimulated spin-off Forums throughout the country, some concentrating on education. Organisers claimed that the Education Forum in São Paulo, in 2004, was the largest educational event in history, with approximately 120 thousand attendees. In 2003, a group of radical, energetic educators in the small rural town of Lins set up the 'Popular Education Forum for the Western São Paulo Region' (FREPOP), which has run annually ever since. Impressively, it brings together movement activists, grassroots organisations, teachers, NGO staff and academics for a four-day residential event. The aim is to promote dialogue and solidarity around a wide range of social concerns, always with 'popular education' as the central 'thematic axis'. Though rooted in its locality, FREPOP invites popular educators from all over Latin America and the world to participate. It is not unusual to find academics co-running sessions with agricultural labourers bussed straight in from the fields, a powerful example of a 'dialogue of knowledges' in action. FREPOP reaches so many people that many see it as a social movement in its own right.

CONCLUSION

This chapter provides a brief overview of popular education in Latin America. In highlighting aspects that may be of benefit elsewhere it also inevitably accentuates the positive meaning, so some qualifications are in order.

First, while it once made sense to talk of 'the Latin American experience', it is now less plausible to locate ideas and practices exclusively in one location. Freire, Boal and the principles of popular education have already impacted worldwide and Latin Americans, in turn, have absorbed ideas from elsewhere. So what is described here is not necessarily unique to Latin America. Second, this account is generalised and its correspondence to particular areas of Latin America will be variable. Third, there are often large gaps between theory and practice. Trying to promote 'subjects' of change is one thing; actually managing to achieve it, another. Training opportunities for activists are also limited and some practitioners are more skilled than others. Fourth, since popular education initiatives are underpinned, consciously or otherwise, by a variety of ideological orientations, it is sometimes difficult to understand what is going on beneath the surface (arguably, the relationship between popular education and ideology receives insufficient analysis). I have met popular educators in Central America who felt little affinity with the region-wide network CEAAL, for example. Similarly, impressed by a particular group of educators in Venezuela, I asked why they were not affiliates of CEAAL, like another centre nearby. The group felt that the centre paid lip service to popular education, was funded by dubious interests and basically engaged in counter-revolutionary activity. Regardless of the accuracy of these claims, there has undoubtedly been dilution and co-option of radical grassroots initiatives in Latin America (Petras, 1999) and it is important to be aware of the difficulty in separating appearance from reality. Fifth, even where there has been success, it may not be easily replicable. The popular education forum FREPOP, for example, requires such extraordinary dedication from so many volunteers that organising a similar event would be a massive undertaking. And even where there is inspiration, we should hesitate to over-romanticise the 'other', putting the Latin American experience on a pedestal: even FREPOP has its limitations and critiques.

While it will not single-handedly sort out the problems of a crisis-ridden world, popular education has an important contribution to make to any movement struggling for social justice. Its recent history in Latin America offers a rich variety of experiences in how to think about, organize and practice popular education. Movements outside Latin America can learn general lessons from this but, depending on their needs, may benefit more from detailed study of particular experiences. In the last analysis movements will have to work out for themselves, in theory and practice, what lessons can be learned as, in the words of the Spanish

poet Antonio Machado, turned into song by Joan Manuel Serrat, now the unofficial anthem of the popular education movement, "traveller there is no path, we create the path by walking".
*Translations from Spanish or Portuguese are the author's

REFERENCES

Alforja. (2011). La Sistematización Participativa para descubrir los sentidos y aprender de nuestras experiencias. http://www.redalforja.net/redalforja/images/stories/PDF-DOCS/SP.pdf
Álvarez, S.E., Dagnino, E., & Escóbar, A. (1998). *Cultures of Politics, Politics of Cultures: Revisioning Latin American Social Movements*, 1–29. Oxford: Westview Press.
Arnold, R., & Burke, B. (1983). *A Popular Education Handbook*. Ontario: CUSO & OISE.
Arnold, R., Barndt, D., & Burke, B. (1994). *A New Weave: Popular Education in Canada and Central America*. Ontario: CUSO & OISE.
Barndt, D. (1991). *To Change This House: Popular Education Under the Sandinistas*. Toronto: Between the Lines.
Barnechea, M.M., Gonzalez, E., & Morgan M.L. (1994). La Sistematización Como Producción de Conocimientos. *La Piragua: Revista Latinoamericana de Educacion y Politica*, (9), 122–128.
Betuto Fernández, F. (1998). Panorama y desafíos de la educación popular en Bolivia. In R. A. Abrio, J. D. Sánchez & A. C. Herrera (coordinadores), *La Educación Popular Ante El Siglo XXI*, 75–77. Sevilla: Librería Andaluza.
Boal, A. (1979). *Theatre of the Oppressed*. London: Pluto.
Boff, L. (1985). *Church: charism and power: liberation theology and the institutional church*. London: SCM Press.
Burgos, A., Gluz, N., & Karolinski, M. (2008). Movimientos sociales, educación popular y escolarización "oficial". La autonomía "en cuestión"'. *Referencia No 24, Boletín del Foro Latinoamericano de Políticas Educativas*. http://www.foro-latino.org/flape/boletines/boletin_referencias/boletin_24/referencias24.htm
Bustillos, G., & Vargas, L. (1993). *Técnicas Participativas para la Educación Popular*. Tomo 1&2. Guadalajara: (IMDEC)
Caldart, R.S. (1997). *Educação em Movimento: Formação de Educadores e Educadoras no MST*. Petrópolis, Brazil: Vozes.
CANTERA http://www.canteranicaragua.org/
Carr, I. C. (1990). The Politics of Literacy in Latin America. *Convergence, 23*(2), 50–68.
CEAAL. http://www.ceaal.org/
CEAAL. (1994). Construyendo la Plataforma de la Educación Popular Latinoamericana. *La Piragua: Revista Latinoamericana de Educacion y Politica*, (8), 3–13.
CEAAL. (1996). *Nuevos Escenarios y Nuevos Discursos en la Educación Popular – Memoria – Taller Sobre 'Refundamentación De La Educación Popular'*. Pátzcuaro, Mexico: CEAAL.
Cendales, G. L., Posada F. J., & Torres C. A. (1996). Refundamentación, Pedagogía Y Política: Un Debate Abierto. In Dimensión Educativa, *Educación Popular: Refundamentación*, 105–124. Santafé de Bogotá: Dimensión Educativa.
Crowther, J., Martin. I., & Shaw, M. (1999). *Popular Education and Social Movements in Scotland Today*. Leicester: NIACE.
de Souza, J.F. (2004). A Vigência Da Educação Popular. In *"Debate Latinomericano Sobre Educación Popular II", La Piragua*, Mayo, (21), 47–55.
Dangl, B. (2010). *Dancing with Dynamite: Social Movements and States in Latin America*. Oakland CA: AK Press.
Dimensión Educativa. (1996). *Educación Popular: Refundamentación* Santafé de Bogotá: Dimensión Educativa.

EZLN (Ejército Zapatista para la Liberación Nacional.) (2008). Cómo Funcionan Las Escuelas Zapatistas. Boletín especial EZLN. *Referencia No 24, Boletín del Foro Latinoamericano de Políticas Educativas.* http://www.foro-latino.org/flape/boletines/boletin_referencias/boletin_24/referencias24.htm

Fieldhouse, R. (2000). The Workers' Educational Association. In R Fieldhouse. *A History of Modern British Adult Education,* 166–198. Leicester: NIACE.

Freire, P. (1972). *Pedagogy of the Oppressed.* Harmondsworth: Penguin Books.

Freire, P. (1974). Education as the Practice of Freedom. In *Education for Critical Consciousness,* 1–84. London: Sheed and Ward.

Freire, P. (1991). *A Educação na Cidade.* São Paulo, Brazil: Editora.

Freire, P. (1993). *Pedagogía de la Esperanza.* Mexico: Siglo Veintiuno Editores.

FREPOP. (2011). http://www.frepop.org.br/mesas_tematicas_programacao.php

Gadotti, M. (1992). Estado e Educação Popular: Bases para uma Educação Pública Popular. In M. Gadotti & C. A. Torres, *Estado e Educação Popular na América Latina.* São Paulo: Papirus.

Gadotti, M., & Torres, C. A. (1992). *Estado e Educação Popular na América Latina.* São Paulo: Papirus.

Garces, D. M. (2010). Moviminetos Sociales y Educación Popular. *La Piragua: Revista Latinoamericana de Educación y Política,* (32), 55–68.

Ghiso, A. (1993). Cuando el saber rompe el silencio... Diálogo De Saberes En Los Procesos De Educación Popular. *La Piragua: Revista Latinoamericana de Educación y Política,* 7, 32–36.

Gibson, A. (1994). Freirian v Enterprise Education: the Difference is in the Business. *Convergence,* 27(1).

Gutiérrez Pérez, F., & Castillo, D. P. (1994). *La Mediación Pedagógica para la Educación Popular.* San José, Costa Rica: Radio Nederland Training Centre (RNTC).

IMDEC. http://www.imdec.net/index.php?option=com_frontpage&Itemid=1

IMDEC. (1994). *Ser Dirigente No Es Cosa Fácil: Métodos, Estilos y Valores del Dirigente Popular.* Guadalajara, Mexico: IMDEC.

Jara, O.H. (1994). *Para Sistematizar Experiencias.* San José, Costa Rica: Alforja.

Jara, O.H. (2004). Resignifiquemos Las Propuestas Y Prácticas De Educación Popular Frente A Los Desafíos Históricos Contemporáneos. In *"Debate Latinomericano Sobre Educación Popular II",* La Piragua, Mayo, (21), 110–114.

Kane, L. (2001). *Popular Education and Social Change in Latin America* London: LAB.

Kane, L. (2010). Universities in Venezuela CONCEPT, Vol 1, No 3. *http://concept.lib.ed.ac.uk/index.php/Concept/article/viewFile/90/100*

Macas, L., & Lozano, A. (2000). Reflexiones en torno al proceso colonizador y las características de la educación universitaria en el Ecuador, *Boletín Rimay,* No 19, octubre. *Quito: ICC* (Quoted in Zibeche, 2008:5).

Magendzo, S. K. (1994). La Sistematización Como Acto Comunicativo y Su Relación Con El Constructivismo. *La Piragua: Revista Latinoamericana de Educacion y Politica,* (9), 136–140.

Mejía, M. R. (1995). *Transformação Social.* São Paulo, Brazil: Cortez.

Mendoza, R. M. C. (coordinación). (1997). *Construyendo Pedagogía Popular: Encuentros de Experiencias Pedagógicas.* Mexico: SEDEPAC.

Núñez, C. H. (1992). *Educar Para Transformar, Transformar Para Educar.* Guadalajara, Mexico: IMDEC.

Núñez, C. H. (1993). Permiso Para Pensar...Educación Popular: Propuesta Y Debate. *América Libre,* No 2, Abril-Mayo, 46–61. Buenos Aires: Liberarte.

Núñez, C. H. (2002). ¿Refundamentación de la Educación Popular? In *"Educación popular: nuevos horizontes y renovacón de compromises".* La Piragua, Mayo, (18).

Olcese, C. (2011). Latin American Movements and Neoliberalism. *Social Movement Studies,* 10(3), 299–303.

Palma, D. (1992). *La Sistematización Como Estrategia de Conocimiento en la Educación Popular.* Santiago, Chile: CEAAL.

Petras, J. (1999). ONGs y movimientos socio-políticos. *PROCESO: El Salvador*, Año 19, número 848, marzo *24*, 6–7.

Ponce, D. (1999). *Interview with author, San Salvador, August.*

Puiggrós, A. (1994). Historia y Prospectiva de la Educación Popular Latinoamericana. In M Gadotti & C. A. Torres, *Educação Popular: Utopia Latino-Americana* 13–22. São Paulo: Cortez.

Rede Mulher. http://www.redemulher.org.br/

Schugurensky, D. (2000). The Forms of Informal Learning: Towards a Conceptualization of the Field. *NALL Working Paper No 19* Ontario: Centre for the Study of Education and Work. https://tspace.library .utoronto.ca/bitstream/1807/2733/2/19formsofinformal.pdf

Schugurensky, D. (2010). *Popular Education: A Snapshot.* http://www.oise.utoronto.ca/legacy/research/ edu20/home.html?cms_page=edu20/home.html

Soethe, J. R. (1994). Educación Popular: Concepciones Históricas, Construcción de Paradigmas y Teoría-Práctica. *La Piragua: Revista Latinoamericana de Educacion y Politica,* 9, 152–159.

Stahler-Sholk, R., Vanden, H. E., & Kuecker, G.D. (2007). Globalizing Resistance: The New Politics of Social Movements in Latin America. *Latin American Perspectives, 2*(153), March, 5–16.

Taylor, P.V. (1993). *Texts of Paulo Freire.* Buckingham: Oxford University Press.

Thwaites Rey, M. (2004). *La autonomía como búsqueda, el Estado como contradicción.* Buenos Aires: Prometeo Libros.

Thomas, G. (2011). Latin American Social Movements: Shaping a New Millenium of Struggle. *Latin American Perspectives, 38*(5), 114–122.

Wilpert, G. (2007). Chávez Announces Nationalizations, Constitutional Reform for Socialism in Venezuela. *Venezuelaanalysis.com. http://venezuelanalysis.com/news/2164*

Zarco, C. (2001). Review of Chapter 1. In L. Kane, *Popular Education and Social Change in Latin America,* 29–32. London: Latin American Bureau.

Zibechi, R. (2008). La Educación En Los Movimientos Sociales. *Referencia No 24, Boletín del Foro Latinoamericano de Políticas Educativas.* http://www.foro-latino.org/flape/boletines/boletin_ referencias/boletin_24/referencias24.htm (All websites accessed October 2011).

SECTION 2

LEARNING THROUGH CULTURAL STRUGGLE

DARLENE E. CLOVER

6. AESTHETICS, SOCIETY AND SOCIAL MOVEMENT LEARNING

ON BEGINNINGS

I am signalling you through the flames…

Civilisation self-destructs. Nemesis is knocking at the door.

What are Poets for in such an age? What is the use of the arts?…

If you would call yourself a Poet, don't just sit there. Poetry is not a
sedentary, not a 'take your seat' practice. Stand up and let them have
it….Through art, create order out of the chaos of living…

Be subversive, constantly question reality and the status quo.

Strive to change the world in such a way that there's no further need to be a
dissident.

Lawrence Ferlinghetti, *Poetry as Insurgent Art*, 2007

Social movements are the unauthorised, unofficial, anti-institutional
collective action of ordinary citizens trying to change the world.

T.V. Reed, *The Art of Protest*, 2005

Visually illuminate. Aesthetically dissonante. Satirically implicate. Theatrically
expropriate. Creatively resonate. Imaginatively educate. This is a chapter about the
positionalities of the arts and the arts as educational practice in society and social
movements. My passion for the arts began with my tenure with the International
Council for Adult Education (ICAE), a Toronto-based non-governmental 'place of
encounter' for adult educators worldwide who shared a commitment to the critical
and social purposes of adult education. Within the ICAE the arts—photography,
popular theatre, music, poetry, dance and the like—were used as enablers of new
understandings, containers for dialogue, and mediums to generate new knowledge.
By extension visual artists, poets, photographers, musicians, and theatre performers
were mediators and agents of critical social learning and change. I also saw the
potential of the arts in social movements when I took part in a women's march in
Ottawa in 1995. Imagine this…

*B. L. Hall, D. E. Clover, J. Crowther and E. Scandrett (Eds.), Learning and Education
for a Better World: The Role of Social Movements, 87–100.*

D. E. CLOVER

Neo-liberalism is in full force as the might-makes-right countries invade those with less power but more natural resources; the competitive market ideology continues to be sharpened on the backs of the poor; environmental justice is shouted from the treetops but ignored at board room tables; and many women, the poorest of the poor who care for the children and communities of famine, war and environmental destruction remain, despite decades of movements for change, just so much collateral damage. But it is a warm and sultry day on the streets of Ottawa and 30,000 women from across Canada and around the world have come together to march towards the parliament buildings, armed with placards, pamphlets, slogans, and a message of change. Swirling in this tide are hundreds of children – for who would look after them so the women could be free to march? – as well as diaper bags, perambulators, squeaky toys, stuffed animals, colourful balloons, lollipops and gushing frankfurters. Lining the banks of this river of defiance and animation is the police, dressed in full riot gear but resting lethargically against their motorcycles, often stifling yawns as the current of thirty thousand strong call for equity, peace and justice for women. But suddenly, things change. Someone is moving through the crowd on stilts announcing – wait for it – a puppet show. Although I am unsure what I am hearing, the police are not. I watch in fascination as they leap to their feet, checking for truncheons, grasping helmets, and gasping furtively in to walkie-talkies: "puppets, puppets, puppets, move!" I watch as some police close in on the puppeteers whilst others position themselves to impede the tidal wave of women and children moving excitedly towards the makeshift stage. Had I misunderstood something? Had I gone mad? Had the police? How could a mere puppet show provoke such a violent reaction when banners, shouting and fist waving could not? How indeed...

I begin this chapter with a discussion of important debates around the place of art in society and in particular, in relation to knowledge and learning. My account does not aspire to be exhaustive but rather to identify some significant and complex metaphysical and epistemological considerations that shape aesthetic discourses and judgements today. Flowing from this, and again in a necessarily truncated form imposed by the limitations of space, I highlight three major challenges embedded in cultural political discourse and outline two contemporary feminist responses – political art and activist art. I then apply these two conceptualisations to two examples of cultural interactions to outline some of key education and learning dimensions of the work of women and men who perform so imaginatively in support of a more just and sustainable world.

ON THE ARTS AND KNOWLEDGE IN SOCIETY

[The arts] are simultaneously emotional, cognitive and sensuous.

Amy Mullins, *Feminist Art and the Political Imagination*, 2003

A plethora of debates exist around the role and place of the arts in human and social development. Indeed, for centuries 'scholars, artists and citizens alike have debated how aesthetic forms engage, refute, undermine, elaborate on, challenge,

88

shock, or counter the social, cultural, and political conditions of society' (McGregor, In Press). Plato is credited with being perhaps the first to articulate a consistent albeit highly derogatory view of the arts in human life and society. To Plato – although others such as the Christian Church took up his arguments with missionary zeal – the arts were 'falsehoods', flawed or inexact imitations of the world with the potential to corrupt by stimulating irrationality and irrigating immorality and associated inappropriate behaviours. This particular understanding derived from a bipartite notion where the rational or thinking element of humanity was seen as noble and aimed towards the greater social good whilst the irrational side – the emotional or 'appetitive' – was highly susceptible to the corrupting forces, making a dangerous "impression on suggestible people" (Belifore and Bennett, 2010, p. 54) by becoming their rulers rather than their subjects. Threaded through these understandings were issues of class and interpretation. Whilst the highly educated classes were understood to have the skills necessary to assess any 'myths' portrayed in and through the arts, the 'susceptible minds' of the non-lettered classes were not. Seen to be lacking in any form of aesthetic judgement or life experience upon which to draw, the masses were unable to interpret artworks 'correctly', discern reality from engineered situations and were thereby mislead into believing things they had "no grounds for believing" (Hospers, 1974, p. 156).

Woven further into the above are questions of the epistemological and educational usefulness of the arts. Russell (2006), reflecting Platonic arguments, suggests arts such as literature, paintings, theatre and poetry lack any ability to supply "real data" that can be judged against any reliable 'scientific' standard. New (1999) concurs, arguing the arts cannot "authenticate the view [they convey]", which means they are neither factual nor reliable sources of knowledge, but he adds that although we may garner some 'truths' from the arts, "they are not shown to be truths by virtue of being persuasively conveyed [through an artwork]" (p. 120). Carroll (2002) takes a slightly different track, concurring the arts can convey universal truths but negating their ability to educate because they simply recycle truisms people already possess. "Consequently, since it makes little sense to claim that people learn [what] they already know…there is little point in regarding the arts as education" (p. 4). The best the arts can hope to do is "activate already possessed knowledge rather than its creation *ex novo*" (Belifore & Bennet, 2010, p. 46).

Scholars such as Adorno (1984) and later, Habermas, however, denounced the winnowing away of the cultural and aesthetic life-world, arguing that this only worked to undermine their potential in terms of democratic public engagement (Duvenage, 2003). Although wary of truth claims in the arts, Habermas argued that aesthetic expressive discourse was the "correct way to interpret one's own and other's needs and desires; the appropriate argumentative form for revealing subjectivity" (p. 55). Further, if "aesthetic experience is used to shed light on individual problems, situation and the striving for solidarity then aesthetics must be seen as part of everyday communicative practice" (p. 118). The arts must therefore be placed within "the formal language of argumentative inter-subjectivity"

(Duvenage, 2003, p. 119) and not simply banished to an affective/emotional homelessness of derision, scorn and condescension.

Yet others argue it is this 'affective' – the sensory, appetitive, and emotive – aspect of the arts that is the one most vital to transforming society. Indeed, Greene (1995) suggests the more serious the problems in life, the more we need the arts to provide us with compassion, empathy and insight. Indeed, it is emotive and affective learning, and not simply the cognitive, that can best challenge today's technically rationalised industrial culture "whose values are brittle and whose conception of what's important [is] narrow" (Eisner in Butterwick and Dawson, 2006, p. 3). Wyman (2004) refers to this as the ability to defy "the constraints of expectation and the everyday…and approach the realm of understanding that lies beyond the mediate and the real" (p. 1). Eisner (2008) walks the emotional-rational tightrope when he suggests the mind operates at its highest level *when* sensory perception and emotion are involved in the process of critical reflection and meaning making:

> To talk about thinking *and* feeling is somewhat of a misnomer, for it segregates feeling from thinking by the inclusion of the word 'and'. The ability to feel what a work expresses, to participate in the emotional ride that it makes possible is a product of the way we *think* about what we see…. Seeing is an accomplishment and looking is a task, and it is through seeing that experience is altered, and when altered, becomes an experience in shaping the kind of minds that people can make for themselves (p. 344).

In other words, emotions do not distract people from thinking about or engaging in 'worthier matters', as Plato and others surmised, but rather, as members of the Frankfurt school believed, liberate our engagement with the world and works "to achieve all we hope for a society" (Wyman, 2006, p. 1).

ON CULTURAL POLITICS

The conflict between politics and art…cannot and must not be solved.

Hannah Arendt, in *The Art of Protest*, 2005

Any discussion of the arts in social movements will ultimately also gives rise to what Reed (2001, p. 303) calls "the difficult question of the relation between politics and aesthetics." Although beyond the scope of this chapter to delve too deeply into these complex concerns, I do want to acknowledge three important concerns because they are relevant to the arts and activism. In doing this I am not trying – nor should one ever try according to Hannah Arendt – to reconcile these struggles. Rather, I am allowing these performative contradictions to remain unanswered although I will in the final sections of this chapter, draw attention to potential of the political purposefulness of art to social movement learning, education and justice-oriented change.

Although speaking predominantly to the commodification and mass production of the arts, Marcuse and Adorno raise the first concern. They believed that if the arts were to make a political impact they needed to be kept free of politics. Their reasons revolved around artistic freedom and a belief that politics would render impotent "art's revolutionary longing and utopian potential" (in Duvenage, 2003, p. 41). A second and linked concern to this troubling of art and politics are questions of use value and instrumentality. Scholars enter this debate from the different corners but the arts for arts sake debates essentially challenge government policies towards the arts [that] fail to recognise their special nature:

> The arts...probably are instruments of social improvement, agents of social change, for social equality or for community harming. Yet...these demands set a list of challenges which are not intrinsic to the arts, are distant from their true nature and all of which could be antithetical to their basic functions and purposes (of beauty, entertainment and enlightenment) (Belifore and Bennett, 2004, p. 8).

Adorno (1984) in particular held the view that any art that attempted to address socio-political issues or directly communicate those in anyway to an audience, was propaganda. Mussolini is an example of what he means. Mussolini argued it was impossible to build a nation without arts and culture and "sought to develop a national culture that engaged directly with the masses [making] cultural instead of political participation" (Doumanis, 2001, p. 146). Doumanis suggests this problematic cultural-political vision may have been "Italian Fascism's most distinctive contribution to modern politics" (p. 146). Finally, and hand in hand with the above, are challenges to concepts such as imagination and creativity. For were it not these faculties that brought us bombs with the capacity to obliterate life on this planet?

ON AESTHETIC POLITICS AND ACTIVISM

Art must become responsible for its politics.

Dot Tuer, in *But is it Art?*, 1995

Notwithstanding these criticisms, and recognising no easy answers exist to the conjunction of art and politics, feminist aesthetic theorists suggest two re-conceptions vis-à-vis social movement struggle that provide a platform for my discussions on learning and education. These are political art and activist art. At their core, both political art and activist art are 'engaged with political issues, questions and concerns' (Mullin, 2003, p. 191). They are a coming together of aesthetic concerns with the socio-political agendas and grievances of social movements. Within both of these categorisations, artists play key roles. Although one's understanding of who an artist is could muddy these waters – many argue we are all artists in our own right – I suggest it raises a key difference between political art and activist art. While the former is artist-centred the later is not. Activist art is a collaboration between artists and other social movement actors that involves "a high degree of...research, organisational activity, and orientation" (Felshin, 1995, p. 10). In other words, the methods of development and execution draw on diverse expertise and creativity beyond the art world/artists 'as a means of engaging the participation of the audience or community in distributing the message to the public' (Ibid, p. 11). Further, Lippard (1984) suggested that 'political art tends to be socially concerned and activist art tends to be socially involved' (p. 349). In other words, political art explores socio-political or cultural issues but it does not involve political action (Mullin, 2003). Moreover, political art is seen to be more product (artwork) oriented and involved more closely with the established art world, although the issues it addresses will have a broader resonance (e.g. Felshin, 1995). Conversely, activist art, in both its forms and methods, is more process, rather than object oriented and "it usually takes place in public sites rather than the within the context of the art world venues" (Felshin, 1995, p. 10). Activist art actively seeks, as alluded to above, broader public participation and therefore is seen to be political in two respects: its process and its content.

ON STORIES

Our strategy should be not only to confront the empire but to mock it ... with our art ... to tell our own stories; stories that are different from the ones we're being brainwashed to believe.

Arundhati Roy, speech at the World Social Forum, 2003

Since their inception, social movements have been rife with creative cultural activities. Indeed, there has never been a viable movement for social change without the arts being central to the movement, make them critical to their tactical repertoire (Reed, 2005; Bogad, 2005). But how can we understand these tactics as educational? What are the education and learning dimensions of the work of women and men who so creatively and courageously "run with brushes and glue", to borrow a metaphor from Chadwick's (1995, p. 7) work on the Guerrilla Girls who dressed in masks and re-painted Master paintings to challenge the gendered nature of the art world. The best way to approach this question is to provide examples of arts-based activities. Although abbreviated, these two stories from Canada in themselves tell us about the potential, and the challenge, of cultural education and learning in social movements.

Carole Condé and Carl Beveridge are political artists in Toronto Canada who have "chosen the labour movement as a primary site of cultural production and reception" (Tuer, 1995, p. 197). Working with men and women in the broad labour movement, these two artists use photography and other visual media to address historical and contemporary labour struggles. For example, *Standing Up* was a visual "chronicle of women workers' fight to win a first contract" (p. 197); *No Greater Power* provided a visual rendering of the impact of industrial globalisation and technological change on the workforce; *No Immediate Threat* was a series of striking and evocative poster-size colour photo-narratives about the nuclear industry in particular and the end of modernism and the illusionary dream of unlimited resources and rising profits. These two artists also create satirical posters and cartoons to draw attention to issues such as class and gender discrimination.

Both the process of creation and dissemination of the product of art are controlled and executed by the artists. Often, although not always the case, the artworks are not exact documentation of people's actual stories but rather, re-creations. The primary reason is that although in the case of *Standing Up*, "the women [are] willing to be interviewed and to discuss the difficulties, both emotional and political, of fighting a first contract, they faced potential reprisals by the company if they could be personally identified in the work" (p. 205). Condé and Beveridge therefore create composite characters and fictional narratives that combine individual testimonies and aesthetic skills. In addition, the artworks combine images and symbols of emotional/personal struggle and collective/political struggle, despair and hope, defiance and loss, imagination and stark reality. They are displayed through exhibitions in union and community halls for members of the labour movement but also, in art galleries to bring exposure of the issues to the art world.

On Vancouver Island, a group of artists, quilters and concerned citizens (e.g. teachers and community workers) and activists came together to develop a community outreach and educational plan to challenge the construction of a gas-fired power plant. The art genre they chose was the quilt because the leader of the team – Kristen Miller – was a quilter. Moreover, although seldom acknowledged, fabric media have a legacy of use in social movement activity such as the Chilean women who created *arpilleras* (small pieces of cloth with images of daily life) depicting the atrocities of the Pinochet regime and smuggled them out of the country to alert the world (Clover, In Press).

The educational outreach process by this group of social movement actors on Vancouver Island began with the group of women sending out hundreds of small squares of cloth to seniors' centres, schools, arts institutions, social service agencies and even local cafes and shops. No guidelines were provided other than the suggestion that people design something on the quilt square – either individually or collectively – to express their feelings and reactions to the plant proposal. As the squares returned the spent a chaotic hours arranging the squares to make the full quilts. This was a challenging process because while some of the women were artists as noted above, others were not so their needs and concerns differed. In addition there was a variety of themes, colours, images, symbols, and textures to work with. In other words, unlike the work of Condé and Beveridge, control was not solely in the hands of two artists although it also meant balancing aesthetic and activist concerns.

Once the squares were in place, sewing them together in to banner-sized quilts began – a practice dubbed 'quilting in public' (Clover, 2009). They quilted on the sidewalks in front of cafés, art galleries, city hall, a local television station, the police station and even the building where the hydro companies were holding a public information session. Through these public exhibitions, the quilters had the opportunity to engage with the hundreds of people who approached them, curious about the collective public quilting (to quilt in public is not commonly viewed in

Canada, however, it is legal according to the police who advanced at one point upon the women!). Some of the images on quilt challenged the need for the plant, stitching instead windmills and solar panels as alternate energy sources. Other images spoke emotionally of the impact the plant would have on children and sea life. Another image depicted a devil gushing from a smoke stack surrounded by words that encapsulated the toxins that would be spewing from the plant (e.g. ammonia and sulphur oxide). Other squares carried bolder, political statements. On one sits the caricature image of Uncle Sam (United States) roasting the world over orange flames from a power plant. Oh, and by the way, in the face of opposition, the hydro companies backed away from the power plant proposal.

ON EDUCATION, LEARNING AND THE ARTS

With such an enriched understanding of the nature of the imagination... arts can be seen as neither servants of some predetermined political message or slogan nor as needing to be above or beyond politics in order to retain their art character.

Amy Mullin, Feminist Art and the Political Imagination, 2003

Together, these two stories highlight a number of inter-woven aspects central to adult education and learning theory and practice. The artworks in both these stories render strikingly visible what are often intangibles in society: struggles between capital and labour, individualism and collectivism, economic and environmental ideologies, gender differences and multiple identities, and people's knowledges. Although these intangibles have profound impacts on people's personal and working lives – not to mention communities as a whole – they often operate subversively yet extremely authoritatively. So engrained are they that although people 'feel' something is amiss they often cannot quite articulate what that is, nor can they always clearly see the link between what feminists call the personal and the political. But the artworks, and the process of art making, can and do. They provide a platform for individual voices to be heard – an elderly man in a seniors home who opposed the construction of the plant or a woman who struggled against patriarchal control in her workplace and her family life. But the individual stories are fragmented and incomplete until the quilt is sewn together; until the individual ideas, concerns and voices become one through a chronicle. Jefferies (1998, p. 113) refers to this as a 'puzzle-picture making' – taking scraps of knowledge, meaning and experience (the squares) and bringing them together in "the overall texture of a quilt" to create a unified pattern and broader, more inter-woven and collective understanding of an issue.

Further, people are often more inclined to speak out in public when there is a sense of safety and anonymity and this is something creative practices can provide. Although not the case for many social movement activists, for others such as women who "are trained from birth to develop social and public personae based on appearances, torn between wanting to be seen and not wanting to appear too visible" disguise and anonymity in public can prove to be enormously empowering

(Chatwick, 1995, p. 9). It is also the sense of collective identity – the quilt rather than a mishmash of squares – that draws attention and becomes a permanent visual reminder of community power and collective struggle.

Picking up some of the threads from above, so to speak, Paulo Freire (1986) once argued that people are not liberated by lectures and slogans because these practices are often simply too passive. Rather, people are liberated when they participate in public dialogue. While many social movement actors have little problem engaging publicly, others do not have this capacity. Fear, apathy and the like can silence voices needing to be heard and marginalise people from engaging openly in activist work. The arts encourage the engagement of the non-actors. By using the process they did, the quilters were able to engage in the public in two very important ways. The first was to reach out, through the squares of fabric, to people around the community who had deep concerns about the proposed power plant but they were not necessarily the type – or at the age such as seniors in care facilities – to participate in rallies or attend public hearings. Just because people are not or cannot be active in more traditional activist ways, does not mean they should be excluded. In fact, they were very much present, their issues and concerns very visibly stitched into the mosaic of the quilt. And by quilting in public in so many diverse locations, the quilters were able to engage many other people in process. In my conversations with the quilters, they argued that it was the soft, gentle approach of the quilting process, the timeliness, the colourful emotional counter-narratives and stories and of course, curiosity at this public project that drew so much attention and worked to educate and engage so many.

The artworks are permanent visual stories and counter-narratives of struggle and despair, power and hope. Stories are important because they are what we use to try to make sense of things difficult to see or comprehend, as noted above, such neoliberalism. The images and stories in the artworks of both projects re-conceptualise, de-construct and ultimately challenge the discourses of, for example, development and unsustainable growth, creating new visual conceptual framings of issues and practices and often illusive analytical opportunities for those who view or engage with them. Importantly, the art works also visually encapsulate 'feelings' and thereby provide an opportunity to respond to 'rationality'. For example, the power plant officials on Vancouver Island were confident with their graphs and charts of increased employment or the prevention of power blackouts, making it virtually impossible for people to fight back using the same rational tactics of fact and debate. But do logic and fact always win the day? Of course not for if this were true the realms of scientific environmental data available to the Canadian government would have closed the tar sands and men would by now have realised the insidiousness of gender inequalities and ended all forms of patriarchy. Rather it is structures of feeling that most often underlay our ability to see and respond to our circumstances in new ways and thereby contributes to new forms of consciousness (Beyer, 2000).

Behind these counter-narratives and stories are creativity and the imagination. Dewey (1934) argued many years ago that the imagination was a powerful faculty that informed daily life in myriad ways, animating and pervading all processes of thinking and observation, a 'blending of interests where the mind comes in contact with the world' (p. 237). Mullins (2003) sees this as "our capacity to think in detailed was about states of affairs with which we are not immediately acquainted" (p. 196). Creativity and imagination help us to imagine the past and the future, possibilities and impossibilities and combine these in ways not generally seen as co-existing. The quilt square of the gushing devil illuminates a deep understanding of the toxic brew to be spewed from the smokestacks in to the global environment in a way that aligns it with morals and the reality of environmental pollution. The standpoint epistemology of the women in the unions illustrated through the photographic projects illustrates what Paulo Freire (1986, p. 58) called "critical reflection on their own lives" – but also demonstrates a deeper political knowledge of the problematic cultural and ideological landscapes of unions. Wyman (2005) takes it further, referring to this in the context of social movements, as the defiant imagination. He believes the defiant imagination is what sparks the passion to act, to speak out, to engage, and equally importantly, "to ask questions we might not voluntarily engage with, uncomfortable questions we might be able to handle in other ways" (p. 15). For as Wordsworth noted in *Prelude*, "Imagination... Is but another name for absolute power" ([1850 1959, p. 491).

While all types of arts from theatre to poetry to photography work well as educational tools in social movements, quilts, to me have a unique quality. Quilts are deeply associated with comfort, warmth, and security and the familiar (Halsall & Ali, 2004). The softness, the familiarity, and the intimations of domesticity are comforting and known (Robertson, 2005). But in the milieu of neoliberal struggle, safety and comfort are an illusion. The quilting project (and many others I have encountered through my research) takes this so-called 'gentle' medium and turns it on its head. So while the shape and construction suggest something in particular, the narrative images and colours tell a very different story. The quilt becomes a comforting and inviting yet brilliantly almost repelling juxtaposition of the conventional (properly quilted) with the unconventional (the critical stories). "Slowed down by this, the view pays attention, is stopped, and enters into a space of criticality, a space represented by the surprising moment" (Robertson, 2005, p. 219) of what Bogad (2005) sees as the "volatile combination of two seemingly incompatible elements."

Picking up a thread from above, making artworks with care and attention – the way artists in the process insist they be done – is a long process, from a stage of imagination and representation in people's minds, to the creative of the final images or product. It is a continuous process of negotiation between initial designs and dreams and the possibilities offered by the chosen form of representation. Choices of materials or techniques are neither passive nor individual; concrete issues rendered metaphoric or symbolic continually call for the altering of designs as the work of art takes on new shapes, forms and meanings It is this slowness and critical/creative thinking about art and about the issues that allows for deeper reflections on aesthetics, on why the quilt or series of posters are being made, on the coherent story they will need to tell and how they will touch the hearts and minds of the viewers. Each time a political/activist piece of art is seen it is re-storied by the viewer, so that the product itself becomes a tool of exploration, of meaning making.

"Because of their power to delight, [artists] teach more pleasantly (and thus effectively) than any philosopher ever could", argued Daniello in *Poetica* back in 1536. Illeris (2003) found that one of the key sub-strategies adult learners develop to deal with complex contradictions is humour. Further, during a speech in the 1990s in Toronto, Canadian feminist Ursula Franklin addressed the propensity by social movements towards doom and gloom by asking, 'Having taken the dim view now what?' These are important views, findings and questions for social movement action. The issues with which social movements deal such as violence against women, undrinkable water systems, or volatile, greedy markets, are simply no laughing matter. Yet pleasure and happiness are and need to be part of our lives and our learning, something social movement artists understand. The quilts and the photography projects are poignant, but they are also imbued with much humour and irreverence. Returning to the defiant imagination, Roy (2004) writes that humour is "a sign of rebelliousness; laughter can defeat the fear of the unknown, [working] as a metaphor for transformation,...a communal response of sensuous solidarity as it implies common understanding with others.. [and helps people] to cope with the situation of the world' (p. 59). Making people laugh, as the arts do so well, has proven to be an effective way to address issues that might otherwise have people shutting down or turning away (Bogad, 2005). This does not mean that they are trivial and mindless, but rather that they are versatile and provide opportunities for creative self and social critique.

ON CONCLUSIONS

What is the purpose of such creative political performance?

L. M. Bogad, Electoral Guerrilla Theatre, 2005

I conclude this chapter by recognising some of the challenges, although they are often mixed with potential, of this cultural work that so adeptly synthesises the cognitive and the emotional, the imaginative and the intuitive, the grim and the comical. To begin, the arts in social movements do not stop neo-liberalism in its tracks – although the quilters did much to stop the power plant – nor are they the only important educational process in social movement activity. Secondly, the arts garner attention, and a lot of it. This can be important in terms of getting the word out about issues and concerns or countering the negative spin the media often puts on protests and other movement activities. The media devoured the visual extravaganza of the quilts and the women and the messages featured on television, radio and in local and regional newspapers. Yet attention is a double-edged sword. For their activist artwork, the women were questioned by the police, threatened by hydro authorities and thrown out of city hall. Not only have those involved in the conceptualising the artworks such as the women union members in *Standing Up* faced reprisal but Condé and Beveridge too have faced opposition from everything from corporate and union management to the formal art world because "it is one thing to be an artist with politics. It is another matter altogether to incorporate a call to social revolution as a transparent theme of an exhibition" (p. 197). People, as Cropley (2003, p. 3) puts it, "who produce novelty in settings that are not open for it, are likely to suffer various kinds of negative sanctions." But many continue to dare to use the arts as a tool of protest, of engagement and learning, of visibility and for this they must be seen as nothing less than courageous. These defiantly public acts are important because it is often from discomfort and challenge, humour and the emotion that we learn the most. And where there is art there is censorship and heavy-handed consequences. This is because, as Griffiths (1993, p. 30) suggests, the arts are understood by those in power to be "far more than mere self-expression or decorative pastime". Their counter-images, humour and life-giving dynamics are nothing less than "vigorously effective" and therefore must be controlled (p. 31). And it is this power that I witnessed at the women's march on the streets of Ottawa through the strings of the puppeteers. Artists will keep on creating even though, or perhaps better said because, the world often violates their deepest values. As the social, economic, and environmental fabrics of so many communities around the world fray under neoliberalism, the cultural work of these social movement actors show us how creativity and the aesthetic dimension can be integral to learning for change.

REFERENCES

Adorno, T. (1984). *Aesthetic theory*. London: Routledge.
Belifore, E. & Bennett, O. (2008). *The social impact of the arts*. London: Palgrave MacMillan.
Bogad, L.M. (2005). Electoral Guerrilla Theatre: Radical ridicule and social movements. London: Routledge.
Butterwick, S. & Dawson, J. (2005). Adult education and the arts. In T. Fenwick, T. Nesbit & B. Spencer (Eds.), *Context of adult education: Canadian perspectives*. Toronto: Thompson Educational Publishing.
Carroll, N. (2002). The wheel of virtue: Art, literature and moral knowledge. *The Journal of Ethics and Art Criticism, 60*(1), 3–26.
Chadwick, W. (1995). *Confessions of the Guerrilla Girls*. New York: Harper Perennial.
Clover, D.E. (In Press). Feminist artists and popular education: The creative turn. In L. Manicom & S. Walters (Eds.), *Feminist popular education: Creating pedagogies of possibility*. New York: Palgrave.
Clover, D.E. (2009). Learning's ecological turn: Citizenship and environmental adult education. In E. Lucio-Viegas (Ed), *Citizenship as politics: International perspectives from adult education*. Rotterdam, NL: Sense Publishing
Cropley, A.J. (2001). *Creativity in Education and Learning*. London: Routledge Falmer.
Dewey, J. (1980). *Art as experience*. New York: First Perigee Printing.
Doumanis, N. (2001). *Italy*. London: Arnold.
Duvenage, P. (2003). *Habermas and Aesthetics*. Cambridge, UK: Polity Press.
Eisner, E. (2008). The museum as a place for education. In *Actas/potencias y communicones*. Madrid: I Congreso Internacional Los Museos en la Educación: La formación de los educadores.
Freire, P. (1986). *Pedagogy of the Oppressed*. New York: Continuum.
Greene, M. (1995). Releasing the imagination. Essays on education, the arts and social change. San Francisco: Jossey-Bass Publishers.
Griffiths, J. (1997). Art as weapon of protest. *Resurgence*, 180, 35–37.

Halsall, E. & Ali, S. (2004). Unravelling Quilted Texts: An Alternate Inquiry into the Social Fabric of Life. *Journal of child and Youth Care Work, 17*(1), 136–140.

Hospers, J. (1974). *Meaning and truth in the arts.* Chapel Hill: The University of North Carolina.

Illeris, K. (2003). Adult education as experienced by the learners. *International Journal of Lifelong Learning. 22*(1), 13–23.

Jefferies, J. (1998). Autobiographical patterns. In I. Bachmann & R. Scheuing (Eds.), *Material matters. the art and culture of contemporary textiles.* Toronto: YYZ Books.

Lippard, L. (1984). Get the message? A decade of art for social change. New York: EIP. Dutton, Inc.

McGregor, C. (In Press). Art informed pedagogy: Tools for social transformation. *International Journal of Lifelong Education.*

Mullins, A. (2003). Feminist art and the political imagination. *Hypathia, 18*(4), 189–213.

New, C. (1999). Philosophy of literature: An introduction. London: Routledge.

Reed, T.V. (2005). The art of protest: Culture and activism from the Civil Rights movement to the streets of Seattle. Minneapolis: University of Minnesota Press.

Robertson, K. (2005). The revolution will wear a sweater. In S. Shukaitis, D. Graeber, & E. Biddle (Eds.), *Constituent imagination: militant investigations/collective theorization.* Oakland: AK Press.

Roy, C. (2004). The Raging Grannies: Wild hats, cheeky songs and witty actions for a better world. Montreal: Black Rose.

Russell, B. (2006). The philosophical limits of film. In Carroll, N. & Choi, J. (Eds.), *Philosophy of film and motion pictures: An anthology.* Oxford: Blackwell.

Shakotko, D. & Walker, K. (1999). Poietic leadership. In P. Begley & P. Leonard (Eds.), *The values of educational administration.* London: Falmer Press.

Tuer, D. (1995). Is it still priviledged art? The politics of class and collaboration in the art practice of Carol Conde and Karl Beveridge. In N. Felshin (Ed.), *But is it art?: The spirit of art as activism,* Seattle: Bay Press.

Wyman, M. (2004). *The defiant imagination.* Vancouver: Douglas & MacIntyre.

ASTRID VON KOTZE

7. COMPOSTING THE IMAGINATION IN POPULAR EDUCATION

INTRODUCTION

True genesis is not at the beginning but at the end, and it starts to begin only when society and existence become radical, i.e. grasp their roots. But the root of history is the working, creating human being who reshapes and overhauls the given facts. Once he (sic) has grasped himself and established what is his, without expropriation and alienation, in real democracy, there arises in the world something which shines into the childhood of all and in which no one has yet been: homeland.' (Bloch, 1986, p. 1376)

Just where, within the current neo-liberal conjuncture and in a world dominated by global capital, American imperialism and quasi-religious fundamentalism, can the progressive activist, including the scholar-activist, find the best entry-points for radical intervention? (Saul, 2006, p. 111)

A narrow alleyway between a brick house and a metal container converted into a cell-phone shop leads to a backyard, neatly divided into different areas for drying washing, having tea, and waiting one's turn at the hairdresser who rents the corner room for his business. The other corner has been turned into a meeting venue: cardboard covering wet patches on the floor, plastic on the walls to keep out the rain, a neon light illuminating a wide assortment of chairs and benches. About 25 people have assembled here, mainly women, and are busy interviewing each other about interests and passions. The owner of the room requests the barber to turn down the thumping music; two women shift their small children from hip to back as they greet each other. All of them label strips of paper with topics they wish to explore in this course. As the strips are laid out and sorted we read 'stop unwealthiness'. This could both summarise the common purpose and indicate how a shift in perspective towards 'enoughness' would be a good beginning.

Through a transparent process of questioning and challenging, negotiation and voting for preferences a course outline for ten weeks emerges, and we have the beginning of another 'popular education school' in the South of Cape Town, an area renowned for poverty and violence. A week later, the group has grown to 28 and there is barely enough space to fit everyone into a converted garage of someone's house. Luckily, it's a dry day, and we can use the outside area to warm up in the winter sun and the wall of the yard to display pictures with speech bubbles that speak of personal concerns about participation and potential obstacles

B. L. Hall, D. E. Clover, J. Crowther and E. Scandrett (Eds.), Learning and Education
for a Better World: The Role of Social Movements, 101–112.

to sustained commitment. Participants draw up community profiles and identify how 'tik' and other drugs, gang violence, crime, and abuse of women and children affect neighbourhoods. These are the daily realities that have been listed as topics for exploration and learning; they are the main concerns that group members wish to address and change.

BACKGROUND

In most 'popular education schools' (PES) such as this one the topics are the same. Not surprising, really, because the one thing that does grow in South Africa is inequality – and PES participants in all corners of and around the city have stories to tell about violence and abuse, crime and fear, economic hardship and social marginalisation. What is surprising is that participants keep on coming, every week – and asked why, they talk about being taken seriously despite not having completed their schooling, about how everyone respects the other so they can take heart and begin to speak up where there was just silence in the past, and about the new knowledge that helps them make sense of their lives, understand when the media speak about globalisation, have new insights into dysfunctional neighbourhoods, unspeakable violence, disaffected youth.

The schools are part of the popular education programme that includes work with organisations around a popular education approach to their work, and popular education practitioner circles that invite dialogue and critical reflection on practice for experienced animators. The programme builds on the history of 'people's education' in the anti-apartheid era; theoretically, it has its foundations in the Freirean *Pedagogy of the Oppressed* (1972), practically it draws on *Training for Transformation l-lV* (Hope & Timmel, 2002), and *Participatory Rural Appraisal* (Chambers, 1983, 2002), and experientially on skills and insights honed in social movement education and learning of recent years, in particular the lessons learnt by the Treatment Action Campaign (TAC) that lobbied successfully for (free) accessible treatment for people living with HIV/AIDS. The programme asserts itself as an education that offers another way of teaching, learning and being together in the world. It has a clear utopian purpose: radical change, both in the way it attempts to model democratic relationships, valuing of the imagination and local knowledge, and in the projected world, both local and global, that is yet to be constructed. In this way, it parallels some of the work described by Crowther (2009) in his 'Stories of real utopia in adult education'.

Participants are what Seabrook (2003, p. 9) would describe as 'invisibles' – people who have historically, politically, economically, socially and geographically been pushed to the margins of society: 'In the rich world the poor have become invisible'. They have been and are also invisible in the sense that Ben Okri has described in his novel *Astonishing the Gods* (1995). Here the main protagonist is introduced as having been born invisible. His mother, too, was invisible, 'That was why she could see him.' Moreover,

It was in books that he first learnt of his invisibility. He searched for himself and his people in all the history books he read and discovered to his youthful astonishment that he didn't exist. This troubled him so much that he resolved, as soon as he was old enough' to leave his land and find the people who did exist, to see what they looked like (p. 3).

He travelled for seven years, and his quest was 'for the secret of visibility'.

Colonised peoples, and black people in particular experience themselves as expendable: as labour they are easily replaced since there is a surplus of unemployed hungry people, as agents of history they have been obliterated, eliminated as creators of cultures and ways of knowing, deleted as inventors of technologies suited and adapted to particular habitats. Their values and worldviews have been denigrated, omitted, excluded or destroyed to a point where we think of western ways as not only the only legitimate but in fact the only existing ones. (Odora-Hoppers, 1999) One important aspect of the popular education programme is to re-affirm cultural, linguistic and social values unique to different participant groups. The quest for visibility and voice and for other knowledges and ways of knowing is a necessary project of the present for the future.

There have been moments in PES when participants uncovered the secret of voicelessness and invisibility and developed a clearer sense of individual and collective identity. Importantly, they found a way out of silence together – as one participant named Gloria described after they had taken to the streets of their neighbourhood to protest police inactivity in response to domestic violence:

> This morning all of us had a voice. And the police were just helpless because we were a lot of women. They were just standing there. One just shouted, 'Give us more money!'. But why are they asking for more money? If you have a passion you don't need money for it.

As non-formal education much popular education is similarly invisible: informed primarily by the commitment towards change it happens in the nooks and crannies of society, driven by belief and passion rather than (financial) resources. And yet it aims high: it wants to contribute to reinventing the world! As Malick (2011) describes:

> The outrage at the social and political inequalities and injustices seems to be a common denominator in the vast majority of (these) popular movements that challenge the "system" or "powers" in place, by opposing destructiveness, passivity and inertia of decades of neoliberal policies. The people have started up (but) a challenge prevails: it is necessary to reinvent the world. But reinventing the world will not come from our current leaders, fed with the capitalist sap, seasoned advocates of neoliberal policies. Reinventing the world is to see the possibilities that the education movement and the civil society movement can bring.

OUTLINE

Here, I focus on the popular education schools in Cape Town as I ponder how to stimulate creative imaginings so that mental images are not clichés of happy people in the sunshine, reproductions of catalogue advertisements, but ideas towards realisable alternatives. How can popular education weave critical analysis with visionary purpose and what does it take to translate ideas rooted in clearly identified values and principles of social justice into sustained joint actions in pursuit of common goals? How do we sew seeds to grow desires for alternative possibilities, and how do we feed the soil so that it might sprout the imagination beyond what is?

I begin by arguing that resistance, defiance, critical analysis and consciousness alone are not enough but we also require what Ernst Bloch (1986, p. 7) called 'anticipatory consciousness': 'Expectation, hope, intention towards possibility that has still not become'. The ability to imagine and project other ways of relating to people and acting in the world are described with the image of a window or gateway that opens. Two examples from the popular education practice will function as illustrations of possible window-openings: The one engaged the imagination in order to construct a new 'country'; the other asked participants to draw on their individual creativity in order to produce a collective moment that might prefigure relationships and ways of production that recall the past and prefigure a future. Both demonstrate some possibilities for a glimpse of the 'not-yet' when members of communities are taken seriously in their quest for information, understanding and action and embark on creative responses to invitations to 'imagine'. However, as I will argue, neither fulfils the potential.

This leads me to propose that we need to 'compost' the imagination if we want it to go beyond reproducing what is (albeit only for some) and fly towards what Bloch called 'homeland': a place/time in which no one has yet been and towards which we strive without quite knowing its shape and colour, size and feel. The seed of this 'not-yet' homeland and new beginning / genesis is always potentially present; according to Bloch (1970, p. 96) we may find it in great works of art that can offer 'the pre-semblance of what, objectively, is still latent in the world.'

I have found inspiration in writings such as those of Mda and Okri; the other fertiliser is the Bolivian manifesto 'Living well' and I give examples of both. I conclude by suggesting that the shift from mere critical to anticipatory consciousness can instil the hope and determination necessary for assuming agency but it requires a slow process to feed and develop a fertile imagination.

DEVELOPING CRITICAL AND ANTICIPATORY CONSCIOUSNESS

Popular educators /activists in social movements would say radical interventions happen through the concerted, purposive building of critical consciousness, through analysing power relations, through fashioning a constantly vigilant attitude. There are many tried, tested and proven strategies for this, from Freirean codes to critical incident studies: We can study the architects of colonialism, neo-liberalism and global capitalism and define how ideologies are spread and reproduced until they become dominant. (Ngugi, 1986) We can examine language and uncover how words that used to express progressive ideas have been taken over to denote quite different things. We can define 'the enemy' and be defiant

(Newman 1999, and 2006); we can develop empathy and exercise 'emotional intelligence' as we learn from song (Martin & Shaw, 2004). We can work descriptively with familiar objects and, by alienating them from familiar associations uncover their histories and uses in order to generate insight about the world we have created, unwittingly or callously (Shor, 1987; von Kotze, 2004). Or we can rave like the writer Eduardo Galeano (2002, p. 18) and come to question habitual ways of being through unexpected propositions such as 'the TV set shall no longer be the most important member of the family and shall be treated like an iron or a washing machine.'

Popular education has been credited with the ability to move people. For example, Tuckett (2012) proposes that Boal's exercises in *Theatre of the Oppressed* (1985) are designed to support analysis, imagine an ideal outcome and strategise how to move towards that outcome, and hence are 'a powerful form of inclusive education for empowerment'. However, even hope and imagination are not inevitably democratic and progressive; they can be instrumentalised and harnessed to values of consumption and competition. How do we get the imagination 'unstuck' when it has itself succumbed to hegemony – when it struggles to break out of normalised values and structures, relations and oppressions? And what of the ethics when radical activists do not affirm but ask uncomfortable questions and confront participants with uncertainties that create a sense of vulnerability and increase the sense of risk in already compromised living conditions?

I believe our popular education schools have laid some foundations of a practice of critical questioning and analysis and in some cases this has already resulted in actions taken. Course participants asserted their rights and dignity when they rejected a counsellor offering 'bucket toilets' and chased him out of the area. They organised and ran the beginning of a public community-based campaign around child abuse, and they have mobilised women of the neighbourhoods to march against violence and abuse of women and children. But to what degree have we managed to go beyond analysing, critiquing and protesting and towards self-consciously imagining alternatives that are radically different from the status quo? Asked what they would like to put in place of the existing reality – how able are participants to articulate another possible world?

The Bolivian indigenous concept of *Living Well* means having all of one's basic needs met while existing in harmony with the natural world:

In the words of the President of the Republic of Bolivia, Evo Morales Ayma, Living Well means living within a community, a brotherhood, and particularly complementing each other, without exploiters or exploited, without people being excluded or people who exclude, without people being segregated or people who segregate.

Bishop (2004, p. 32) has distinguished usefully between a 'politics of imagination' and 'political imagination': the politics of imagination critiques the way in which imagination has become harnessed to economic, social and political interests. *Living Well* takes issue with the 'existing inhuman capitalist system that brings selfishness, individualism, even regionalism, thirst for profit, the search for pleasure and luxury thinking only about profiting, never having regards to brotherhood among human beings who live on planet Earth.' Political imagination, on the other hand, engages with questions of power, wealth and justice. This is the imagination we need in order to envision another world built on principles of equality and justice, of *all* living well rather than *some* living better. Illich (1973) has called this conviviality and as Crowther (2009, p. 87) argues, 'conviviality involves a deeper, underlying ethical impulse, which understands that freedom and interdependence are mutually constitutive.' The following two examples describe moments in PES when the politics of imagination and political imagination were engaged.

Example 1: A Human Rights Activity

Each PES had sessions on human rights and participants whose own experiences have generally been of the violations of basic rights began by establishing the difference between rights and needs, having versus enjoying rights and how responsibilities and rights were tied together. Each time we could have spent the rest of the day telling tales about lack of service delivery and the flouting of basic rights with regards to water, sanitation, and energy. But instead of recycling what we already knew participants settled into two groups to design a 'new country'. Their task was to individually, then collectively decide on what basic ten rights they would enshrine to ensure that in the new country all can 'live well'. Once each group had negotiated a list of ten they came together and tried to consolidate their final ten.

This raised questions such as: Is employment the same as work? Do we have to have employers in the new country? What will we work for – indeed: what is the relationship between food security and work – and what is the difference between people as producers or consumers of food? Other questions touched on the right to decent health care – and as we explored what that might mean we also examined the causes of unhealthiness, such as poor nutrition and dangerous sexual behaviour. Invariably, discussions included an analysis of power and interest in relation to the rights demanded, and they involved painful and joyful uncovering of hegemonic power that requires deliberate shifts in perspective. Participants tried to drown each other out trying to make themselves heard – and this raised the question of how people in the country would make decisions that are agreeable and binding to all? We discovered that there were no 'first generation rights' on the list and that 18 years after the election of our first democratic government we have already forgotten the long hard struggle for the vote in South Africa.

Invariably, discussions moved towards re-defining jobs as work and work as inclusive of reproductive tasks and not just income generation, and as decent, useful and self-determined. Leadership was to be shared, education would be de-institutionalised and happen on a need-to-know basis with all assuming roles as both learners and educators. Of course, land would have to be distributed fairly ensuring all could grow food, and health would be a collective responsibility. As participants began to dream their way out of what is they also began to formulate another world without ever labelling it as such. The process of thinking out of the box, being creative, daring and path breaking generated much energy and laughter. Reviewing the sessions in the following week brought up stories of how some participants had reproduced a lot of the process in their homes, generating much debate. In the end, asked why the participation of all had been so high in spirit and active in contributions and discussions there was consensus: 'Because we were making something new!'

Example 2: The Pipe-blowers of Steenberg

At the end of the PES all participants from six different areas came together in one place for a celebration. The event began with a music-making workshop that turned into an extended metaphor for popular education. The hall exploded with noise as people held bits of plumbers' pipe to their lips and blew. Some forgot to close the pipe with a finger or thumb and they strained to produce a sound; two older women were holding on to each other bent in laughter, the children left their games and joined in and people who had never before met nodded to each other in rhythm or stamped their feet in unison. All were totally absorbed in the attempt to 'make music'. Pedro 'the music man' alerted us that this was truly a democratic moment: everyone participated – depending on the length of pipe all with a different note, but each trying to contribute to the cacophony. He demonstrated that single notes can produce a rhythm but not a tune, and that it would take the effort of all, in coordinated fashion, to turn noise into melody. But, he cautioned, the pauses, the silences were as important as the making of the sound– and participants agreed: this is so, in life, also: if you speak all the time it is but a noise – and only the listening allows us to create dialogue and make meaning together.

We played to a rhythm, and then: Can we hear a tune emerging? He asked, and various participants hummed or whistled what they heard. Each had their own version and each, as he pointed out, was equally valid: this is what it sounded like from where you played your note!

Would we all like to contribute our notes and produce melodies, music that is pleasing to the ear and heart? Pedro called on 'conductors' to help him orchestrate and thus we began to make real music together. It was a magic moment of creation and as one tune followed another we became more accomplished and attuned to each other – until, breathlessly, we exploded into exhilaration and delight, applauding each other, ourselves, the conductors, the moment.

Creative Impulses Towards Alternatives?

Three observations suggest themselves: firstly, the sessions demonstrated the importance of interdependence, away from individualistic thinking and acting towards collective efforts; secondly, they shifted emphasis away from participants as consumers towards participants as producers and creative agents; thirdly, they demonstrated 'enoughness' as a virtue to pit against the too-much of consumerism. All these are important contributors towards vision-building but not, I will argue, clear enough ideas, imaginings of alternatives.

A. V. KOTZE

Firstly, the value of collectivity: through a process of negotiating and dialogue participants in the human rights sessions arrived at the insight that their 'new country' would have to be founded on communal values, on collective demands and visions and that interdependence meant not 'each one for him/herself' but 'all together for the common good.' Having internalised how conditions of competition for scarce resources translate into competitive behaviour rather than sharing it took a while to recognise just how deep the 'cut-throat' mentality had permeated all aspects of their lives to the degree that it had become naturalised as normal. Re-imagining relations as cooperative and reciprocal was a major step – and one that had to be made over and over again, in different sessions. In the pipe-blowing session the collective making of music became a powerful metaphor. When labelled 'democratic' with deliberate allusions made to relations and cultural practices of the past the process turned into a sustained experience of the pleasure and possibilities of collective activity – a precursor to action.

Secondly, agency as producers rather than consumers: through the negotiation of rights it became obvious how we are constantly at risk of falling for the happiness conspiracy suggested in our consumer society. At every corner the ideal citizen is described and celebrated as the consumer: of more bigger, better, newer goods the production of which eats up water, air, natural resources. In the initial round of defining rights for the 'new country' participants were bound to the familiar and listed 'rights' denied by the state without questioning their own ability to produce and meet needs if given access to and availability of resources. Bit by bit they explored how fundamental needs for sufficient food, shelter, clothing, good health, family security and meaningful lives might not have to be enshrined as rights if our utopian country was built on the basic values of strong community engagement and access to a thriving natural world that could offer the means to meet needs.

Playing the pipes was a visceral experience of our creative productive selves. Music is part of everyday life – but rarely do we play the part of making rather than just consuming it. Processes of creative productivity re-assert us as human beings, and not just parts of an ever-faster stress-inducing working machinery. Importantly, creative activities also remind us that as much as we can make new things we can change existing ones – and this belief in our power to affect change is a necessary ingredient in working for alternatives. These are insights that should have been named and explored further if the utopian dimension, the composting of the imagination for envisioning alternatives was to be realised fully.

Thirdly, enoughness: Increasingly, in community development circles enoughness is suggested as a concept that expresses satisfaction and saturation. It is seen as embracing principles of 'living well' without the necessity of exploitation of others and the environment. Participants realised that it would take a major, fundamental re-think to establish this 'new country', away from consumerism as a value and way of being and towards embracing sufficiency for all as more important than competitive 'advantage'. They struggled to imagine the possibilities of houses being built and food grown by all, of a convivial society in which all relate as both teachers and learners, of caring without domination and each one helping the other to live well. But they got animated at imagining themselves in this reinvented country in which relations amongst people and the environmental would be harmonious and free from want. The pipe-blowers experienced change as a process rather than outcome. They expressed surprise at how much can be achieved with a small piece of plumbers pipe: beyond the music itself there was the moment of collective exhilaration and joy, the bending-over and helping each other, the listening and voicing.

The recognition of one's ability to affect change, to produce another world is a crucial first step. Creative collective experiences can help the break through from seeing others as barriers rather than essential allies and make conscious the potential of solidarity in action. Bloch (1986, p. 35) reminded us

> (because) our fellow human man (sic)is no longer the barrier to our own freedom, but rather the means by which this freedom is truly achieved. Instead of freedom of acquisition, there shines freedom from acquisition, instead of imagined pleasures of cheating in the economic struggle, there shines the imaginary victory in the proletarian class struggle. And even higher above this shines the distant peace, the distant opportunity of being in solidarity and being friendly with all men.

However, we failed to name the moments as demonstrations of how the production of creative moments and objects can be a political way of counter-acting the saturated satisfaction induced by consumerism, and filling the vacuum left when acquisitions fail to really satisfy the craving for happiness. I wish I could say we had clearly articulated how the human rights sessions and the pipe blowing had shown up the value of 'enoughness' rather than overindulgence and wastefulness. We did not reflect on our creations and made conscious why and how the process imbued us with joy and kindled desire. We stopped just beyond the experience without considering how those images and feelings, the process and the outcome we created can function as models, prefiguring what it is we wish to build.

Composting the Imagination

Composting is a slow process in which organic matter breaks down and individual components mix with each other as they turn into nutrients for soil. Adding compost to soil means feeding seeds and seedlings to grow into healthy plants. Similarly, the imagination needs to be fertilised, enriched with ideas and words, images and values that must be allowed to break down and mingle until they become the compost that fertilises the imagination. If we wish to build vision that is not simply the denial or reversal of what is but goes way beyond and in other directions we need to draw inspiration from various sources and begin a deliberate process of transformation in which individual components combine to form something new. Our daily experiences with people or organisations that act wisely are one such source, and often this may have involved delving into past histories and ways of living. Other sources are writers, artists, musicians who have the ability to transcend the mundane and transport us into dreams. Sometimes inspiration is a document with forgotten or new ideas. For me, such inspirations are the values often referred to as part of indigenous knowledge systems, the early writings of Zakes Mda, and the Bolivian 'Living Well' manifesto.

In Mda's 'Ways of Dying' (1997) the professional mourner, Toloki, turns the makeshift one-room mjondolo (shack) he has constructed into a home by sticking pages from advertising brochures and catalogues of 'home and gardens' onto the walls. At night, he takes Norias hand and slowly walks her through the landscape of shrubs and trees, lawns and fountains and for a moment they imagine themselves in a beautiful surrounding far removed from the reality of the squatter camp. Mda describes an integrity of being and acting with care that is consistent with a definition of development for a 'small planet' or the principle of 'enoughness'. The meaning of life comes from a sense of community based on being-with and through others rather than reckless consumerism and exploitative relations enmeshed in power and status. Here is a story that describes and paints the principle of ubuntu (being through the other) for what it is: not social capital but humanity /humaneness and human solidarity.

The Bolivian Living Well manifesto spells out clearly these values and echoes the principles of Bloch's 'homeland':

Living Well means living within a community, a brotherhood, and particularly completing each other, without exploiters or exploited, without people being excluded or people who exclude, without people being segregated or people who segregate...Living Well rather means complementing one another and not competing against each other, sharing, not taking advantage of one's neighbour, living in harmony among people and with nature. It is the basis of the defence of nature, of life itself and of all humanity, it's the basis to save humanity from the dangers of an individualistic and highly aggressive, racist and warmongering minority.

To create this new life we must assume agency, together:

We have to wake up community energy, boost community energy in our communities, which is the main capacity we've got to transform society and build a Living Well vision. We have to follow the example of these people and communities, starting to rebuild our communities and nations OURSELVES, with our own hands, our own hearts and our own brains, starting to take responsibility for the building of a Living Well Life for all within the limits of nature. We cannot rely only on governments and international movements to solve our problems.

CONCLUSION

Moments of opening in which alternatives appear as real possibilities are crucially important. The physical change observed in people as they performed their music together, the affirmation of a young women reporting how she took the inspiration of creating the 'new country' as a model to engage her household in the evening are some testimonies to the importance of experiencing oneself as a producer of alternative visions and a creative being.

Thus, the missing dimension in much popular education such as PES, I would contend, is a self-conscious deliberate effort to define where we want to go. 'Where people cannot name alternatives or imagine a better state of things, they are likely to remain anchored or submerged', suggests Greene (1995, p. 52) Once we have de-naturalised what has come to be accepted as normal, analysed the principles that make it appear such and shone light on power relations and agendas and the forces that militate against the interests of the invisibles, we must open that imaginary window and throw our imaginations beyond what is towards what could be. While we need to strategise and hone our action skills we also must be directed by a clear sense of the homeland we wish to create. If our visions are blurred, our core values lack clearer definition, our short-and long-term goals seem to be anchored on lighthouses moored on ships we should stop for a moment, mobilize energies, and look for 'compost'. Our hopes and passions become more sustained when our visions are deeply rooted in collective beliefs and agendas and precise in the simple images and sounds, the feels and smells we desire. This requires sustained energy and time fuelled by a continuous process of critical questioning, analysis and also feeding, nurturing and firing the imagination.

Once we have clarified our quest, integrity is key: we require a daily commitment to the philosophy and practices of living well – and this must be owned and modelled by all. As Salgado (2011) reminds us: 'It is necessary that each member of the community lives the ethical, political and philosophical values that frame the paradigm and thus, that the community he/she belongs to vibrates and communicates in hope to other communities its doing in this "new" paradigm'. Utopia is not a place and time but a process of becoming. On his travels the protagonist in Okris novel sees a bridge that he has to cross, but it seems insubstantial and he is afraid to step on it 'lest he would plunge down below'.

'What holds up the bridge?' he asked his guide.

'Only the person crossing it', came the reply' (1995, p. 16)

We are forever crossing fragile bridges; they come into being through our awareness and it takes some courage and determination to keep the transition, the process of making that 'other', alternative, alive. Freire and Horton suggested *We make the road by walking,* Nelson Mandela spoke of *The Long Walk to Freedom.* Popular education processes need to ensure that critique and the creative imagination fertilise one another, that values and new idea are activated and become visible in the work of the imagination towards creating the homeland.

REFERENCES

Bishop, P. (2004). Pedagogies of hope: education, utopian imagination and the corporatizing university. In: Willis, P. & Carden, P. (Eds.), *Lifelong learning and the democratic imagination. Revisioning justice, freedom and community.* Adelaide, PostPressed.

Bloch, E (1970). *A philosophy of the future.* New York, Herder and Herder.

Bloch, E (1986). *The Principle of Hope.* (3 vols) Cambridge, MIT Press.

Chambers, R (1983). *Rural development: Putting the Last First.* Longman, Harlow.

Chambers, R (2002). *Participatory workshops. A sourcebook of 21 sets of Ideas and Activities.* Earthscan Pubications, London.

Crowther J. (2009). Real Utopias in adult education. In: Flecha Garcia, R & Steinberg, S. (Eds.), *Pedagogía Crítica del S.XXI.* Re-vista Electrónica Teoría de la Educación: Educación y Cultura en la Sociedad de la Información. *10*(3). Universidad de Salamanca, pp. 74–89.

Finger, Mathias &Asun, JM (2001). *Adult education at the crossroads: learning our way out.* London, Zed Books.

Freire, P (1972). *Pedagogy of the Oppressed.* London, Penguin.

Galeano, E (2002). The right to rave. In: *New Internationalist* 342, 2002, p. 18.

Greene, M. (1995). *Releasing the Imagination: Essay on Education, the Arts, and Social Change.* San Francisco, Jossey-Bass Publishers.

Hope, A & Timmel, S (2002). *Training for Transformation. A handbook for community workers.* (Vols 1–4) Training for Transformation Institute, Keinmond.

Illich, I. (1973). *Tools for conviviality.* New York, Harper & Row publishers.

Malick, S.Y. (2011). Education Movement and Civil Society Movement. In: *Virtual Exchange "Education in a World in crisis: Limitations and Possibilities with a view to Rio+20".*

Martin, I. & Shaw, M. (2004). Songs for learning, songs for yearning. In: Willis, P. & Carden, P. (Eds.), *Lifelong learning and the democratic imagination. Revisioning justice, freedom and community.* Adelaide, PostPressed.

Mda, Z. (1997). *Ways of dying.* Oxford, Oxford University Press.

Newman, M. (1994). *Defining the enemy. Adult education in social action.* Paddington, Stewart Victor Publishing.

Newman, M. (2006). *Teaching defiance. Stories and Strategies for Activist Educators.* San Francisco: Jossey-Bass.

Ngugi Wa Thiong'o (1986). *Decolonising the mind. The politics of language in African literature.* Harare, Zimbabwe Publishing House.

Odora-Hoppers, C. A., Moja, T. & Mda, T. (1999). Making this our last passive moment: The way forward. In: MW Makgoba (Ed.), *African Renaissance.* (pp. 233–243) Cape Town, Mafube Publishing & Tafelberg.

Okri, B. (1995). *Astonishing the Gods.* London, Phoenix Paperback.

Salgado, A. (2012). The change of paradigms in the context of multiple crises. Good living as an essential element in the paradigmatic substitution. In: *Virtual Exchange "Education in a World in crisis: Limitations and Possibilities with a view to Rio+20".*

Saul, J. (2006). *Development after Globalisation. Theory and Practice for the embattled South in a new Imperial Age.* London & New York, Zed Books and Scottsville, UKZN Press.

Schumaker, J. F. (2006). The happiness conspiracy. *New Internationalist,* 391.

Seabrook, J (2003). *The no-nonsense guide to world poverty.* Oxford, NI, Verso.

Shor, I. (1987). *Critical teaching and everyday life.* Black Rose, Montreal.

The Concept of "Living Well" – http://www.energybulletin.net/stories/2010-10-08/concept-%E2%80% 9Cliving-well%E2%80%9D-bolivian-viewpoint Accessed 20.04.10

Tuckett, A. (2012). Lessons learnt needed to root democracy in diversity and sustainability. In: *Virtual Exchange "Education in a World in crisis: Limitations and Possibilities with a view to Rio+20".* 10 Jan 2012

von Kotze, A. (2004). Life would be a fair alternative: engaging the democratic imagination. In: Willis, P. & Carden, P. (Eds.), *Lifelong learning and the democratic imagination. Revisioning justice, freedom and community.* Adelaide, PostPressed.

STEPHEN BROOKFIELD

8. RADICAL AESTHETICS: KEN LOACH AS SOCIAL MOVEMENT EDUCATOR

In *The Aesthetic Dimension* (1978) Herbert Marcuse argued that in advanced industrial societies the aesthetic dimension represented the last best hope for challenging the stifling constraints of one-dimensional thought. For him, "art subverts the dominant consciousness, the ordinary experience" (p. ix) through introducing into life a dimension of experience that does not conform to the prevailing logic. Hence, "the political potential of art lies only in its own aesthetic dimension" (p. xii). What art offers us is a chance of breaking with the familiar, of inducing in us an awareness of other ways of being in the world. Art "opens the established reality to another dimension; that of possible liberation" (1972, p. 87). If social movements are focused on creating "a world different from and contrary to the established universe of discourse and behaviour" (1969, p. 73) then working to create such worlds therefore "involves a break with the familiar, the routine ways of seeing, hearing, feeling, understanding things so that the organism may become receptive to the potential forms of a non aggressive, non exploitative world" (1969, p. 6). Lester Bangs, the American rock critic, captures what Marcuse means in one of his essays on punk band The Clash: "for once if only then in your life, you were blasted outside of yourself and the monotony which defines most life anywhere at any time, when you supped on lightning and nothing else in the realms of the living or dead mattered at all" (2004, p. 90).

Building on Marcuse's analysis, this paper argues that social movement educators need to concern themselves with the radicalising function of art, the way in which artistic creation politicises artists and consumers. To illustrate this I focus on the work of the British director Ken Loach, who has a five-decade career as a political filmmaker. Although not all Loach's films are set within social movements, those that are (for example *Days of Hope, Hidden Agenda, Land and Freedom, Carla's Song, The Flickering Flame, The Wind that Shakes the Barley, Bread and Roses*) perform several of the educational functions that T.V. Reed identifies in his book *The Sound of Protest* (2005). They sound warnings, inform internally, inform externally, historicise, and critique movement ideology.

To take just one example, the 12-minute sequence in Loach's *Land and Freedom,* in which villagers and Republicans during the Spanish Civil War debate whether or not to collectivise their village, works as social movement education on several levels. Although explicitly concerned with teaching viewers about the history of the disparate groups in the Republican movement, it also serves other

B. L. Hall, D. E. Clover, J. Crowther and E. Scandrett (Eds.), Learning and Education for a Better World: The Role of Social Movements, 113–124.

important educational purposes. It teaches about the difficulties of escaping a dominant ideology of individualism, it provides an effective dramatisation of the confusion, overlapping and simultaneous contributions, and tangential elements of discussion, and it illustrates how power plays itself out in the micro-politics of decision-making. This paper will explore this scene in detail as an example of how Loach's films can be used for education about, and within, social movements.

A 'SELECTIVE' FILMOGRAPHY

If this section reads somewhat like Loach's Wikipedia entry, this is because I have plagiarised myself, having written a chunk of that entry! Loach's personal history is important because it represents the narrative of individual improvement much championed by British Prime Minister, Margaret Thatcher – a narrative Loach both loathes and critiques. As a schoolboy in the English midlands he was a pupil at King Edward VI Grammar School in Nuneaton and then did National Service in the Royal Air Force before studying law at Oxford University. He worked as an actor in repertory theatre and then joined the BBC as a director of television dramas such as *Z-Cars*, a police drama. In 1966, Loach directed *Cathy Come Home* portraying working class people affected by homelessness and unemployment, and presenting a powerful and influential critique of the workings of the Social Services. This was revolutionary for its time and created vigorous debate in the UK, remarkable for a TV program. Two films quickly followed; *Poor Cow* (adapted from a Nell Dunn novel) in 1967 and *Kes*, the story of a troubled working class teenager who trains a kestrel he takes from a nest. In 1999 the British Film Institute listed *Kes* as the seventh best British film of the twentieth century.

During the 1970s and '80s, Loach's films were less successful, often suffering from poor distribution, lack of interest and political censorship. His film *The Save the Children Fund Film* (1971), commissioned by that charity, disturbed its sponsors so much they attempted to have the negative destroyed. It was only screened publicly for the first time in September 2011. In 1982, the British TV Channel 4 commissioned Loach and Central Independent Television to make *Questions of Leadership*, a documentary series exploring the British trades union movement's response to the policies of the Conservative government. Presaging several of his later fictional films, the documentary featured union members criticising their own leaders as well as the Tory government. Channel 4 refused to broadcast the series; a decision Loach claimed was politically motivated. In 2004, for the first time, the real reason for this censorship was revealed, in Hayward's book, *Which Side Are You On? Ken Loach and His Films,* where it emerged that media tycoon Robert Maxwell, a director of Central Independent Television, had put pressure on Central's board, to withdraw *Questions of Leadership.* At the time he was buying the *Daily Mirror* newspaper and needed the co-operation of union leaders criticised in the series. The banning continued with Loach's film *Which Side Are You On?* (1985), a film about the songs and poems of the UK miner's strike commissioned by Channel 4. The film was eventually transmitted on Channel 4, but only after it won a major prize at the Berlin International Film

Festival. This disappointed Loach who expected it to be shown in the middle of the strike and not towards its end.

These repeated brushes with TV companies moved Loach to return full time to cinema. The late 1980s and 1990s saw the production of a series of critically acclaimed and popular films such as *Hidden Agenda*, one of the rare films dealing with the political troubles in Northern Ireland, *Carla's Song* set partially in Nicaragua, and *Land and Freedom* examining the Republican resistance in the Spanish Civil War. During this period he was also awarded prizes at the Cannes Film Festival on three occasions. He directed the Courtroom Drama reconstructions in the docudrama *McLibel* concerning a couple's battle to distribute accurate information about the McDonald's fast food chain. Interspersed with overtly political films were smaller dramas such as *Raining Stones* a working class drama concerning an unemployed man's efforts to buy a communion dress for his young daughter.

In 2006, Loach won the prestigious Palme d'Or prize at the Cannes Film Festival for *The Wind That Shakes the Barley*, a film about the Irish War of Independence and subsequent civil war during the 1920s. In characteristic fashion this sweeping political-historical drama was followed by *It's a Free World* a story of one woman's attempt to establish an illegal placement service for migrant workers in London. Throughout the 2000s Loach continued to intersperse wider political dramas such as *Bread and Roses* (which focused on the Los Angeles janitors strike) and *Route Irish*, set in the Iraq occupation, with smaller examinations of personal relationships. *A Fond Kiss* explored an inter-racial love affair, *Sweet Sixteen* a teenager's relationship with his mother, and *My Name is Joe* an alcoholic's struggle to stay sober. His most commercially successful recent film is 2009's *Looking For Eric*, featuring a depressed postman's conversations with the ex-Manchester United football star, Eric Cantona (played by Cantona himself). A measure of Loach's difficulties gaining broad release for his work is the fact that this film ended up making only £12,000 profit (The Guardian, 2011).

In 2011 he released *Route Irish*, an examination of private contractors working in the Iraqi occupation. A thematic consistency throughout his films, whether they examine broad political situations, or smaller intimate dramas, is his focus on personal relationships. The sweeping political dramas examine wider political forces in the context of relationships between family members (*Bread and Roses, The Wind that Shakes the Barley, Carla's Song*), comrades in struggle (*Land and Freedom*) or close friends (*Route Irish*). In a 2011 interview for the *Financial Times*, Loach explains how "The politics are embedded into the characters and the narrative, which is a more sophisticated way of doing it" (Slate, 2011 p. 67).

Loach argues that working people's struggles are inherently dramatic: "They live life very vividly, and the stakes are very high if you don't have a lot of money to cushion your life. Also, because they are the front line of what we came to call the class war, either through being workers without work, or through being exploited where they were working. And I guess for a political reason, because we felt, and I still think, that if there is to be change, it will come from below. It won't come from people who have a lot to lose, it will come from people who will have everything to gain" (*The Guardian*, 2011). As we shall see, his particular genius is to be able to portray how the vivid pursuit of high stakes decisions plays itself out in particular dramatic situations.

LOACH'S CINEMATIC METHOD

In a 2010 interview with *The Observer* newspaper's Tom Lamont, Loach outlined how three continental films shaped his own approach to filmmaking. The most influential was Vittorio De Sica's *The Bicycle Thieves*: "*The Bicycle Thieves* was the one that did it for me first. The story is just of a man and his son, looking for work on a bicycle and what the consequences are for their family. It only tells the story of this one family and doesn't go beyond, but in doing that it tells you everything you want to know. I love this idea of telling a story in microcosm; if you get the story right and the characters right, the film will say everything about the wider picture without having to generalise. Of course, that's how I rationalised it later. At the time, I just thought: wow" (The Observer, 2010, p. 29). Milos Forman's Czech film *A Blonde in Love* "endorsed everything that I was trying to achieve with my own work, but hadn't managed to. It was about people and families, observed in a way that was full of humanity and humour, but was still astringent, not soft" (p. 29). His third choice, Gillo Pontecorvo's *The Battle of Algiers* "took a political event and made it cinematic, but did so without resorting to the traditional ways of heavy-handed film-making (vast armies). It had a lightness about it, but it was very immediate. I was beginning to become politically engaged at the time, so it really fitted the moment" (p. 29)

The influence of these three films is apparent in Loach's approach to film-making. All of them emphasise the importance of the narrative, the story, and the writing. This reverence for writers and scripts may seem surprising, given the apparently improvised nature of many of his scenes. But Loach's final script and final film are usually very close. In a 2010 symposium I attended at London's Curzon cinema Loach said quite unequivocally that the most important elements of any of his film were the writer, the story and the script. But in transferring the story and script to film he is always looking to make the interplay between actors seem as natural as possible and encourages a measure of improvisation around the script to ensure this happens.

Second, in contrast to almost every other contemporary filmmaker, Loach's films are shot in narrative sequence. His intent is to have the story unfold for the actors in real time, in the same way it unfolds for the viewer. Filming scenes in order from first to last, Loach believes, helps the actors find a natural and spontaneous response to their circumstances. Many actors in his films are often not given the full script at the beginning of a shoot, but rather they experience the story just as a fictional character might do. He will often give actors their scenes a couple of days in advance so they can learn their lines, but they still won't know what comes after that. If a scene involves shock or surprise for a character, the actor might not know what is about to happen. In *Kes* the boy actor, discovering the dead bird at the end, believed Loach had killed the bird, which he had become fond of during the filming (the crew used a dead bird found elsewhere).

In the same film the scene where the school headmaster is searching the schoolboys, the small first year boy holding everybody else's cigarettes was under the impression that he was to give the headmaster a note and leave the office. Subsequently, when he is searched and found to be "a right little cigarette factory", he is caned alongside the other boys; hence, his look of shock and tears of pain are real. In *Raining Stones* one of the actresses visited at her house by a loan shark had no idea that he was going to force her to take off her wedding ring and give it to him as part payment. In *Carla's Song*, the bus driver, played by Robert Carlyle, knew nothing of Carla's attempted suicide until he discovered her in the bath. In *Looking For Eric*, the main actor discovered that footballer Eric Cantona was in the film only when he turned around to face him in a scene, with the camera rolling.

Third, instead of using well-known professional actors, Loach generally prefers using unknown talent and 'real' people with experience of the situations portrayed in the film. Many films involve a mix of professional actors and actors drawn from the communities that are the focus of the film. In *Bread and Roses*, a film about immigrant cleaners in Los Angeles, many of the extras were themselves immigrant cleaners whilst others were also labour and grassroots activists. Some knew from their own experience the dangers of crossing the border into the US. His use of young untrained actors in films such as *Kes, Looks and Smiles, Tickets, Looking for Cantona* and *Sweet Sixteen*, has also drawn praise for the naturalistic performances he coaxes from them.

LAND AND FREEDOM: THE DECISION

I want now to focus on Loach as a social movement educator by exploring in detail one scene in one film. This is the scene titled 'The Decision' in 1995's *Land and Freedom*, Loach's film concerning the struggle of the Republican, anti-fascist revolutionary forces in the Spanish civil war. The film is told through the experiences of David, a young unemployed man and Communist party member who leaves Liverpool to join the struggle. About a third of the way into the film David and his colleagues reclaim a village held by the fascists, during which members of the militia and villagers are killed. The villagers bury their dead and sing the 'Internationale' at the funeral. The villagers, observed by the militia, then hold a meeting to decide whether or not to collectivise the village's resources and abolish private land ownership.

The scene is important to all adult educators for one particular reason. As a 12-minute sequence it is, in my estimation, the best portrayal of the tumultuous rhythms of discussion I have ever seen in a feature film. Multiple speakers are tripping over each other's words, people struggle to speak spontaneously trying to get their words out concerning issues that they are extremely emotional about, and the meeting leader struggles to keep order as people respond to each other. Conducted mostly in Spanish, people shout at each other, become passionately engaged, stumble over words, have difficulty articulating what they are trying to say in the heat of the moment, and alternate individual contributions with group conversation. The ebb and flow of the conversation, with pauses between arguments, and with rationality alternating with fevered emotion, capture the inherent unpredictability of discussion.

Hill (2011) explains how the camera work in the scene seems to be responding to actual events, trying to catch up to a conversation that is so vigorous and spontaneous that it feels unrehearsed. It moves onto characters heard off screen, and shows people's reactions to speech as much as focusing on the speakers' faces themselves; "compositions are rarely tidy and characters, who are speaking different languages, are allowed to talk across each other or interrupt what other characters are saying" (p. 207). Although it appears to have been shot in one take the sequence took two full days of shooting and a week's editing to arrive at the 12 minutes seen on screen (Hayward, 2004, p. 209).

To social movement educators, the scene is important because it crystallises in one specific conversation fundamental questions concerning the dynamics and tensions of all social movement activism. How should short-term goals be balanced against long-term aims? When should abstract principle be sacrificed for immediate expediency? How are revolutionary ideas lived out in practice? How do you balance individual freedom against collective wellbeing? In what ways can activists struggling within one specific context draw on the experiences of those outside? How do you balance the benefit of taking a risk and inspiring others against the prospect that this could lead to sacrifice, even death?

Critics and commentators have agreed "the discussion of land ownership…is central to the literal and figurative meaning of Land and Freedom" (MacFadden, 1977, p. 150). As in most of his films, Loach explores these questions not as an abstract debate that focuses only on ideas, but as conflicts embedded within the clash of very specific characters and their worldviews. In Leigh's (2002) words "it presents both individual drama and social analysis without breaking the rhythm of the story" (p. 177). Loach explained it to Graham Fuller as follows; "it was very important to us that these conflicts were reflected through the relationships, that they didn't exist in the abstract, that it wasn't a film about 'ologies' or 'isms', that it was really a film about David and the betrayal of his group, and his relationship with Blanca and why she felt betrayed. All that has more resonance with people than a lecture would" (Fuller, 1998, p. 99). To Loach the debate "seemed great drama, great conflict, a very human struggle put forward in concrete terms…it's not a battle of ideologies. That would be a major turn-off, and nobody would want to go and see it. The scene shows people struggling in a very practical, human way, just to see how they can move" (ibid.).

Loach uses film to explore these questions, but we should always remember that it is his writer on the film, Jim Allen, who takes equal credit, at the very least, for this particular scene. Loach captures the hurly burly of real time discussion, but Allen's words, spoken seemingly off the cuff and seemingly extemporaneously by the actors, show the universal nature of social movement dynamics. This is such an authentic scene for three very specific reasons. First, Loach cast actors with a political conscience so that their characters' ideologies matched their own. Hence, the positions their characters take in the discussion actually reflect the actors' own personal beliefs. Hill quotes Loach as saying "all of the positions taken by the actors corresponded to their actual positions" (Hill, 2010, p. 207). The only person 'acting' his viewpoint was the actor playing Gene Lawrence, the most vociferous opponent of collectivisation. Second, the scene features actual villagers drawn from the village where the sequence was shot. Third, immediately before filming Loach told the actors to forget the script to achieve a greater spontaneity. So what we see is Allen's words filtered through the actors' own spontaneous efforts to express positions they believe in off-camera.

To appreciate how Loach explores social movement dynamics in one 12-minute sequence I will do a detailed explication of the scene. The scene opens in the house of Don Julian, a wealthy landowner. Most of the villagers are delighting at being in the landowner's house but the camera concentrates on the worried and apprehensive face of Pepe, a farmer who we find out fears collectivisation. The chair calls the meeting to order by declaring Don Julian's house to be now a house of the people, to the sound of assorted cheers and applause. A villager, Teresa, is the first to speak. She argues that the village must collectivise immediately so people can pool their resources and produce food for the whole village and for the militia members at the front. Pepe, the farmer responds by saying 'to each his own', that he supports collectivising Don Julian's land, but that each farmer should retain a little bit of land for themselves. He argues persuasively for the value of his own craft knowledge, saying that he knows his land's particularities and works it his own way to get the most from it. He declares passionately that he has poured his whole life into his land, and that's what has made it what it is today.

An elderly peasant, Miguel, then speaks to say it would be better for everyone to work the land together to help keep the revolution going. He asks Pepe rhetorically "will you eat all the wheat and potatoes you harvest?" and then compares the revolution to a pregnant cow; without help the cow and calf will die and all will go hungry. A women villager then interjects to support Miguel by pointing out how people have died for the revolution. For their deaths to mean something the revolution must be continued and collectivisation will support this by ensuring everyone can eat. On the defensive now, Pepe then moves to another line of justification, one to do with judgments about whether or not human nature is determined at birth. Arguing an essentialist line he declares "there are those who are what they are". Some just work harder, and are more capable, than others he says, and some just don't work at all. He also briefly returns to his earlier espousal of craft knowledge saying his land is as good as it is because he is the one who has worked it.

Another villager, Paco, jumps in to say that the village must grow more and improve its harvest and that by working the land together they will be able to do that. He is supported by another farmer who states that with a tractor available to all the village they can accomplish five times more in a day than one farmer can with a mule. He is supported by another villager who cites outside experiences in his support of collectivisation. He says that other villages have done this and that it works. He then expresses the communist principle of 'from each according to his ability, to each according to his needs' expressed by Marx in his *Critique of the Gotha Program* (Marx, 2008/1875). If the village abolishes private property and pools its resources, then, depending on the situation of each farmer, they can take what they need. If they need a cow, then they will get one. He rejects Pepe's essentialist argument that some just work harder than others, declaring that they all work hard and have all got four or five children to feed.

At this point Pepe suggests that the members of the militia be allowed to speak, hoping they will support his viewpoint. He points out that their fighting has taken them to multiple locations and this means they have seen what's happened in other villages, an argument the chair supports. At first Gene Lawrence, an American who is the senior militia leader, throws the argument back to the villagers, saying it's their village to do with what they will. Upon being pressed, however, he offers his perspective. It is at this point that all the questions of tactics and strategy, the individual's rights against the collective's need, and the opposition of short term-objectives and long term goals really start to be explored more deeply.

Lawrence begins by acknowledging that a decree issued by the Republican government specifically authorises the collectivisation of lands owned by those who supported Franco's attempt to overthrow the democratically elected government. But he then argues that collectivising all land against the will of individual farmers who are themselves anti-Franco and anti-fascist will only divide and weaken the movement. Moreover, these petty divisions and squabbles between those for and against collectivisation will endanger the production of food. So collectivisation should be placed on the back burner to ensure the solidarity of the movement against Franco.

A Spanish militia member who says that private land must be completely cancelled because while it exists it keeps people in a capitalist mentality, contradicts Lawrence. Lawrence responds by saying this is no time for textbook arguments on socialism and land reform because the overwhelming priority is to defeat Franco and fascism. He declares "you can't collectivise anything if you're dead". Blanca, the chief female character in the film speaks against him saying her people did not wait for the government to announce a program of collectivisation, but that they took it for themselves. Lawrence counters by saying the villagers need to hold the big picture in mind and to think beyond the confines of their own private lives. He acknowledges that on their own the Spanish people would have had no difficulty in defeating Franco, but that the Spanish military is now supported and armed by Mussolini and Hitler. He argues passionately that the rest of the world (other than Russia and Mexico) has turned their back on Spain by refusing to sell arms to the Republican forces. He then articulates an argument expressed sooner or later in every social movement conversation about strategy; if you want to win broad external support you need to moderate your slogans otherwise you will scare potential outside supporters away. Specifically, Lawrence argues, if you want capitalist countries to sell you munitions to help you to arm the revolution, you must keep them on your side. At these arguments Pepe nods his head approvingly and smiles in agreement, sensing his argument is won.

A German militia member then speaks up. "In Germany", he says, "there were six million members of the Trade Union movement who together made up the strongest, best-organised workers' movement anywhere in the world." The movement wanted revolution but when Hitler's National Socialist party ascended to power the Socialist and Communist leaders told them to hold off and make revolution later. This was a mistake he says, we must make revolution now. Another peasant farmer then interjects to take Lawrence's plea to look outside the village and turn it against Lawrence. He says that when villagers see that collectivisation can be reality then word will get out and people in Italy and Germany will follow the Spanish example. For him the important thing is to show the world that although materially they have nothing as individuals, as a collective they have power. "We must not be seized by fear" he ends.

A French militia member, Bernard, clearly nervous at having to speak, then interjects. The French people are looking to Spain, he says, so peasants shouldn't be fighting each other they should be fighting together. In a reference to his recently dead militia comrades he says: "we know the price of freedom" and "we have lost friends" as the camera cuts to a distraught Blanca whose lover, an IRA member, has just been killed capturing the village. The scene then moves to a Scottish militia member who directly opposes and challenges Lawrence by questioning: "Whom are you trying to appease?"

The Scot follows this up by saying that in seeking to pull back from revolutionary language and practices Lawrence is appeasing foreign bankers and foreign governments. In a key declaration he defines what a radical, revolutionary change really is – a fundamental change in privilege, wealth and power. He then argues that foreign bankers and governments will only really be appeased when the movement's ideas are diluted and watered down to mean absolutely nothing. He acknowledges Lawrence's point about needing to look to the world outside of the village, but twists it to say we need to look at what's happening to working people elsewhere, not to foreign bankers and governments. Outside this room, he says, are two million landless peasants living lives of misery with no hope. We need to harness the energy of that two million, otherwise the ideas that have inspired the revolution will be worthless and the deaths of comrades will have been in vain. He ends by declaring that ideas are at the basis of everything people are working for.

At this point we hear from the main character, David. He sides with Lawrence arguing that if Franco wins then at least one million of those two million landless peasants will be dead because their lives mean nothing to Franco. David argues that what the revolutionary militia needs to focus on is winning the war; otherwise there will be no point to all the ideology being discussed. He then expands his view of ideology. Ideology doesn't exist in a book, he declares, it has to exist in a real place, to be a living real entity for real people. A village woman then contributes. We have to take risks, she declares, otherwise the misery, hunger and hopelessness will continue. Franco may indeed come back and kill them, but that risk is worth it to collectivise and thus improve the quality of their lives. At this point the chair calls for a public vote by raised hands and the majority of the villagers decide they will, in fact, collectivise their land. That decision is greeted by cheers, delight and hugs from its supporters.

The tensions explored in this sequence, particularly that around choosing whether to place the necessity to defeat Franco over the importance of staying true to revolutionary collective ideas (with the accompanying risk of losing that struggle) surfaces further in the film's narrative as Lawrence leaves the anarchist-inclined POUM militia to command a unit in the Stalinist-supported International Brigade. In a situation presaging the situation in a later Loach film exploring a revolutionary movement – *The Wind that Shakes the Barley* – comrade turns on comrade as an International Brigade unit requires the surrender of POUM members, during which Blanca is killed. This theme of how the leaders of the left constrain and sabotage their members' revolutionary actions is close to Loach's heart.

THE EDUCATIVE DIMENSION OF 'THE DECISION'

The debate scene, in my opinion, is an important teaching tool for social movement educators. It presents a rare realistic approximation of what a contentious movement discussion looks like. The only other filmic depiction of a small meeting discussion I can recall that even comes close (and it is much less exhaustive) is the meeting of Texas teachers in John Sayles film *Lone Star*, who debate what should count as the official curriculum of school history. The characters in the *Land and Freedom* scene are talking about what to do about the most precious and fundamental resource in their lives – their land. They stand to both gain and lose a great deal by taking a leap into the uncertainty of a new political economy. Since, by definition, social movement activists are passionate about their involvements the scene can be a good teaching tool for encouraging activists to consider how they will themselves comes to similarly momentous decisions over charged and contentious issues.

You can ask activists a number of pointed questions about the scene. Did the chair ensure there was a basic fairness to the discussion? Did all those who wished to speak up get their chance? Was the decision in effect made before the meeting, meaning that the conversation was, in Paterson's (1970) terms, a counterfeit discussion, one appearing free and open but actually predetermined? Were all viewpoints presented in fact respected? Loach himself observed that "it was important that even the most vocal opponent of full collectivisation, Lawrence, should not be a 'caricature' and that his position was accorded proper respect" (Hill, 2011, p. 207). Did Loach ensure this happened? As a viewer I have to say I was persuaded by both Lawrence and David's arguments that debates about land reform and socialism are pointless unless/until Franco is defeated.

In a book I co-authored on *Discussion as a Way of Teaching* (Brookfield and Preskill, 2005) I argued that discussion leaders should help groups develop their own ground rules to guide their discussions, particularly those geared toward decision-making. One approach I advocated was to use videos of discussions to do this. The *Land and Freedom* discussion about collectivisation is a video excerpt particularly suited to working with activist groups to help them decide what they want their own decision-making meetings to look like. Many such groups reject overly formalistic procedures to run meetings such as *Robert's Rules of Order* (2011) but many also become frustrated and disillusioned with discussions that seem to continue interminably without ever reaching a consensus, or with dogged participants who will not let an issue go simply because they have the energy to keep arguing. After watching the collectivisation discussion people can consider the questions I raise above about fairness, equity, respect and inclusion and use their responses to generate some basic ground rules for how they wish to go about making decisions about the role of their group in the wider movement.

I also believe that this excerpt crystallises so many social movement tensions and dynamics that it can be a useful training or induction tool for those committing to a movement for the first time. It illustrates enduring tensions such as the ways personal biographies and theoretical convictions are fused, the inherently emotional nature of attempts to reach agreements on contentious movement issues, the need to balance the short-term necessity of dealing with specific problems and impediments against the long term broad goals of the movement, and the need to work on achievable local goals by learning from wider relevant experiences. As a helpful tool to prepare new movement members for what they can expect in the months and years ahead, this collectivisation sequence is an excellent educative tool.

But this is just one sequence in just one of Loach's film. For more examples of how movement members deal with these eternal dynamics I urge readers to look at his whole body of work. The TV miniseries *Days of Hope* and the films *Bread and Roses* and *The Wind that Shakes the Barley* are good places to start.

REFERENCES

Bangs, L. (2004). 'The Clash' In A. D'Ambrosio (Ed.), *Let fury have the hour: The punk rock politics of Joe Strummer*. New York: Nation Books.

Brookfield, S. D. & Preskill, S. J. (2005). *Discussion as a way of teaching: Tools and techniques for democratic classrooms*. San Francisco: Jossey-Bass, (2nd ed.).

Fuller, G. (Ed.) (1998). *Loach on Loach*. London: Faber and Faber.

Hayward, A. (2004). *Which side are you on? Ken Loach and his films*. London: Bloomsbury Publishing.

Hill, J. (2011). *Ken Loach: The politics of film and television*. London: Palgrave Macmillan/The British Film Institute.

Leigh, J. (2002). *The cinema of Ken Loach: Art in the service of people*. London: Wallflower Press.

MacFadden, P. (1997). Saturn's feast, Loach's Spain: Land and Freedom as filmed history. In, G. McKnight (Ed.), *Agent of challenge and defiance: The films of Ken Loach*. Westport, CT: Greenwood Press.

Marcuse, H. (1969). *An essay on liberation*. Boston: Beacon Press.

Marcuse, H. (1972). *Counterrevolution and revolt*. Boston: Beacon Press.

Marcuse, H. (1978). *The aesthetic dimension: Toward a critique of Marxist aesthetics* Boston: Beacon Press.

Marx, K. (2008). *Essential writings of Karl Marx: Economic and philosophic manuscripts, Communist manifesto, Wage labour and capital, Critique of the Gotha program*. St. Petersburg, Florida: Red and Black Publishers.

Paterson, R. W. K. (1970). "The concept of discussion: A philosophical approach" Studies in Adult Education, *1*(2).

Reed, T. V. (2005). *The art of protest*. Minneapolis, MN: University of Minnesota Press.

Roberts Rules of Order. http://www.robertsrules.org Retrieved December 15th, 2011.

The Observer. "Ken Loach: The film that changed my life". The New Review Section, May 15th, 2010, p. 29.

The Guardian, 2011. http://www.guardian.co.uk/film/2011/aug/28/ken-loach-class-riots-interview?INTCMP= SRCH

Slate. http://www.slate.com/id/2302617/pagenum/2

SECTION 3

CHANGING THE WORLD

BUDD L. HALL

9. 'A GIANT HUMAN HASHTAG': LEARNING AND THE #OCCUPY MOVEMENT[1]

INTRODUCTION[2]

'Are you ready for a Tahrir moment? On September 17, we want to see 20,000 people flood into Lower Manhattan, set up tents, kitchens, peaceful barricades and occupy wall street for a few months…'. So read the challenge issued by *AdBusters*, the Vancouver based cultural activists in their blog of July 13, 2011. They provided the original #OCCUPYWALLSTREET hashtag and a poster of a ballerina dancing on the back of the charging wall street bull. This spark, reheated and propelled through social media such as the hacker group Anonymous, ignited some 200 activists who then worked for 47 days to prepare for the first occupation of Zucotti Park resulting in what we now know as the Occupy Movement.

This chapter looks at the revolutionary pedagogies of #OWS, the Occupy Wall Street movement. In doing so, it builds on and contributes to an increasing interest in the centrality of theories and practices of social movement learning to the understanding of the transformative power of social movements. The focus of the #OWS movement has been on inequality both within our communities and nations and between them. It has looked in particular at economic inequality and the role of finance capital in driving this growing inequality. In drawing attention to the corrosive nature of inequality, I suggest in this chapter that learning and education have played a more central role in achieving these goals than arguably is true for the vast majority of movements that we are familiar with in the 20th Century. While I would argue that democratic knowledge and learning frameworks are extremely helpful in understanding the impact and power of any social movement, the Occupy movement has drawn more attention to the processes of learning, to collective thinking, to active listening and to the creation of new physical, intellectual and political spaces than movements that have preceded it. This chapter and indeed this book extend the conversations amongst a growing number of scholars some of whom were involved in the special issue on social movement learning of the journal *Studies in the Education of Adults* that the four editors of this book were responsible for in late 2011 (Hall, Clover, Crowther and Scandrett). For this chapter I am looking at both the learning within the #OWS movement and the learning from or as a result of the movement. In doing so I associate myself with John Holst in noting that for too long, social movement learning scholars have tailed or copied social scientists in their analyses of social movements and that it is time for those of us coming from radical adult education traditions to advance our

B. L. Hall, D. E. Clover, J. Crowther and E. Scandrett (Eds.), Learning and Education for a Better World: The Role of Social Movements, 127–140.

own theoretical positions (2011). I am hoping in this to extend and deepen my own earlier conceptualisations of social movement learning (Hall, 2004, 2006, 2009).

The sources that I have drawn on for this chapter are the very sources that account for the rapid growth of the #Occupy Movement itself. Like the movements of the Arab Spring, the #Occupy Movement has gained inspiration, shared organising strategies, set collective agendas and informed the world at key moments using the instruments of the social media. Twitter, Facebook pages, web pages, e-mail lists have played particularly critical roles in all aspects of the movement, not the least of which has been its learning activities. As someone who has been active within the 140 character messages of the Twitter world, I have been able to follow our own local Occupy movement, learn of the activities of the world-wide movement, gain access to both internal and external commentators and analysts and feel part of the movement through my own 'tweets'. Virtually all the sources that I have used for this chapter have come directly or indirectly from the thousands of messages founded in the Twitter universe of #OWS, #OCCUPYWALLSTREET, #Occupy and other similar hashtags. And although articles and books of a more academic nature are emerging daily, they will not replace the hashtag world in the hacking of our consciousness.

THE #OCCUPY MOVEMENT

'The proposed rules that we would like to share tonight about working by consensus were developed and refined by a group in Madrid associated with the protests there. They are rules associated with the creation of a People's Assembly for the Occupy Movement'. These words were spoken in Victoria, British Columbia in late September of 2011 by a volunteer from the logistics team to a group of about 40–50 people who had gathered in Centennial Square, alongside the Victoria City Hall, to discuss the establishment of an Occupy camp in our city. The persons who explained the rules for raising issues, considering amendments, being allowed to speak, voting and other procedures for making decisions by consensus were not elected leaders. Indeed one of the first acts carried out was to choose a number of facilitators from amongst those who had come out to the first meeting. Once a group of facilitators had volunteered, the conduct of the very first organising meeting was turned over to them and the evening's debates and discussions began.

Scenes like these were occurring around the world beginning with the September 17 first General Assembly of the Occupy movement in the heart of Wall Street in New York City itself and spreading throughout the world at the speed of Twitter #hashtags and Facebook linkages over a period of days and weeks so that at the peak of the tented occupations, there were about 1500 cities around the world with physical occupations of some kind. Galvanised by the clarity of the call for justice in a world where 1 per cent of the world's rich dominate and exploit 99 per cent of world's people, the spark of the Occupy movement caught fire and spread throughout the rich countries of the world. The Occupy Movement was born with a speed and a unity of both purpose and process that have set it apart from most social movements of the 20th Century. It is a quintessentially 21st century movement born in the realisation that global capitalism has widened the gap between the rich and the poor, has robbed the working classes and the middle classes of their dreams, and has made the rhetoric of democracy even in wealthy countries seem empty and powerless. The #OWS movement has drawn strength from the revolutionary energies of the Arab Spring which was itself sparked by reactions to the self immolation of the 27 year old Tunisian fruit vendor in December of 2010. The Occupy Movement drew as well from and the massive protests of Europe and from the 'encampadas' or tented occupations in Madrid and Barcelona.

Murray Dobbin, a veteran Canadian left-wing writer and activist has captured the freshness of the 'Giant Human Hashtag' eloquently in noting that,

> The Occupy movement has been like a powerful cleansing wind blowing over the political landscape—exposing not just the obscenely rich, and criminally irresponsible political elite, but almost every other political player too: cowardly liberals, cautious social democrats, the strangely silent churches, social movements stuck in the past, and a moribund labour movement. Indeed, that is what is most striking about this movement: It owes nothing to anyone. (2011, 1)

While the #OWS movement seems to have arrived in the public sphere seemingly 'from nowhere', this is not of course the case. Indeed the 1980s, 90s and early 2000s have seen a series of protests and movements that we generally refer to as anti-globalisation protests of the anti-globalisation movement. Beginning with the protests associated with the Seattle World Trade discussions, there have been a series of actions that have targeted the locations where the leaders of the global capitalist system have been meeting. We are also familiar with the World Social Forum which has sprung up to support the idea that 'another world is possible' in opposition to the Davos World Economic Forum where the heads of governments and corporations meet each year. Added to this are the various campaigns such as the 'Make Poverty History' campaign that has set specific targets on governments for debt reduction and redistribution. The #OWS movement has taken well-known critiques of global capital and found a way to bring them to a broader public.

The #OWS movement has succeeded in putting the issue of the corrosive reality of economic inequality on the front pages of mainstream media and has influenced the political agenda in countries like the United States where it can be argued that in the 2012 Presidential election, that the ballot question of job creation has if not been supplanted by the inequality agenda, at least influenced it. Corporate greed, corrupt political processes, a flawed system of capitalism no longer able to offer enough 'trickle down' to the middle classes to sustain their modest dreams are being discussed by broad publics and analysed by scholars and politicians everywhere. The Editorial in a local newspaper in Vancouver is an example of what national and global mainstream and even conservative media are saying, 'Politicians need new economic narrative to preserve democracy' (Vancouver Sun,

Tuesday, January 31, 2012, p. A10). Of course readers will say that much more is needed than a new narrative to break with the form of rogue capitalism that has been allowed to run wild for far too long.

CHARACTERISTICS OF THE MOVEMENT

While the focus of this chapter is on the learning dimensions of the Occupy movement, the learning dimensions of the movement are so intricately tied up with the very fabric of the movement, with its qualities and specific organising strategies, that it important to devote some space to a description of what the distinctive characteristics of the movement are. Terms and concepts associated with the Occupy movement include: consensus-based, decentralised leadership, collective thinking, direct democracy, non-violence, non-ideological, anarchist, creating replicas of the society we want, creating new knowledge. Many of the characteristics of the movement owe their origins to the work done by the Group Dynamics of the Puerta del Sol Protest camp in Madrid. The *Quick Guide on Group Dynamics in People's Assemblies* (July 31, 2011) provided a unifying organisational, strategic and learning framework for the global movement. Designed by the Puerta del Sol team from practices originating with the revolutionary pedagogies of the Tahrir Square occupation in Egypt, the *Quick Guide* captures a way of organising political work based on a desire for direct democracy rather than representative democracy, an interest in the self-organising principles of anarchist scholar activists such as David Greaber (2007) and presents a set of practical tools for organising consensus with large groups of people. The goal of people's assemblies, according to the *Quick Guide*, is to promote 'collective thinking' (2011). Collective thinking is in contrast to a more traditional sense of political discussion where persons with diverse points of view argue their positions until a majority of persons are with them. Consensus is rare in this form of political discourse. Collective thinking calls for persons with diverse perspectives to listen to each other and come up with not a winning or losing idea, but a new idea which represents consensus. People's Assemblies are,

> Participatory decision-making bodies which work towards consensus. They must be pacific, respecting all opinions: prejudice and ideology must be left at home. An assembly should not be centred on an ideological discourse: instead it should deal with practical questions: What do we need? How can we get it? (Commission for Group Dynamics, 2011, p. 1)

The people's assembly processes are fundamentally pedagogical and can be recognized by adult educators, popular educators and others as similar to principles of progressive adult learning that the radical tradition from the Antigonish Movement of Canada to Freire's *Pedagogy of the Oppressed* and more.

Of course the dynamics in each of the occupy locations differed somewhat according to the numbers of people available and the personalities of those who were there. The suggested roles needed to achieve consensus with large groups of people are innovative and helpful. In the guidelines there was to be no permanent central coordinator or even a central coordinating team. All roles were to be rotated and include a moderator who's job is to keep focused on the issue around which consensus is to be built.. A Floor team takes lists of people who wish to speak to a topic with a floor team coordinator to help organise the interventions to keep the debate moving forward, avoiding repetitions and so forth. A minutes team records the discussions and decisions. In addition a set of gestures to provide participants with a capacity to convey their feelings such as agreement, disagreement, and come-to-the-point without shouting or speaking are outlined.

THE IMPORTANCE OF THE SPACE

Luis Moreno-Cabulard, an Assistant Professor at the University of Pennsylvania who participated in the Madrid camps said that the objectives of the emphasis of the occupations were on, 'being inclusive, setting aside strong ideological identities that could divide and also, of course, the idea of taking the square to try a do a replica of what you would like to see' (quoted in Sledge, 2011, np). The importance of the actual occupation of physical space cannot be over emphasized. From the symbolism of the occupation in the Wall Street district itself to the choice of locations for the hundreds of other occupy sites, the notion of symbolically taking back space stolen from the 99 per cent by the 1 per cent has played a critical role. The idea of creating a small-scale community that could operate with a sense of inclusiveness, fairness and justice has been another one of the deep pedagogical experiences of the movement. Almost all of the occupy sites had a number of physical characteristics. They had tents or shelters of some kind. They had kitchens for the preparation and serving of meals to the community. They had health services including support for safe sex and often for safe drug and substance use. They also all had libraries! Books on anarchism, Marxism, feminism, queer theory, arts-based revolutionary stories, the poetry of struggle, histories of struggle, critiques of capitalism appeared quickly in the Occupy Victoria space and in all of the sites around the world. The irony in countries like Canada and Britain and elsewhere where funding for public libraries is threatened but the occupying communities would include libraries as a central focus of the new democracy that they call for, is not lost.

In calling for occupations of space as a symbolic or metaphorical device to promote the message of action needed, the movement in North America has come face to face with a very different response to the notion of occupation. In downtown Victoria, where I live and where I have described the first meeting of the People's Assembly of Victoria, a number of Indigenous activists brought our attention to the fact that Victoria and indeed all of Canada and the United States are build on the occupied traditional territories of the First Nations Peoples of this part of the world. European settlers colonised and occupied our part of the world. What is more once the early years of contact were finished when the Indigenous Peoples had helped the settlers to survive in these new and strange parts of the world, the powerful and aggressive processes of colonisation, displacement from lands, genocide, forms of assimilation, residential schooling and destruction of languages and cultures began. The question raised is how can we occupy a space already occupied? A thoughtful discussion ensued on the first night of the Victoria People's Assembly with a decision that it was useful to associate with the 'brand' and solidarity of the Occupy Movement, that we would prefer to refer to our actions as being part of the People's Assembly of Victoria. And while this discussion may seem from a global perspective as relatively minor, it underscores the violent and aggressive nature of European colonialism. There are deep implications as well from an epistemological perspective about parallels between the ways that white European colonialism occupied the territories of the worlds Indigenous Peoples, but also how they colonized and occupied the intellectual, scientific, and spiritual spaces as well.

IN THE WORDS OF THE OCCUPIERS

The Occupy movement has no Commandante Marco, the mysterious and charismatic leader of the Zapatisa movement in Mexico. But perhaps because of that hundreds and thousands of participants have created blogs, tweeted and in other ways found ways to share their insights about their own experiences. Raimundo Viejo of Pompeu Fabra University in Barcelona and a participant in the Barcelona camps was quoted in the July 13 call to action by *adbusters*. He highlighted the differences between the Occupy movement and earlier anti-globalisation campaigns.

> The anti-globalisation movement was the first step on the road. Back then our model was to attack the system like a pack of wolves. There was an alpha male, a wolf who led the pack, and those who followed behind. Now the model has evolved. Today we are one big swarm of people (AdBusters, 2011)

Yotam Marom is a participant in the Wall Street occupation. Marom was one of the organisers of the Bloombergville two-week occupation in New York that preceded the Wall Street actions. He participated, not in a leadership position, in the planning meetings that took place over the summer of 2011 leading up to the September 17 Occupation. Speaking of the new form of organising that has emerged with the Occupy movement, Marom tells us,

> I have to admit I was sceptical. I saw too many white young college kids and not enough grassroots organizers, not enough of those communities hardest hit by neoliberalism and austerity. I was pushed away by some of the cultural norms being adopted and found myself at odds with the lack of demands, not to mention the sometimes over-emphasis on process...But I was wrong about some of those assumptions, and—though we are still far from being a huge, unified movement, with clear goals, led by the most oppressed layers of society, with the capacity for long-term struggle—things have steadily improved (Marom, 2011, p. 1).

He speaks to not only a new way of organising, but a new generation of activists with new tools and new imaginations about how to create a better world. His comments also speak to the diversity of the Occupy movement. The Occupy movement is an inclusive community of young and not-so-young who are brought together by the sheer ugliness of a world where corporate greed is celebrated and middle class and the poor are left to try to hold their lives together in any way that they can. Veteran organisers of the 60s and 70s are sprinkled in amongst the anti-globalisation activists of the 1990s and early 2000s. The young include middle class higher education students weighted down by crippling debt paying for their university tuitions, Black activists, Latino and Indigenous Peoples, libertarians who support the 2012 USA Republican nomination candidate Ron Paul, anarchists, socialists, Marxists, neo-Marxists, artists, small business owners and more. The 99 per cent includes virtually everyone expect the super rich. A very important caveat does need to be made as we keep the power of the 99 per cent formulation in mind. There are dramatically different privileges and conditions of life and hope between the middle class 99 per cent in the rich countries of the world and the bottom billion, the poorest billion people in the world. At some point, these differences will become important to deal with. In the case of our Victoria People's Assembly there was an important discussion about the use of the 1 per cent vs. 99 per cent meme as the picture is more complex and nuanced. Many among the 99 per cent in fact support political regimes that keep the 1 per cent on the top for example. As the movement matures the nuances will undoubtedly gain more visibility.

THEORY AND THE MOVEMENT

The role of theory in the Occupy movement to date is subject to much discussion. There are no shortage of scholars, public intellectuals and commentators willing to make the links between their own intellectual roots and the Occupy movement. David Graebner is one of the academics whose work has been most often associated at least with the emergence of the New York Wall Street Occupation. He is an academic, a Reader in Anthropology at the University of London's Goldsmith's College. An anarchist, his 2007 book, *Lost People*, draws lessons from the lives of the Betafo People of Madagascar that he studied between 1989 and 1991. He observed a process of consensus decision-making in a part of the world where there was no state apparatus to depend on at all. People were 'Basically managing their own affairs autonomously'. It is also acknowledged that Joseph Steiglitz, the Nobel laureate and Professor at Columbia University, is the person who first formulated the 1 per cent – 99 per cent illustration of economic inequality (2011). A still less publically acknowledge intellectual whose work has influenced the commitment to and tools of non-violence is Gene Sharp. In 1993, the elderly Sharp, the Director of the Albert Einstein Centre and a world authority on non-violent revolutions based in Boston, Massachusetts wrote a book for the Burmese democracy struggle headed by Ang San Suu Kyi. The book, *From dictatorship to democracy: a conceptual framework for liberation* contained 198 examples of what Sharp called non-violent weapons (1993). He believes that if people do not have non-violent alternatives, they will be forced to turn to violence and war. His list of 198 non-violent weapons has been translated into scores of languages and has been used throughout former Eastern Europe and in Egypt itself.

What is not as clear however is how much most of those involved in the Occupy movement know about what academics in particular claim to be the intellectual foundations. Evan Calder Williams, a Doctoral candidate from the US studying in Italy notes that the blogs and other social media sites where protestors have been recording their thoughts and reflections have had more impact on the movement. This kind of 'street theory' he says,

> Isn't anti-intellectualism: It is simply to say that the relevant theory is that which will be developed from struggling to grasp the obscure shape of the past few years. It is safe to say that…the many-month occupation of a Chilean girl's school, and Occupy the Hood are—and deserve to be—of far greater intellectual import than any contemporary theorist will be (Williams as quoted in Berrett, 2011, p. 5)

PEDAGOGIES OF OCCUPATION

The de-centralised and shared leadership model of the Occupy Movement requires an attention to learning and education that might take a very different form in other movements. It is a movement that takes Paulo Freire's admonition to 'Read the World' to a mass scale. It is also a pedagogical movement that blurs the lines between education that is consciously focused within the movement and education that is designed for the broader public. And like principles of anarchism that have deeply influenced the movement itself, there is a spirit of support for autonomous learning, for the self-organisation of learning and the open and transgressive learning that might bring revolutionary change closer. As one of the occupiers in the London St. Pauls #OccupyLSX movement has said, 'The Occupation is a physical and mental learning process for all those who seek to change society' (Lotz, 2012) For the sake of simplicity, I want to divide the remaining discussion into education at the occupations and education beyond the squares or plazas.

The fundamental learning principles guiding the physical occupations of the squares emanate from the *Guidelines* of people's assemblies that I have described earlier in this chapter. The process of creating consensus amongst a large and diverse group of persons who have no history of working together requires a clear pedagogical model. The first tool required is one which will allow the crowds to be able to hear speakers without resorting to loudspeakers that in the case of the Wall Street occupation were banned by police and in any case depend on external sources of easily disrupted electrical energy. The 'human loudspeaker' or 'human microphone' is the process that has arisen in the occupying camps around the world. 'Mic check' will be heard from a speaker at the front of the crowd and the words 'mic check' will be repeated to all the groups in the space. The use of this form of speaking serves two additional pedagogical purposes beyond the technological one. It means that the speakers need to consider carefully what they will say and divide their thoughts into audible sound bytes for transmission by human loudspeaker. For listeners it also means that the message is heard in short phrases and is heard several times over as the message is passed along to the back of the square. The effect can be quite disarming for those experiencing it for the first time. When Naomi Klein stood to address the crowd in Zucotti Park in New York, she began by saying, 'I love you' only to hear the words 'I love you' repeated back to her more loudly and repeatedly. Taken aback, but not unpleased, she noted that she did not just say those words so hundreds of people would shout 'I love you' back, but it does illustrate the power of a pedagogical tool invented by the occupiers who had been faced with a communications challenge because the were not allowed to use power for amplication (Klein, 2011).

Referring again to the *Guidelines*, they set out a number of learning parameters, the kinds of which many of might use in our own workshops or classrooms particularly when dealing with highly charged, sensitive or political kinds of topics. The *Guidelines* call on participants to work towards a new form of knowing, to collective knowing. And engaging in collective knowing means learning to listen to each other in a deep and respectful way as the goal is to transform our learning from a competition for ideas into the construction of new knowledge that will be practical and advance us in the specific tasks that are at hand. Setting aside our ideological baggage, respecting all contributions, giving us the time to come to a point of consensus.

Another support for social movement learning in the squares has been the establishment of 'people's libraries' in virtually all the occupied sites. One of the purposes of an actual occupation is the opportunity to create small and temporary alternative societies that allow us to at least imagine different ways of organising our entire community. In spite of the spirit that the occupy movement is a different form or organising than has gone on before or by older organisers, the interest in a huge range of theoretical and inspirational literature has been remarkable. The libraries like the kitchens where occupiers are fed are also spaces where occupiers and visitors engage in the thousands of conversations that provide the deepest form of informal social movement learning within the camps themselves. Living together, struggling together, arguing, caring, helping, solving problems, singing, and comforting each other all provides an extraordinarily rich epistemological environment. People learn through sharing their reflections, reactions, dreams and frustrations. And all this happens without any structured learning processes whatsoever. Indeed this kind of social movement learning is at the heart of all social movements written about in this book, but needs to be illuminated in particular in the contexts of the Occupy Movement.

TENT CITY UNIVERSITY

In many of the large Occupy sites, more organised forms of adult education have emerged. Tent City University is Occupy London's educational arm. Defining the Occupy Movement as a movement designed to change the debate about how we organise ourselves throughout the world from an economic point of view, Tent City University says that it is important to keep moving forward 'provoking thought and forcing debate' (Tent City University, 2011). They continue, '...Under neoliberalism, free flows of information were impeded, as public media became concentrated in the hands of a very wealthy few and universities found their funding slashed' (2011, np). Everyday at the site near St. Paul's Cathedral speakers from the world of academia, banking, business, politics, activism, the arts and more shared their ideas with the occupiers and the many passers-by interested in new debates about alternatives to the globalised economy as it is currently structured. But Tent City University goes beyond this.

'But education isn't just about eye-opening debate. It represents, in our understanding, a radical platform for challenging the very legitimacy of power relations' they proclaim (Tent City University, 2011, np). These words might easily be imagined as having been said by Raymond Williams, Paulo Freire, Paula Allman, Moses Coady, Myles Horton, Gandhi-ji or Julius Nyerere. Tent City University says that the construction of radical education programmes faces three challenges: a new approach to learning, breaking down communications barriers between people and a new pedagogy of place. The motto of Tent City University is 'anyone can teach, everyone can learn' and acknowledges the work of Paulo Freire in this regard. 'We seek to promote an approach to learning that prioritises process over end-point and values these skills all of us have to share and the capacity all of us have to learn' (2011, np).

'Empathy is reduced [between people] by lack of interaction and mobility across social groups' say the Tent City pedagogues thus leading to the second educational challenge. If the divisions between social groups are especially acute, they explain, this is a 'significant contributing factor to injustice and inequality' (2011, np). So learning from migrant workers cleaning the building of The City financial district that surrounds the educational space, learning from bicycle mechanics, former bankers, students, the homeless, the poor and the middle class sharing the same space and listening to each other in fresh ways creates a pedagogical space where new collectivities and new communities can emerge. Building on the idea of space leads to the third challenge, a new pedagogy of space.

Public space, especially in the heart of our major cities has disappeared over the years as the value of the land has risen so high that virtually all space near the economic sectors in our cities has been privatised. Tent City University exists to challenge the closing of the physical and pedagogical commons and for the opening up of spaces for public free debate and discussion in the very heart of the city of London. In rejecting the right of the state to create laws which exclude people from what should be public spaces, they have created 'flash teach-outs'—a combination of education and direct action. Flash mobs are the social media mass spontaneous gatherings that have been springing up all over the world in recent years for both political and celebratory purposes. A flash teach-out is a sudden large gathering in front of for example the Bank of England for the purposes of staging public lectures, hosting open debates and other educational events. As formal education becomes more and more commoditised and inaccessible, Tent City University, is offering popular alternatives through workshops, lectures, debates, films, games, praxis and action. In doing so they are challenging not only the neoliberal status quo, but also the educational status quo. They are creating a vibrant new chapter in a rich tradition of social movement learning.

SOCIAL MEDIA LEARNING SPACES

As with the Arab Spring stories told in another chapter in this book, the social media are at the heart of both the operational organising strategies and at the heart of the pedagogies of the occupations. This is true both for those who are participants living in the camps, drop-in day visitors and for the thousands of persons who because of their work, families or locations could not be part of the actual occupations. #OCCUPYWALLSTREET, #OccupyLSX, #OWS, #Occupy are all hashtags on Twitter that anyone can access. There are hundreds of local occupy hashtags such as #Occupyvictoria or #PAOV in my community. Simply log into your Twitter account and do a search for any of these hashtags and you will be in touch with the living and breathing heart of the movement. These streams of information provide times for meetings, names of speakers, links to important commentaries in blog form, links to what the mainstream media is saying about your own community or the larger world community, stories from Egypt, stories from Europe and much more.

When one combines the learning resources available via Twitter, Facebook, web sites, blogs, wikis and even image sites such as Tumblr or Instagram, we have living social movement encyclopaedias, but ones that are 'written' by each one of us as we choose what and where to read. Newspaper like formats have sprung up, *The Occupation Times* or @*Occupy London*. Graphic presentations in the form of Graphic comics such as 'Stories of the 99%' by Occupy Comix are yet another creative way that new forms of social movement learning are springing into our minds (2011).

Inevitably the on-going physical occupation of the various sites ended. For security reasons, cold weather, changing strategies the camps themselves were shut down, the tents taken away or confiscated and the occupiers evicted. But the social media that have been the heartbeat of the movement have continued and even expanded. Occupy 2.0 is alive and well and providing the movement with access to flash mob actions, on-going educational spaces, strategic discussions and deepened forms of de-centralized leadership.

HACKING YOUR CONSCIOUSNESS

Time, the ultimate power, will determine what the long-term influence of the occupy movement will be. Will the critiques about not having a specific political agenda be proved right? Will the fact that life within some of the camps themselves was not free from issues of harassment of women for example detract from the grander vision? The occupy movement throws up new concepts, new frameworks, and arguably new theories. Theories and perspectives that have been created in the very processes of deep listening, collective knowing and practical direct and non-violent action that are the occupy movement itself. Doyle Canning from the Boston based narrative strategy centre smartMeme talks about how the bold actions of occupy movement have harnessed the 'psychic break', which she understands happens when, 'The dominant narrative unravels and there is an opening for a new story to be take hold on a massive scale' (2011:3). Another insight into how the educational side of the movement works, comes from the Matador Network who say,

It's impossible to pinpoint when the shift occurs—when you go from being an observer of the various occupations around the world, to becoming a participant. Perhaps it was when you realized the thriving vitality that emerged when you walked onto the grounds of an occupation: the drum circles, the creative signs, and the passionate dialogue…Or perhaps you're still convinced the Occupy Movement is a waste of time. No matter the *hacking of your consciousness has begun* (emphasis added). When people recognize a different way of being, they realize they can choose their experience in life. The implications are profound (MacKenzie,2011, p. 1)

NOTES

[1] The hashtag # is the symbol used in Twitter social media accounts to allow users to find postings related to the word or letters so indicated. #OCCUPYWALLSTREET and #OWS are the hashtags most often used for 'tweets' related to Occupy Wall Street. The phase, *a Giant Human Hashtag* is from Eric Sanders on December 19, 2011 writing in Big Think.

[2] Thanks to Darlene Clover, Eurig Scandrett and Simon Zukowski for very helpful comments.

REFERENCES

AdBusters (2011). *AdBusters Blog* of July 13, 2011 http://bit.ly/n4v4T

Berrett, Dave (2011). 'Intellectual Roots of Wall Street Protests Lie in Academe' in *The Chronicle of Higher Education* October 16, 2011 pp 1–6.

Canning, Doyle (2011). 'Can the #Occupy Movement Be a Turning Point' Op-Ed in *Yes Magazine* posted Oct 3, 2011 pp 1–4 retrieved November 12, 2011 from http://www.yesmagazine.org/people-power/can-the-occupy-movement-be-a-turning-point.

Commission on Group Dynamics (2011). *Quick Guide on Group Dynamics in People's Assemblies* retrieved February 2, 2012 from http://takethesquare.net/2011/07/31/quick-guide-on-group-dynamics-in-peoples-assemblies/

Graebner, David (2007). *Lost People: Magic and the legacy of slavery in Madagascar* Bloomington, Indiana: Indiana University Press, pp 469.

Hall, Budd (2004). 'Towards transformative environmental adult education: lessons from social movements' in Darlene Clover (Ed). *Global Perspectives on environmental adult education*, pp 152–168, New York: Peter Lang.

Hall, Budd (2006). ''Social Movement Learning: Theorizing a Canadian Tradition' in Tara Fenwick, Tom Nesbit and Bruce Spencer (Eds). *Contexts of adult education. Canadian perspectives*, pp 230–238 Toronto: Thomson Educational Publishing.

Hall, Budd (2009). 'A River of Life: Learning and environmental social movements', *Interface: A Journal for and about Social Movements 1*(1)*, 46–78.*

Hall, B., D. Clover, J. Crowther and E. Scandrett (Eds.). Special Issue of *Studies in the Education of Adults, 43*(2), Autumn 2011.

Holst, J. (2011). 'Frameworks for Understanding the Politics of Social Movements' in *Studies in the Education of Adults, 43*(2, Autumn), 117–127).

Klein, N. (2011). 'Occupy Wall Street: The Most Important Thing in the World Now' delivered October 7, 2011 and retrived December 18, 2011 from http://informationclearinghouse.info/article29332.htm

Lotz, C. (2012). 'St Paul's Occupation makes its mark' in Jan 23 *A World to Win Blog* retrieved on January 25, 2012 from http://www.aworldtowin.net/blog/st-pauls-occupation-makes-its-mark

Marom, Y. (2011). 'A Brief Analysis from a Wall Street Occupier' October 4, 2011 posted in *Current Articles, Occupy Wall Street* and retrieved on December 4, 2011 from http://www.afreesociety.org/a-brief-analysis-from-a-wall-street-occupier

MacKenzie, I. (2011). 'How the Occupy Movement is hacking your consciousness' *Matador Network* Dec 30, 2011 pp 1–2 retrieved on January 6, 2012 from http://matadornetwork.com/bnt/occupy-movement-hacking-consciousness/

Occupy C. (2011). *Stories of the 99 %* Occupy Comix, *1*(1), December 2011.

Sanders, E. (2011). 'Occupy Wall Street: A Giant Human Hashtag' *Big Think* web site of December 19, 2011 Http://bigthink.com/ideas as retrieved on December 28, 2011.

Sharp, G. (1993). *From Dictatorship to Democracy: A Conceptual Framework for Liberation* Boston: Albert Einstein Centre.

Sledge, M. (2011). 'Reawakening the Radical Imagination: The Origins of Occupy Wall Street' in *Huffington Post* 11/10/11 retrieved February 2, 2012 from http://huffingtonpost.com

Steiglitz, J. (2011). 'Inequality: Of the 1 %, By the 1 %, For the 1 %' in *Vanity Fair* May 2011 retrieved February 2, 2012 from http://vnty.fr/i4n84g

Tent City University (2011). '@Occupy London' Nov 8, 2011 retrieved on December 8, 2011 from http://www.zcommunications.org/occupy-london-by-tent-city

AZIZ CHOUDRY

10. BUILDING COUNTER-POWER FROM THE GROUND UP: CONTESTING 'NGOISATION' THROUGH SOCIAL MOVEMENT LEARNING AND KNOWLEDGE PRODUCTION

INTRODUCTION

The chapter reflects upon tensions over learning and knowledge production in international non-governmental organisation (NGO) and social movement networks contesting global free market capitalism, now widely known as the 'global justice movement'. It discusses aspects of NGO/social movement activist networks opposing the Asia-Pacific Economic Cooperation (APEC) forum during the 1990s, and more recent activism against bilateral free trade and investment agreements, (FTAs) both in the Asia-Pacific region. It compares and contrasts the dominant forms of professionalised NGO knowledge/action with knowledge/action emerging from grounded social struggles against FTAs, and critiques the trend towards the NGOisation/NGO management of social change with particular focus on its knowledge/learning implications. The chapter argues that movements can create counter-power and radical alternatives to the prevailing world order by looking beyond dominant models of transnational NGO-driven campaigns and modes of action, drawing on the intellectual/conceptual resources produced in the course of grounded local struggles against global capitalism but informed by understandings of global political and economic power dynamics.

In doing so, the chapter draws from insights from critical adult education (Foley, 1999, Novelli, 2010, Holst, 2002, 2011), political activist ethnography (Kinsman, 2006; G. Smith, 2006) and the author's involvement in these activist networks (Choudry, 2009; Choudry and Kapoor 2010, Choudry and Shragge, 2011). Drawing additionally from knowledge and learning produced in the course of social struggles, it identifies and questions hegemonic NGO practices, arguing that hierarchies of power and knowledge within 'alternative' milieus often reproduce, rather than challenge dominant practices and power relations, and serve elite interests rather than those of constituencies which these organisation claim to represent.

Feminist, Marxist, critical race and other critical scholars, have advanced critiques of NGOs and what I call "NGOisation". These include Kamat's (2002, 2004) work on the impacts of NGOisation and the growth of NGOs on political space and development in India and internationally, and INCITE!, Women of Color Against Violence's (2007) recent analyses of the 'non-profit industrial

B. L. Hall, D. E. Clover, J. Crowther and E. Scandrett (Eds.), Learning and Education for a Better World: The Role of Social Movements, 141–154.

complex' in the Americas. For Petras and Veltmeyer, (2005), and others, the professionalisation of community-based NGOs and their de-politicisation works well for neoliberal regimes, keeping 'the existing power structure (vis-à-vis the distribution of society's resources) intact while promoting a degree (and a local form) of change and development' (p. 20). Moreover, if we trace the lineage of existing scholarly critiques of NGOs and institutionalisation or demobilisation, such analyses of NGOisation often owe a debt to collective forms of critical knowledge production, learning and debates emerging from within social movements and activist networks committed to progressive social change. Often these tensions and critiques are raised and even worked out in practice before being subjected to academic scrutiny.

Bob (2005) argues that 'in their role as gatekeepers, major NGOs may act as brakes on more radical and exceptional ideas emanating from the developing world, and for that reason some important challengers eschew foreign ties' (p. 194). There is a relationship between the NGOisation of social change and its impact on knowledge production and learning. Elsewhere (Choudry, 2009, 2010a, 2010b, Choudry and Shragge, 2011), I explore in detail how, within supposedly "alternative" global justice networks, a relatively small NGO elite attempts to claim positional superiority for forms of professionalised knowledge and advocacy that attempt to side-line, filter, or erase more critical positions emerging from social movement activism opposed to capitalism and colonialism. Petras and Veltmeyer (2001) contend that the vast majority of NGOs feed off mass-based social movements and displace or serve as a buffer against more critical challenges to state power and capital. They charge that while NGO professionals put themselves forward as spokespeople for the poor and marginalised, with NGO conferences and parallel summits ideal vehicles and venues for this practice. While emphasising the importance of context-specific approaches to understanding NGOs and social movements and wary of over-simplistic binaries of "good" grassroots activists versus 'bad' international NGOs, I contend that the dominant tendency of many development and advocacy NGOs is to compartmentalize the world into "issues," and "projects", and the practice of an "ideology of pragmatism" which entails an unwillingness to name or confront capitalism directly. These positions, which replicate, rather than challenge dominant power relations, serve to undermine and contain more critical forms of knowledge production and action in relation to confronting global capitalism. Even within movement networks purportedly committed to 'global justice', many NGOs in both the North and South replicate dominant approaches to hierarchies of knowledge by favouring academic, professionalised knowledge forms over learning developed in social struggles. But these processes are also being challenged by ideas and mobilisation strategies arising from learning and knowledge production occurring in many past and present struggles. At the start of the 21st century, one set of sites for this movement knowledge production is taking place in diverse locations among movements confronting FTAs.

DYNAMICS AND DISCONNECTS INSIDE THE GLOBAL JUSTICE MOVEMENT

Considerable scholarly research (e.g. Starr, 2000; Goodman, 2002; McNally, 2002; Polet and CETRI, 2004; Bandy and Smith, 2005; Day, 2005) has gone into examining popular struggles against capitalist globalisation, including campaigns against the World Bank, the International Monetary Fund (IMF), the WTO and the Free Trade Area of the Americas (FTAA). Some studies have discussed the emergence of the APEC forum in the Asia-Pacific and the networks of opposition that arose to contest its agenda (Pue, 1998, Kelsey, 1999, Choudry, 2008). The anti-APEC networks of NGOs, social movements and activist groups in the 1990s, along with networks and coalitions opposed to the North American Free Trade Agreement (NAFTA) in the Americas foreshadowed what came to be dubbed the 'anti-globalisation' or 'global justice' movement, especially after the mobilization in Seattle against the WTO Ministerial Meeting in November/December 1999. The claims of newness surrounding "globalisation" and "anti-globalisation" obfuscated the fact that in many contexts, particularly in the Third World, there had been long and on-going resistance to neoliberalism in its different manifestations spanning several decades (Flusty, 2004; Choudry, 2008). Yet relatively little attention has been paid to newer bilateral free trade and investment agreements (FTAs) which have spread in the wake of the breakdown of multilateral (WTO) and regional (e.g. FTAA) negotiations, and the rise in social movement activism against these agreements. Such movements have often been mass-based (e.g. opposition to the recently-ratified US-Korea FTA has regularly brought out tens of thousands of Korean farmers, workers and other activists, while 200,000 Costa Ricans rallied against a free trade agreement with the US (part of the Central American Free Trade Agreement) in February 2007), yet have been largely off the radar of the transnational NGO networks which coalesced around the WTO.

Rather than grounding my analysis of these movements and networks in dominant strands of social movement theory or policy discussions put forward by professionalised NGOs this chapter is informed by my engagement in activism against APEC and bilateral FTAs. In situating my analysis in this way, I concur with Flacks (2004) and Bevington and Dixon's (2005) critiques of the shortcomings of much social movement theory as being driven by attempts to define and refine theoretical concepts which are likely to be "irrelevant or obvious to organisers" (Flacks, 2004, p. 147), and the latter's call for the recognition of existing movement-generated theory and dynamic reciprocal engagement by theorists and movement activists in formulating, producing, refining and applying research. This body of theory also pays little attention to significance of learning in struggle. There is a further disjuncture or tension between top down impositions of alternative policy platforms articulated by international NGO and trade union elites and the visions and strategy/analysis coming out of grounded struggles.

Kinsman (2006) is right to challenge the "standard binary oppositions of theory versus practice and researcher versus activist constructed through academic disciplines, professionalisation and institutionalization" (p. 134). Smith (2006) suggests that for activist researchers, there is a wealth of research material and signposts derived from moments of confrontation to explore the way that power in our world is socially organized. He contends that being interrogated by insiders to a ruling regime, like a crown attorney for example brings a researcher into direct contact with the conceptual relevancies and organising principles of such regimes. Significant learning takes place in moments of confrontation within and among NGO/social movement networks over position, tactics, analysis, priorities etc.

There is a tendency among scholars of social movements and social movement learning to underestimate the significance of incremental informal learning, which takes place in the course of campaigns and activist organising contexts on the ground and in the course of movement building, – by contrast with the often higher-profile teach-ins, alternative "peoples'" summits and other non-formal modes of education in these contexts. As Kinsman (2006) notes, research and theorising

> Is an everyday/every night part of the life of social movements whether explicitly recognized or not. Activists are thinking, talking about, researching and theorizing about what is going on, what they are going to do next and how to analyse the situations they face, whether in relation to attending a demonstration, a meeting, a confrontation with institutional forces or planning the next action or campaign (p. 134).

NGOISATION, KNOWLEDGE POLITICS AND "PEOPLE'S SUMMITS"

During the 1990s, in the course of participating in numerous NGO conferences and activist teach-ins, and as an organiser and educator in a small Aotearoa/New Zealand-based activist group opposed to APEC, the WTO and the global free market economy, I began to wonder increasingly about the ways which these activities, the documents produced and the discourses employed serve to create and reify 'experts' and 'leaders', particularly through writing, speeches and narratives. These writers, leaders, and spokespeople were frequently academics and/or professional NGO analysts and researchers, rather than organizers or people engaged in grassroots struggles. These often-charismatic NGO professionals and scholar-activists tend to produce texts prolifically, and claim power to speak for and represent movements and mobilizations, with a ring of credibility and authority. Yet in doing so, they can contribute to the silencing and marginalisation of voices from grassroots movements and organisation.

Once people are validated as authorities or resource people in these settings, they are also asked to formulate alternatives. This is contradictory. On the one hand, there is often a talking up of alternative knowledge(s) and the importance of voices from below. On the other, there is often a deep reticence among both scholar-activists and professionalised staff of NGOs to meaningfully support these marginalized and excluded voices – including stepping back to allow some space for people from grassroots struggles to talk on the same terms as they do. Sometimes a mobilised mass opposition movement is precisely what is needed to create political space to challenge power relations, rather than ungrounded formulae for 'alternatives' contained in conference declarations and NGO charters and teach-in presentations (Petras and Veltmeyer, 2001 and 2003; McNally, 2002). Kress (1982) and Clark and Ivanic (1997) note that there is unequal distribution of access to 'socially prestigious and socially shaping' (p. 55) forms of writing, and that this has its roots in a society's economic, political, ideological and social structures. Kress argues that this has economic, political and ideological effects: 'those able to produce meanings and messages are few by comparison with those who consume meanings and messages. Hence the control of messages and meanings is in the hands of a relatively small number of people' (p. 3).

The status accorded to policy analysts and NGO researchers, and their powers of interpretation pose some challenges for any movement or network, which espouses democracy and community. In the context of building 'alternatives to globalisation', I wondered if anti-globalisation networks really needed their own school of high priests to interpret both policy and put forward alternatives? In turn, why would these professionalised 'experts' be best placed to propose a program of action? Once again, within movements or networks that advocate democratic organisation tend to reproduce the same hierarchies that structure broader societal relations. In efforts to uncover the meanings and implications contained in the text of trade and investment agreements, for example, do NGO policy analysts not also frequently create their own elitist discourse, or, indeed, internalize a discourse and a language from the agreement itself? Narrow textual analysis of trade agreements by NGO policy analysts frequently fail to take account of questions of broader social and political context(s) and underlying ideologies that lie beneath the texts. They assume particular kinds of literacy in readers that can comprehend the technical jargon of trade and economic policy, rather than adopting a popular education orientation. Moreover, they are rarely oriented towards supporting the building of social movements on the ground, but rather towards the lobbying efforts of professionalised NGOs.

The emergence of a class of "anti-high priests", and the epistemological privilege accorded to policy analysis is of concern for those committed to putting democratic forms of organisation and non-hierarchical values into practice in work to build social movements. Michels (1978) and Ostrogorski (1964) warn of the dangers to organisational democracy posed by the technical specialization associated with leadership roles within the organisation that they examined. We must ask whether such specialized technical discourse – in written texts and in public forums and teach-ins – empowers others, or whether it merely reifies the power, status and language of professional 'experts' in the context of the movements? Why are the words of this professionalised NGO stratum valourised over the analyses of people with more direct, everyday/every night experience of resistance to neoliberalism? What are the implications for building mass movements if the words of writers and 'experts', who often lack any social movement base, mediate popular understandings of the contents of neoliberal agreements, economic arrangements or policies?

Activities in NGO/activist circles can be highly formalised and institutionalised – from internal staff or membership meetings and trainings, to conferences, teach-ins, media events, speeches at rallies, reporting and other relationships with funders. Tensions exist between the possibilities for transformation and space for critical reflection and action, and vested interests in maintaining order, authority and the institution itself. NGO Summits on APEC did not prove conducive for much critical reflection in my experience. For all of the claims that NGO conferences on APEC were democratically organized 'people's' spaces, they were tightly controlled, and quite hierarchical, with a preponderance of academic and NGO professionals addressing the meetings, rather than grassroots activists. In many anti-APEC networks, the richness of movement conversations, often in informal spaces and places was reflected neither in many of the publications and campaign literature of the well-resourced NGOs that campaigned on 'free trade' nor in academic or journalistic accounts of these activities. Debates, which questioned hegemonic NGO practices, power, knowledge, mandate and representation, were either shut down or avoided (see Choudry, 2010a and 2010b).

KNOWLEDGE, LEARNING AND STRUGGLE IN MOVEMENTS AGAINST
BILATERAL FREE TRADE AGREEMENTS

Despite a multitude of such movements and mobilisation's against these agreements, particularly (though not exclusively) in the Third World, the transnational NGO/activist networks that have actively contested APEC the WTO and FTAA have largely failed to connect such struggles with each other, and are largely inconsequential in relation to anti-FTA activism. The trajectory of transnational networks of NGOs and trade unions contesting free trade that has accompanied mobilizations against global (WTO), and regional (APEC) institutions and processes operates on a different track from the locally grounded struggles against FTAs. There has been a disconnection between major mobilisations against FTAs and established NGO networks on globalisation, which have generally been slow to react or seriously address the bilateral deals. On the contrary, some of these NGOs which have focused on the WTO have issued triumphalist statements responding to the state of WTO talks which have suggested that neoliberalism is on the defensive, which completely ignore the commitments being made in bilateral free trade negotiations (e.g. IATP, 2008; Menotti, 2008) which go further than existing agreements.

There are specific challenges for education and mobilisation campaigns against bilateral free trade and investment agreements by comparison to activism targeting more established global agreements and institutions such as the WTO, the World Bank and the IMF. In spite of commonalities of these agreements, and the fact that activists in, for example, Thailand and Colombia had been campaigning against bilateral deals with the US, there has been little opportunity to learn from each other's struggles. However connections are being made between movement activists fighting FTAs. On the one hand, the pursuit of bilateral trade and investment negotiations is a divide and rule tactic pursued by more powerful economic and political actors. Yet, by the same token, it has led to less hegemonic capture of the framing of the analysis and opposition/alternatives platforms by international NGOs as we have seen with APEC, WTO, and FTAA campaigns. This break has meant that analysis and learning in resistance to bilateral FTAs has tended to emerge from below, rather than through construction by regional or global NGO coalitions. While it might be overstating the case to argue that the diverse sites of learning/knowledge production in the bilateral FTA resistance movements all directly contrast with or speak back to the positions and platforms of the NGO-dominated global justice movement which has focused on APEC or the WTO, for example, there are nonetheless differences between the kinds of knowledge produced in these struggles, not least the incremental, grounded knowledge and learning produced in the anti-FTA movements.

Bilateral agreements represent an intensification of capitalist globalisation. On the ground, in countries where movements have been struggling against them, the comprehensiveness of many FTAs has engendered the building of common fronts of struggle at national levels in many countries. Internationally, however, there is a tendency of NGO campaigns on economic globalisation to be compartmentalized around individual institutions, and "issues" (agriculture, human rights intellectual property rights, labour, and women). There is another tendency for a rather standard formulation or platform of opposition to be mounted against the WTO, IMF/World Bank but still relatively little focus placed on FTAs although these impose more immediate threats. There remains a reticence to reconceptualise 'globalisation' to include threats detached from the global institutions such as the WTO, World Bank and IMF, and to see dangers inherent in what appeared to be smaller deals. The question remains how to conceptualise capitalist globalisation equally driven by a web of smaller agreements and to target this process in a concerted manner.

Just as there is a great diversity in positions, ideologies, perspectives and tactics among opposition movements against the WTO, so too, we can find among opposition to bilateral FTAs those who call for reform of these agreements (largely major trade union bureaucracies and Northern NGOs) and those who reject these agreements altogether. NGO technical policy analyses of these agreements, institutions and processes are often detached from political economy/geopolitical factors, and lack a systemic critique of capitalism and imperialism which understand all of these institutions, agreements and processes – global regional, sub regional, bilateral, national and sub national (i.e. state/province/municipal level) as demanding oppositional responses.

Compartmentalised approaches that do not confront the systemic nature of capitalism can only be of limited effectiveness. For many NGO campaigns, this compartmentalisation occurs around issues (e.g. agriculture, services), sectors (women, workers, farmers, Indigenous Peoples) and institutions and agreements (such as WTO, FTAA,) without a broader underlying framework of analysis necessarily informing action against global capitalism *per se*. This tends towards a rather fragmented analysis. Certainly, in some anti-FTA struggles, particular aspects of these agreements attract more attention than others, such as intellectual property provisions of the US-Thailand agreement, and the toxic waste dumping provisions of the Japan-Philippines Economic Partnership Agreement, but many of the most vibrant and sustained anti-FTA mobilisations have seen broad fronts of opposition grow through an understanding of the comprehensive threats posed by these agreements. For example, movements of people living with HIV/AIDS in

Thailand found common cause and forged alliances with farmers because of the intellectual property chapter in the proposed US-Thai FTA. Meanwhile, the Korean government's removal of the film quota (to promote Korean films) as part of FTA negotiations, and commitments to further liberalise Korean agriculture brought film actors, directors and producers together with farmers and trade unionists in the streets against the US-Korea FTA. Another example of building a common understanding among farmers arose in Thailand. Thai people – especially farmers – mobilised against the Thailand-China FTA as it became clear how much harm it would cause to Thai farmers, especially fruit or garlic producers in the north of the country. But the reality of the struggle took on a different dimension when they went to China and talked to garlic farmers there. Contrary to what they imagined, the FTA, which had put many Thai garlic growers out of business, was of no benefit to Chinese garlic producers.

People's movements to stop FTAs are often isolated from each other, a direct reflection of the "divide and conquer" strategy that bilateralism thrives on. A number of anti-FTA movements have made it a priority to break the isolation and link with others fighting such agreements in order to share analysis and learning's from each other's struggles. The Thai anti-FTA movement has been quite proactive in this respect, organising several events that have brought activists from different countries together to strategise on FTAs (Similar collaboration has also taken place in Latin America among movements fighting bilateral deals). FTA Watch, a Thai coalition, invited bilaterals.org, GRAIN and the Bangkok office of Médecins Sans Frontières to help co-organise a global strategy meeting of anti-FTA movements. Dubbed 'Fighting FTAs', the three-day workshop was held at the end of July 2006 in Bangkok. It brought together around 60 social movement activists from 20 countries of Africa, the Americas and the Asia-Pacific region to share experiences in grassroots struggles against FTAs and to build international strategies and cooperation. For many participants, it was the first time they had been able to physically sit down with other movement activists fighting FTAs and discuss strategy and experiences. In February 2008, GRAIN, bilaterals.org and BIOTHAI (Biodiversity Action Thailand) produced a collaborative publication and launched a multimedia website called "Fighting FTAs: the growing resistance to bilateral free trade and investment agreements" which provides both a global overview of the spread of FTAs and maps the growing resistance and *Fighting FTAs, Education for Action: The Challenges of Building Resistance to Bilateral Free Trade Agreements.*

FTA struggles highlight the importance of resistance firmly grounded in local and national contexts, but which connects to regional and global perspectives. Strategies that emerge from strong local organisation are the ones most able to map the terrain of struggle, to identify key local and international players pushing specific agreements and specific provisions of agreements to know their weak points, histories, styles of operating and how they are connected, and to oppose expose and challenge those pushing FTAs and their strategies. Alongside this, technical policy analysis needs to be informed by and connected to the realities of people's struggles, not the other way round. These forms of knowledge are increasingly important as potential resources for other movements, which find themselves confronting the same strategies and players in different parts of the world.

BUILDING KNOWLEDGE, ANALYSIS AND POWER FROM THE GROUND UP

I now turn to discuss alternative ways to organise and build power, including grassroots, bottom-up approaches and leadership from below. An integral part of building this power is connected with how knowledge, learning, and conceptual resources for struggle developed and mobilised in social action settings can inform, orientate (and in turn be informed and orientated by) practice in ways that counter dominant trends of professionalisation. As Kelley (2002) puts it: 'Social movements generate new knowledge, new theories, and new questions. The most radical ideas often grow out of a concrete intellectual engagement with the problems of aggrieved populations confronting systems of oppression' (p. 9). Participation in social activism offers activists and the wider movement(s) opportunities to learn and create knowledge, through informal activities that take place in the daily life of organisation/movements. This happens if the place created is not overly controlled by professionalism and offers social interaction. This "social learning" is embedded in social interaction between participants in social movements and organising, or between organisation/movements. This learning is often unanticipated, incidental (though not insignificant), and dynamic in nature. Holst (2002) notes how the importance and nature of learning in social movements tends to be dismissed in the literature. For him, social movements, through public protest that can take various forms, attempt to educate and persuade the larger public and politicians. Second, there is much educational work internal to social movements, in which organisational skills, ideology, and lifestyle choices are passed from one member to the next informally through mentoring and modelling or formally through workshops, seminars, lectures, and so forth.

A wealth of knowledge can be brought forth from social struggles. Yet relatively few attempts have been made to theorise informal learning through involvement in social action. One exception is Foley (1999), who validates and analyses the importance of the incidental learning in a variety of social struggles. Foley argues that to do this analysis 'one needs to write case studies of learning in struggle, making explanatory connections between the broad political and economic context, micro-politics, ideologies, discourses and learning' (1999, p. 132). Holst (2002) refers to the 'pedagogy of mobilization' to describe the learning inherent in the building and maintaining of a social movement and its organisation:

> Through participation in a social movement, people learn numerous skills and ways of thinking analytically and strategically as they struggle to understand their movement in motion ... Moreover, as coalitions are formed, people's understanding of the interconnectedness of relations within a social totality become increasingly sophisticated (pp. 87–88).

Such forms of knowledge can directly challenge professionalisation and technicism which permeates NGO-dominated global justice advocacy, and can help to inoculate organisation against disconnection from potential movement sites of contestation and building opposition. Novelli (2010) highlights the dialectics of strategic learning through struggle and contestation that includes incidental, formal, informal, and non-formal education. This implies an engagement in 'strategic analysis, which in turn leads to strategic action, and then to intended and unintended consequences of action, and to further reflection/analysis and action' (p. 124). Foley (1999) emphasizes the importance of 'developing an understanding of learning in popular struggle' (p. 140). His attention to documenting, making explicit, and valuing incidental forms of learning and knowledge production in social action is consistent with others who understand that critical consciousness and theory emerge from engagement in action and organising contexts, rather than ideas developed elsewhere being imposed on "the people" (Bevington and Dixon, 2005; Choudry and Kapoor, 2010; Kelley, 2002; Kinsman, 2006; Smith, 1999).

CONCLUSIONS

As Bevington and Dixon (2005) note, important debates and learning inside movement and NGO networks often simply do not enter the literature about social movements, or indeed social movement learning itself. The critical learning that takes place in grounded movements against free trade agreements is gained informally, through experience, by acting and reflecting on action, rather than in formal courses or non-formal teach-ins. Many scholarly, NGO and activist accounts pay inadequate attention to the significance of low profile, long-haul political education and organising work. Gupta (2004) notes, it is not easy for activists 'to sit down and record their work, but in this age of information overload you need to record in order almost to prove that you exist' (p. 3). It is important to document the articulation of challenges to hegemonic NGO and "civil society" positions to challenge their status as the definitive "alternative" discourses to be referenced by future movements and academic inquiry. In doing so, grassroots groups can contest professionalised NGO forms of knowledge and power and other hegemonic positions within NGO/movement milieus and contribute to building a body of knowledge and resources for struggle.

Scholars who seek to understand social movement and NGO networks need to attend to questions coming out of social movements and activist research in regard to power dynamics and the valuing of certain forms of knowledge. These questions are often based on sophisticated macro- and micro- analyses of what, to an outsider, might seem a baffling network of relations, and shifting power dynamics. This is not to argue that evaluation and analysis from the standpoint of being embedded in activism is *necessarily* rigorous or adequate, Smith (2006) and Kinsman (2006) both warn of a need for activist researchers to go beyond the 'common sense theorising' which often goes on in these settings, but which does not attend to actual social practices and organization. Reflexivity is crucial when starting from, engaging with, and analysing activist knowledge(s). In a similar vein, Foley (1999) writes that the

> Process of critical learning involves people in theorising their experience: they stand back from it and reorder it, using concepts like power, conflict, structure, values and choice. It is also clear that critical learning is gained informally, through experience, by acting and reflecting on action, rather than in formal courses (p. 64).

In examining the knowledge being produced and shared in grounded struggles against bilateral FTAs, we can discern a different forms of knowledge production and learning in struggle that can trouble disconnected transnational professionalised NGO forms of knowledge, and contribute to building a body of knowledge and resources for struggle. The fact that so much of this anti-FTA resistance has happened in the global South, without strong connections to transnational NGO networks is undoubtedly a factor in its relative absence from both NGO and scholarly purview. In the context of transnational social movement/NGO networks, as Thayer (2000) notes, 'barriers to South-North conceptual migration are both economic and discursive. On the one hand, the periphery and its intellectual products are constructed as both exotic and specific, while the centre and its discourses and theories enjoy all-embracing, universal status' (p. 229). The privileging of Western, professionalised epistemologies of knowledge manifests itself within NGO and activist networks with the reification of 'experts' and the dominance of professionalised forms of knowledge such as technical policy analysis of official texts which are decontextualised from the political and economic structures of power in which they exist. It positions certain kinds of knowledge, individuals and organisation as authoritative, and devalues or ignores others.

Scholarly analyses of social movements and NGOs and the learning that occurs within them owe a debt to collective forms of critical knowledge production, learning and debates emerging from within social movements and activist networks committed to progressive social change. We need further research into the possibilities for forms of critical intellectual leadership and knowledge production and sharing that play supportive roles to, rather than claiming to speak and strategise for, social movements. Further, if we agree that academic work on NGOs, NGOisation and social movements requires some level of political investment on our part as scholars, we must critically engage with the intellectual work taking place within these social action settings, and, take up Bevington and Dixon's (2005) call for movement-relevant theory – to produce research which is useful and accountable to movements for social change. As Marx (1968) once put it, all social life is essentially practical. All mysteries, which lead theory to mysticism, find their rational solution in human practice and in the comprehension of this practice.

REFERENCES

Allman, P. (2001). *Critical education against global capitalism: Karl Marx and revolutionary critical education.* Westport, CT.: Bergin and Garvey.

Bandy, J., & Smith, J. (2005). *Coalitions across borders: Transnational protest and the neoliberal order.* Lanham, MD: Rowman and Littlefield.

Bevington, D. & Dixon, C. (2005). "Movement-relevant theory: Rethinking social movement scholarship and activism," *Social Movement Studies, 4*(3).

Bob, C. (2005). *The marketing of rebellion: Insurgents, media and international activism.* New York: Cambridge University Press.

Choudry, A. (2011). On knowledge production, learning and research in struggle. *Alternate Routes. 23,* 175–194.

Choudry, A. & Shragge, E. (2011). Disciplining dissent: NGOs and community organisation. *Globalisations, 8*(4), 503–517.

Choudry, A. (2011). Learning in struggle, Sharing knowledge: Building resistance to bilateral FTAs. In Kapoor, D. (Ed), *Critical Perspectives on Neoliberal Globalisation, development and education in Africa and Asia/Pacific,* (pp. 31–48). Rotterdam: Sense.

Choudry, A. (2010a). What's left? Canada's 'global justice' movement and colonial amnesia. *Race and Class, 52*(1), 97–102.

Choudry, A. (2010b). Global justice? Contesting NGOisation: Knowledge politics and containment in antiglobalisation networks. In Choudry, A, & Kapoor, D. (Eds.) (2010) *Learning from the ground up: Global perspectives on social movements and knowledge production* (pp. 17–34). New York: Palgrave Macmillan.

Choudry, A. (2008). NGOs, social movements and anti-APEC activism: A study in knowledge power and struggle. Unpublished Ph.D. thesis, Concordia University.

Clark, R. & Ivanic, R. (1997). *The politics of writing.* London and New York: Routledge.

Day, R. J. F. (2005). *Gramsci is dead: Anarchist currents in the newest social movements.* London: Pluto Press.

Flacks, R. (2004). Knowledge for what? Thoughts on the state of social movement studies. In Goodwin, J. & Jasper, J. M. (Eds.), *Rethinking social movements: Structure, culture, and emotion* (pp. 135–153). Lanham, MD: Rowman and Littlefield.

Flusty, S. (2004). *De-coca-colonization: Making the globe from the inside out.* New York: Routledge.

Foley, G. (1999). *Learning in social action: A contribution to understanding informal education.* London and New York: Zed Books.

Goodman, J (Ed.) (2002). *Protest and globalisation: Prospects for transnational solidarity.* Sydney: Pluto.

Gupta, R. (2004). Some recurring themes: Southall Black Sisters 1979–2003 and still going strong. In Gupta R. (Ed.), *From Homebreakers to Jailbreakers: Southall Black Sisters* (pp. 1–27). London: Zed Books.

Holst, J. D. (2011). Frameworks for understanding the politics of social movements. *Studies in the education of adults, 43*(2), 117–127.

Holst, J. D. (2002). *Social movements, civil society, and radical adult education.* Westport, CT.: Bergin and Garvey.

Institute for Agriculture and Trade Policy (IATP), (2008, 29 July). "Trade talks collapse, new direction needed". Press release. Retrieved from http://www.tradeobservatory.org/library.cfm?reflD=103455.

INCITE! Women of Color Against Violence. (Eds.) (2007). *The revolution will not be funded: Beyond the non-profit industrial complex* Boston, MA.: South End Press.

Kamat, S. (2004). The privatization of public interest: Theorizing NGO discourse in a neoliberal era. *Review of International Political Economy, 11*(1) (February), 155–176.

Kamat, S. (2002). *Development Hegemony: NGOs and the State in India.* Oxford: Oxford University Press.

Kelley, R. D. G. (2002). *Freedom dreams: The Black radical imagination.* Boston: Beacon Press.

Kelsey, J. (1999). *Reclaiming the future: New Zealand and the global economy*. Wellington: Bridget Williams Books.

Kinsman, G. (2006). "Mapping social relations of struggle: Activism, ethnography, social organization" in *Sociology for changing the world: Social movements/social research*, (Ed.), Frampton, C., G. Kinsman, A.K. Thompson, and K Tilleczek. Black Point, N.S.: Fernwood.

Kress, G. (1982). *Learning to write*. London: Routledge.

Marx, K. (1968). Theses on Feuerbach. In *Karl Marx and Frederich Engels: Selected Works*. New York: International. Accessed online at: http://www.marxists.org/archive/marx/works/1845/theses/theses.htm

McNally, D. (2002). *Another world is possible: Globalisation and anti-capitalism*. Winnipeg: Arbeiter Ring.

Michels, R. (1978). *Political parties: A sociological study of the oligarchical tendencies of modern democracy*. Gloucester, MA.: Peter Smith.

Menotti, V, (2008, 30 July). "Derailing Doha and the pathway to a new paradigm: How WTO's collapse clears the way to solve today's food, fuel, and financial crises". International Forum on Globalisation. Retrieved from www.ifg.org/programs/derailing_doha-vmenotti-30july08.pdf

Newman, M. (2006). *Teaching defiance: Stories and strategies for activist educators*. San Francisco, CA.: Jossey-Bass.

Novelli, M. (2010). Learning to win: Exploring knowledge and strategy development in anti-privatization struggles in Colombia. In Choudry, A, and Kapoor, D. (Eds.), *Learning from the ground up: Global perspectives on social movements and knowledge production* (pp. 121–137). New York: Palgrave Macmillan.

Ostrogorski, M. (1964). *Democracy and the organization of political parties*. Volume I: England. Chicago: Quadrangle Books.

Petras, J. & Veltmeyer, H. (2005). *Social movements and state power: Argentina, Brazil, Bolivia, Ecuador*. London: Pluto Press.

Petras, J., & Veltmeyer, H. (2001). Globalisation unmasked: Imperialism in the 21st century. New Delhi: Madhyam.

Polet, F, and CETRI (2004). *Globalizing resistance: The state of struggle*. London: Pluto.

Pue, W. W. (Ed.) (1998). *Pepper in our eyes: The APEC affair*. Vancouver: UBC Press.

Smith, D.E. (1987). *The everyday world as problematic: A feminist sociology*. Toronto: University of Toronto Press.

Smith, G. W. (2006). Political activist as ethnographer. In *Sociology for changing the world: Social movements/social research*, ed. G. Kinsman, A. K. Thompson, & K. Tilleczek, pp. 44–70. Black Point, NS: Fernwood.

Smith, L.T. (1999). *Decolonising methodologies: Research and Indigenous Peoples*. London: Zed Books.

Starr, A. (2000). *Naming the enemy: Anti-corporate movements confront globalisation*. London: Zed Books.

Thayer, M. (2000). Traveling feminisms: From embodied women to engendered citizenship. In Burawoy, M., et al. *Global ethnography: Forces, connections, and imaginations in a postmodern World* (pp. 295–338). Berkeley: University of California Press.

Wallace, T. (2003). NGO Dilemmas: Trojan horses for global neoliberalism? In Panitch, L., and Leys, C. (Eds.), *Socialist Register 2004: The New Imperial Challenge* (pp. 202–219). London: Merlin.

CATHERINE ETMANSKI

11. INCH BY INCH, ROW BY ROW

Social movement learning on Three Oaks organic farm

INTRODUCTION

On the south-western tip of Vancouver Island, Canada, sits one of many organic farms found in this part of the world. In passing, you might not imagine the depth of learning – indeed the wonder – that transpires on this land; that is of course unless you already understand the language of the morning dew drops as they refract shades of purple, green, and silver off the winter leeks. For me, a new way of communicating and interacting with "the rest of nature" (Clover, de Oliveira-Jayme, Follen & Hall, 2010) grew from the year I worked part-time on Three Oaks organic farm. Not only did I learn a little about the skill of turning seed into dinner, I also *learned about learning* in the context of a contemporary social movement led by small-scale organic farmers.

Social movement learning has been characterized as the learning that "occurs informally and incidentally, in people's everyday lives" (Foley, 1999, p. 1), by people both inside and out of social movements (Hall & Clover, 2005). The work of organic farming necessitates persistent praxis—a constant cycle of action and reflection prompted by the turning of seasons and the emergent needs of the field. Like other social movements, then, the organic farming movement can be understood as inherently educational in nature (Hall, 2006). The farmers at the centre of this work are situated in the context of a global movement of "grassroots food security initiatives—the foundation of an alternative food system premised on local subsistence and fair trade—[that] are springing up everywhere in the North and in the South" (Conway, 2004, p. 3). The purpose of this chapter is to examine the learning-centred role of organic farms in this movement, and to understand farmers as more than food producers, but also as educational leaders who are planting seeds for a better future.

Using my own experience as a point of departure, and drawing largely from conversations with Rachel Fisher[1] of Three Oaks Farm, I will begin by situating this one small farm in the context of global movements centred on food. I provide an overview of the farm in which I participated and the collaboratively run business (Saanich Organics, 2011) of which it is part. I then outline literature related to alternative farming movements before moving into a discussion of the learning I experienced and observed while working on the farm. I conclude by suggesting that organic farmers provide hope for a more sustainable definition of

B. L. Hall, D. E. Clover, J. Crowther and E. Scandrett (Eds.), Learning and Education
for a Better World: The Role of Social Movements, 155–168.

progress, one that moves beyond sustainability in word only, toward a truly equal valuing of social, ecological, and economic prosperity.

Before going further, it is important for the reader to understand that I am not a farmer, nor am I purporting to be an expert voice on the matter of all things organic. I am a relative urbanite, who had the luxury of time to explore an interest in organic farming that had been put aside while I completed my studies. Although urban agriculture is on the rise (e.g. see Rau, this volume), and it certainly is possible for anyone to learn how to grow food, I realized rather quickly that achieving a similar level of expertise as my farming mentor would be equivalent in time and study to completing a Ph.D.—*at least*. I am nevertheless sincere in my desire to highlight and celebrate organic farmers' work because, as an educator, I appreciate that learning in this movement is holistic and effective, and as a citizen, I believe that the small-scale organic farming movement might just hold clues for reinvigorating our collective social, environmental, economic, spiritual, cultural, and intellectual well-being. Let me be clear that in focusing on attributes, it is not my intention to ignore or minimize the often harsh reality of physical labour, economic uncertainty, debt, or bankruptcy, and dangers stemming from dependency on an unpredictable and ever-changing climate. Moreover, I am certainly not romanticizing the tireless efforts of thousands of landless peasants and migrant workers who toil under unjust conditions in crops (organic or otherwise) destined for Western bellies. Instead, this chapter has a narrower, place-based focus and should be understood as lessons *about learning* derived from my exposure[2] to a particular organic farmer. Caveat aside; I turn now to an overview of the farm on which I worked.

THE LEARNING CONTEXT: THREE OAKS FARM AND SAANICH ORGANICS

Rachel Fisher is an organic farmer who runs Three Oaks Farm, located near Victoria, in the Canadian province of British Columbia (BC). Rachel collaboratively operates and co-owns a small business, called Saanich Organics, along with Heather Stretch of Northbrook Farm and Robin Tunnicliffe of Feisty Field Organic Farm. Together, these three farmers strive to sustain their agricultural land, their community, their families, and themselves by growing and marketing top quality organic fruits and vegetables and selling them at a fair price to families in and around Victoria. Their prices reflect the unsubsidized cost of food production, a fair wage for workers, and a low mark up to ensure their own economic viability. The business of Saanich Organics currently provides a weekly or bi-weekly food box delivery programme for approximately eighty families. Each food box contains in-season produce (not pre-selected by customers), and a homemade newsletter with recipes, tips for eating the more uncommon produce, and updates about the farming community. Saanich Organics also supplies twenty-five local restaurants and shops, and sells at two farmers' markets.

None of these three women started with a background in agriculture, but have each learned the skills of the trade, and forged ahead to build successful farms. They recently documented their unique business model and individual narratives in a book (Fisher, Stretch & Tunnicliffe, 2011) and previously released a shorter handbook about their work, published by the British Columbia Institute for Cooperative Studies (Tunnicliffe, 2008). In addition, one of the farmers, Robin, completed a Master's thesis exploring the economics of organic farming in the Saanich Peninsula (Tunnicliffe, 2011) and has given multiple guest lectures (Tunnicliffe, 2009, for example). I had the opportunity to work alongside Rachel on Three Oaks farm in 2008, and learn a little more about the larger movement of farmer-educators with similar values, a movement to which I now turn.

DIVERSE PERSPECTIVES ON THE ORGANIC FARMING MOVEMENT

The organic farming movement has emerged largely in response to the current state of global industrial agriculture. The list of social, economic, and environmental problems – indeed crises – associated with the dominant agricultural paradigm is extensive and I will not go into detail about all aspects of it here. To name but a few examples: the extensive use of natural gas and oil in fertilizers, pesticides, farming infrastructure, machinery, and food transportation (particularly in the face of Peak Oil); damages associated with growing mono-crops, cash crops, and agro-fuels; depletion of soils and rainforests, as well as groundwater pollution leading to oceanic 'dead zones'; displacement of Indigenous peoples and other unethical treatment of both people and animals; subsidies and product dumping, which create an increasingly unequal global marketplace; and finally, the multiple ways in which industrial agriculture contributes to Climate Change. Many challenges stem from the technological and chemical changes to agriculture during the Green Revolution, which ultimately "proved to be unsustainable as it damaged the environment, caused dramatic loss of biodiversity and associated traditional knowledge, [favoured] wealthier farmers, and left many poor farmers deeper in debt" (Altieri, 2009, p. 102). Kesavan & Malarvannan (2010) suggest that "today, it is widely acknowledged that the 'yield gains' associated with the green revolution of the 1960s and 1970s have tapered off largely because of deterioration in the structure, quality and fertility of the soil" (p. 908). In addition, the spread of patent-protected, fertilizer-dependent seeds through neo-liberal globalization policies has created debt and dependency on foreign aid amongst poor farmers around the world (Altieri, 2009, p. 103). The use of certain pesticides in treating seeds was recently linked to the worldwide decline of the honeybee population (Krupke, Hunt, Eitzer, Andino & Given, 2012), and scientists have been calling for further investigation into links between the general use of pesticides or herbicides and the occurrence of cancer in both children (Hoar Zahm & Ward, 1998) and adults (Dich, Hoar Zahm, Hanberg & Adami, 1997). The list goes on.

People in many parts of the world have been taking action at both the local and global level to resist and transform the dominant agricultural system. Of particular note is a transnational peasants' movement called *La Via Campesina* (the peasant road), which emerged during discussions at the 1992 Second Congress of the Nicaraguan Farmers' Union, and was established in 1993 in Mons, Belgium

(Schuurman, 1995). It is a peasant-led network that has grown to represent 200 million farmers in 70 countries in Africa, Asia, Europe, and the Americas, and encompassing approximately 150 local and national organizations (La Via Campesina, 2012). The Mons Declaration outlined three fundamental rights, which essentially were (1) farmers' rights to self-organize, (2) rights to diversified agriculture, and (3) each country's right to autonomous decision-making power over agricultural policy, in consultation with peasants and Indigenous peoples (Schuurman, 1995). Various authors have documented and analyzed the birth and evolution of this movement (Aurelie Desmarais, 2007; Borras, Jr., 2008; Martínez-Torres & Rosset, 2010; Schuurman, 1995; Torrez, 2011), suggesting that it has moved through various phases from emergence and protest, to representatives taking their rightful place at the table in global trade and policy debates, to internal strengthening and gender analysis, to defining themselves more clearly in terms of food sovereignty in opposition to neo-liberal capitalist policies and global corporations. Interested readers can find many publications and position statements on *La Via Campesina's* website, included in the references.

At the same time, in North America, the drive to support local, organic agriculture and eat in season produce is gaining momentum through such bestselling books as Michael Pollan's, *In Defense of Food* (2008) and *The Omnivore's Dilemma* (2006), as well as through popular documentary films such as, *Supersize Me* (Spurlock, 2004) and *Food Inc.* (Kenner, 2008; helpfully critiqued by Flowers & Swan, 2011). The gap between food producers and consumers is also narrowing through such food-centred movements as the *100-Mile Diet* (Smith & MacKinnon, 2007), or the international *Slow Food Movement,* which promotes good, clean, and fair food for all (e.g. see Slow Food Canada, 2012). In parallel, the number of organic farms in Canada is on the rise, particularly in BC, which moved from 154 certified producers in 1992, to 430 in 2001 (MacNair, 2004, p. 10). Kerton and Sinclair (2010) assert that "organic food has become the fastest growing agricultural sector within Canada, and is being recognized for its potential to revitalize communities, boost rural economies, save the family farm, and simultaneously protect the environment, creating diverse, resilient ecosystems" (p. 401). The Certified Organic Associations of BC (COABC, 2012) lists 68 certified organic farms on Vancouver Island and the Gulf Islands, and this number is complemented by an abundance of non-certified farms, farms in transition, and backyard, community, or school gardens (LifeCycles, 2012).

Scholarly literature related to organic, alternative, and local agriculture has been approached from multiple perspectives. Many authors have discussed the gendered nature of sustainable agriculture practices (Chiappe & Flores, 1998; *McMahon, 2001; 2002; 2011*; Prügl 2008; Sumner, 2003; 2005a). McMahon (2011), for instance, reports that 37% of farmers in BC are women—the highest number in Canada—and that women grow 60–80% of the food in the Global South.[3] Sumner (2005b) adds that women hold the majority of executive positions in organic farming organizations. Women farmers around the globe are at risk for multiple reasons—not least of which because they own less than 2% of property worldwide. Nevertheless, the idea of women as farmers disrupts "the North American cultural association of masculinity, farming and technology, [and the associated] paternalistic notion that hunger will be solved by global-market focused, capital and technology intensive agriculture" (McMahon, 2011, p. 402). Rather, "research shows that small farms are much more productive than large farms if total output is considered rather than yield from a single crop" (Altieri, 2009, p. 105). This suggests that rather than continuing to look to the dominant agri-food business for solutions, we could increase support for the women and other small-scale farmers who are already provisioning for their families and communities.

In his book about cooperative economic models, Restakis (2010) argues that, in North America at least, many popular movements "have been gravely weakened by a lack of contact with economics—as if anything might be gained by turning our backs on that discipline, flawed though it is" (p. 6). He suggests instead "economics is *everybody's* business" (p. 6). Though not all farmers employ a cooperative model similar to that of Saanich Organics, several scholars, many of whom argue that such businesses contribute to strengthening the social economy, have explored the economic side of farming. Authors approach this topic from diverse perspectives. For example, as mentioned above, Tunnicliffe (2011) recently conducted interviews with twenty-five farmers on the Saanich Peninsula of BC to better understand how (and whether) they 'make it work' financially. Donald and Blay-Palmer (2006) contend that small and medium-sized specialty, local, ethnic, and organic food businesses represent a growing and dynamic industry in Toronto, Canada. Legun (2011) is reassured by the infusion of socio-ecological values into the bottom line, and the pursuit of organic farming as a feasible means of supporting one's family. Shiva (2005) has argued that "the globalized free market economy, which dominates our lives, is based on rules that extinguish and deny access to life and livelihoods by generating scarcity" (pp. 13–14), but Schor (2010) suggests that organic farmers' work contributes to a needed paradigm shift toward economic plenitude. Schor's Plenitude model, of which she claims the small-scale organic farming movement is a clear example, advances a four-pronged approach of (1) freeing up time through moderation in working hours; (2) self-provisioning through a do-it-yourself mentality; (3) so-called, 'true materialism' through an environmentally aware approach to consumption, including understanding environmental and social impact throughout the lifecycle of a product; and (4) an investment in social capital through fortifying community networks beyond one's immediate family. Connelly, Markey, and Roseland (2011) report that food-centred initiatives in the Canadian cities of Edmonton and Vancouver have helped to integrate the issue of sustainability into the social economy; though, they also recognize that more work is needed to create structural, systemic, and infrastructure level change. While farmers continue to endure competition in the marketplace in the era of global capitalism, the above authors suggest that increased emphasis on alternative agriculture is helping to both humanize (Restakis, 2010) and re-localize the economy.

Nevertheless, it is important to recognize that while organic farming may be on the rise, so too is global hunger. The World Food Programme reported that the number of undernourished people worldwide increased to 1.02 billion in 2009, the highest number reported to date (Hansen, 2009, p. 3). "Today, one in seven people do not get enough food to be healthy and lead an active life, making hunger and malnutrition the number one risk to health worldwide—greater than AIDS, malaria and tuberculosis combined" (World Food Programme, 2012, section 5). As such, organic agriculture and its related counterparts in alternative, artisanal and niche food production are frequently critiqued as elite practices (Buck, Getz & Guthman, 1997; Guthman, 2003; Pilgeram, 2011). Yet, many members of the organic food movement are fully cognizant of this tension, and argue that their "work as food activists is not done until it is made accessible to all" (Rainbow Chard Collective, March, 2011, n.p.). Such scholars and activist groups acknowledge the challenge presented by the ideal of 'good, clean, and fair food for all' and the reality that so many go hungry (see also the BC Food Systems Network, 2012).

A related body of scholarship has looked at the role local farms play in ensuring food security for island residents in Canada. At one time, Vancouver Island food producers supported over 85% of the food needs of the population, but this has dropped to less than 10% today (MacNair, 2004). *In the event* of conflict, natural disaster, or fuel scarcity, whole communities on Vancouver Island and the surrounding Gulf Islands are at risk of food shortages due to transportation (especially ferry) interruptions. Moreover, the changing climate is affecting global food supplies and local food production (Ostry, et al., 2010; Puska, Clements & Chandler, 2011). These scholars call for increased advocacy and scholarship around local food production, as well as support for local meat and poultry processing infrastructure (McMahon, 2011; Tunnicliffe, 2011).

The above literature demonstrates that the organic farming movement is integral to debates around climate change, the intersection of gender, race, and class in food production, and the overall health, well being, and security not only of Canadians, but of peoples around the world. While the scholarly perspectives outlined above provide the context for this movement, I now turn to the practical, philosophical, transformative, and spiritual insights around learning I gained by working in the dirt on the farm.

LEARNING IN ACTION

During my time on Three Oaks Farm, I encountered a range of farmers, who had different motivations and objectives. Some were working there full-time, while others were there in a more part-time, casual capacity. Among them were committed apprentices who were interested in eventually starting their own farms; others were more short-term workers who were exchanging their labour for lodging, home-cooked meals, access to fresh food from the garden, and the opportunity to learn from an experienced farmer. Some approached Rachel via organized internship networks such as World Wide Opportunities on Organic Farms (WWOOF, 2012; sometimes referred to as 'willing workers on organic farms') and Stewards of Irreplaceable Land (SOIL, 2012), while others got in touch with her on their own. I met both novice and experienced farmers from across Canada, as well as from Malaysia, New Zealand, Germany, and Spain.

While a WWOOF or SOIL placement, or other work arrangement, may provide the structure in which knowledge is shared, as scholars of social movement learning and informal education know, learning can and does happen at any time, in any place. This section on learning in action refers to the spontaneous conversations that arise during a day's work, or unplanned lessons gleaned through repetitive actions, exposure to the land over time, sustained opportunity for question and answer, or through symbolic connections drawn between the task at hand and a prior understanding (Etmanski & Barss, 2011). I will provide a few examples to illustrate this point.

While I was working with her, Rachel began raising chickens for her family's own consumption. This experience led to a variety of conversations, for example the difference between free run and free range, and where to set up the chicken pen. Rachel placed a movable pen in a fallow area where the birds would fertilize the land and prepare it for the next planting season. Once they had been in one area for a certain period, this pen was then moved to a new location. This ordinary activity on the farm launched us into conversations around Permaculture and measures for setting up energy-saving, reciprocal relationships on the land, such as those employed by the Salatin family of Polyface farm.[4] These conversations led us further into the harsh reality of human intervention with nature: In spite of the relatively humane life chickens might lead on an organic as opposed to a factory farm, so-called 'meat birds' have been bred to the point where their legs can no longer support the weight of their disproportionately large torsos (i.e. they have been bred to produce more breast meat). The average poultry eater would not normally have the opportunity to see a chicken that could no longer stand due to the weight of its torso. Indeed, observing these birds was an eye-opener for me in spite of any prior knowledge I may have gained from literature and film. It also led us to productive conversations around where to purchase local, organic feed, the real cost of each chicken, how that cost incorporates a farmer's learning over time, regulations for slaughtering and selling meat, the challenge of learning how to butcher chickens, and the lack of meat processing infrastructure on Vancouver Island (also discussed by McMahon, 2011; Puska, Clements & Chandler, 2011; Tunnicliffe, 2011).

As this example reveals, a simple demonstration on 'how to' complete a certain task was often accompanied by discussions around why this particular farmer made the choices she did, the experiences or literature that informed her choice, the other options that were available, and philosophical musings related to the work at hand. Similarly, a mundane task of weeding led to practical conversations around the merits and controversies surrounding the very practice of weeding in organic farming—as well as more philosophical conversations around the dominance of the human species and our ability to choose which plants have a right to survive in the garden, and which do not. Such a conversation also led some of my co-workers and me to more serious dialogue around ethical dilemmas and controversies associated with human control over death (under a variety of circumstances).

These kinds of conversation could take place while working side by side in the field, over lunch at the kitchen table, at a farmers' market, at an event that showcases local food,[5] or at any point where people interested in the organic farming movement come together. While similar tangents could certainly emerge in contexts not directly related to the organic farming movement, the purpose of these examples is to provide a small window into the depth of conversation that occurred on a daily basis in the field. In my experience, conversations here were as rich as any graduate level classroom, and, for me, they provided a safe space to ask questions, share my own knowledge and observations from an outside perspective, and get to know previously unexplored elements of my physical strength and identity. The key difference was that these conversations simultaneously engaged my body as well as my heart and mind, allowed me to experience the seasons more fully, and solidified theory into practice through the everyday actions of the farm. In addition to enriching my knowledge, this kind of learning work—like other work practised in community, such as cooking or building—provided the pure satisfaction of observing the tangible outcomes of the day's efforts.

TRANSFORMATIVE AND SPIRITUAL LEARNING WITH NATURE

Canadian scholar Jennifer Sumner (e.g. 2003; 2005a; 2005b; 2008; 2009) has developed the most direct links between learning and the organic farming movement, claiming first and foremost "eating is a pedagogical act" (2008, p. 1). In her 2008 study of forty-one organic farmers in South-Western Ontario, she came to understand how farmers conceptualize their own knowledge production and meaning-making systems. She first analysed findings according to a Habermasian framework, and then documented expressions of farmers' *spiritual* knowledge, which could not be immediately classified within Habermas' (1978) model. It is these spiritual and indeed transformative dimensions of learning in the organic farming movement to which I will give further attention here.

Kerton and Sinclair (2010) have suggested that the simple act of buying organic food can serve as a catalyst for transformative learning. Participants in their study reported that buying organic food was a point of entry for more engaged citizenship since consumers began questioning the practices behind other industries and goods. They suggest that in some cases, people were transformed into food activists through their engagement with farmers and local, organic foods—a finding that transforms consumers into learners in this social movement. I propose that organic farmers already see this transformative potential, which is why many of them are explicit about direct marketing through farm-gate sales and farmers' markets. These face-to-face encounters provide the opportunity for consumers to ask questions, clarify concerns (particularly around the cost of organic produce), and develop a closer relationship to their food by building relationships with its producers.

For me, another element of transformation stemmed from the potential experience of awe derived from working directly with nature. The artist, Paul Cézanne, famously mused that *the day is coming when a single carrot, freshly observed, will set off a revolution* and I wholeheartedly concur. Debates abound about whether and how, exactly, aesthetic experiences can lead to personal or societal transformation (see chapters by Clover; and Brookfield in this volume). These debates notwithstanding, through the experience of working on the farm I have come to appreciate that the sheer beauty and vitality of the Earth holds tremendous power and transformative potential. I can distinctly remember my first experience harvesting bunches of radishes. As I rinsed them under the cold-water tap, and their full colour emerged from beneath the dirt, the brightness of their fuchsia skin struck me as profoundly beautiful. From that moment forward, I began to see radishes—and indeed carrots and other plants—in a new light; not only for their beauty, but for their texture, their taste, their unique preferences, and the labour involved in planting the seeds, thinning the seedlings, weeding and covering the rows, and harvesting them one by one. This was the first of many profound, sensory experiences; transformative moments that culminated in a deeper appreciation for the beauty of nature, the aesthetics of farming, and for Mother Earth as a supreme artist.

Finally, it has been suggested, "some of the most powerful learning occurs as people struggle against oppression" (Foley, 1999, p. 1). While I affirm that this work is grounded in a struggle for a healthier, more ecologically and socially just planet, my observations propose that it is a joyful struggle, better represented by the sentiment: "I'm not fighting my fight; I'm singing my song" (M. Labelle, personal communication, September, 2010). Outrage against injustice plays a critical role in driving social action, of course (see, for example, Von Kotze, this volume), and Rachel, too, spent years as an environmental activist, working on protests to draw attention to clear-cut logging in old growth ecosystems such as the Walbran Valley. However, she now goes about her work quietly, creating a new world by living it every day, and leading by the example of her life choices. She describes a feeling of satisfaction and 'rightness' derived from her work, knowing that it is healthy for the earth, for her body and mind, and for her family and community. She has been intentional in choosing a life path that is mindfully sustainable rather than one bound in thoughtless consumption. Farmers can speak for themselves regarding their own spiritual or transformative experiences, but for me, not only did working close to the land help to heal a body suffering from the privileged ailment of too much time spent in front of a computer, moments spent observing and appreciating the beauty found in Rachel's garden helped cultivate a new, more grounded way of relating to the world's innumerable—and seemingly insurmountable—injustices.

CONCLUSION: FOOD AS A POINT OF ENTRY

Whether we live in the Global South or North, our daily encounters, if we care to notice them, push us up against the limits of an old paradigm—an out-dated way of thinking, doing, being, and knowing. Gross injustices within and between countries, over-consumption, toxic waste, and widespread depression and oppression indicate that we must change the fundamental ways we relate to one other and to the Earth if we are to survive as a species. Yet, today's social, environmental, economic, and spiritual challenges have become so deeply interconnected that it can be difficult to find an entry point for addressing any given issue. In this increasingly complex global context, the small, local, open, and globally connected (Manzini, 2009) organic farming movement may represent an interdisciplinary leap into a new paradigm. Its proponents draw clear links from agriculture to physical and psychological health, environmentalism to economics, community development to education, technology to spirituality, and philosophy to action research. These values-based leaders are attending to local, grassroots concerns, while simultaneously promoting global democracy and social justice.

This chapter has sought to provide an introduction to the small-scale organic farming movement, and the diverse kinds of learning that propels this movement forward. School-based educators and organizational leaders in many sectors can benefit from greater understanding of the experiential learning strategies as well as the knowledge produced within this alternative agriculture movement. Through workshops, courses, learning tours, and short and long term apprenticeships, farmers are training a new generation of food activists. On a daily basis, they are innovating for the well being of their families and communities, redefining prosperity according to socially and ecologically based values, and tilling the soil for a better world to emerge. There is still more work to be done, it's true, but inch by inch, row by row, they are planting the seeds for a more sustainable, healthy, and socially just future.

NOTES

[1] Rachel's name is used here with permission and I would like to thank her for her comments on an earlier draft of this chapter. Marc Labelle and the reviewers provided most helpful feedback as well.

[2] To be clear: I spent one day per week on the farm from April to June, 2008, and then two to four days per week between September and December, 2008. I have since brought three groups of graduate level Educational Leadership students out to Rachel's farm in the context of a class site visit.

[3] The term 'Global South' is used with caution and is meant to denote Majority World countries, whether they are in the North or in the South.

[4] Polyface farm is discussed in depth in Michael Pollan's bestselling book, the Omnivore's Dilemma (2006). For a discussion of the Salatins' complex, synergetic farm design, see section two, chapter eleven in particular.

[5] Examples include annual events such as the Island Chefs' Food Fest, or Feast of the Fields hosted by Farm Folk City Folk. More information on these events can be found online.

REFERENCES

Altieri, M. A. (2009). Agroecology, Small Farms, and Food Sovereignty. *Monthly Review (July-August)*, 102–113.

Aurelie Desmarais, A. (2007). *La Via Campesina: Globalization and the Power of Peasants*. Halifax, NS: Fernwood.

Borras, Jr., S. M. (2008). La Vía Campesina and its global campaign for agrarian reform. *Journal of Agrarian Change, 8*(2/3), 258–289.

British Columbia Food Systems Network. (2012). [Official website]. Retrieved from: http://fooddemocracy.org/about.php

Buck, D. C., Getz, C. & Guthman, J. (1997). From farm to table: The organic vegetable commodity chain at Northern California. *Sociologia Ruralis, 37*(1), 3–20.

Certified Organic Association of BC. (2012). [Official website]. Retrieved from: http://www.certifiedorganic.bc.ca/

Chiappe, M. & Flores, C. B. (1998). Gendered elements of an alternative agriculture paradigm. *Rural Sociology 63,* 372–393.

Clover, D. E., de Oliveira-Jayme, B., Follen, S. & Hall, B. (2010). *The nature of transformation: Environmental Adult Education* (3rd ed.). Victoria, BC: University of Victoria.

Connelly, S., Markey, S. & Roseland, M. (2011). Bridging sustainability and the social economy: Achieving community transformation through local food initiatives. *Critical Social Policy, 31*(2), 308–324.

Conway, J. (2004). *Identity, place, knowledge: Social movements contesting globalization.* Black Point, NS: Fernwood Publishing.

Dich, J., Hoar Zahm, S., Hanberg, A. & Adami, H-O. (1997). Pesticides and cancer. *Cancer Causes & Control, 8*(3), 420–443.

Donald, B. & Blay-Palmer, A. (2006). Growing innovation policy: the case of organic agriculture in Ontario, Canada. *Environment and Planning C: Government and Policy, 23,* 557–581.

Etmanski, C. & Barss, T. (2011). Making Pedagogy Explicit in Ecological Leadership Praxis. *Action Learning and Action Research Journal, 17*(1), 4–36.

Fisher, R., Stretch, H. & Tunnicliffe, R. (2011). *All the dirt: Reflections on organic farming.* Victoria, BC: Touchwood Editions.

Flowers, R. & Swan, E. (2011). 'Eating at us': Representations of knowledge in the activist documentary film Food, Inc. *Studies in the Education of Adults, 43*(2), 234–250.

Foley, G. (1999). *Learning in social action: A contribution to understanding informal education.* London: Zed Books.

Guthman, J. (2003). Fast food/organic food: Reflexive tastes and the making of 'yuppie chow'. *Journal of Social and Cultural Geography 4*(10), 45–58.

Habermas, J. (1978). *Knowledge and Human Interests.* (J.J. Shapiro, Trans.) Boston: Beacon Press.

Hall, B. L. (2006). Social movement learning: Theorizing a Canadian tradition. In T. Fenwick, T. Nesbit & B. Spencer (Eds.), *Contexts of Adult Education: Canadian Perspectives* (pp. 230–238). Toronto: Thompson Educational Publishing.

Hall, B. L. & Clover, D. (2005). Social movement learning. In L. English (Ed.), *International encyclopaedia of adult education* (pp. 737–747). London: Palgrave MacMillan.

Hansen, R. (2009). *Foreword to Food Aid Flows 2009 Report.* World Food Programme. Rome, Italy: wfp.org. Retrieved from: http://www.wfp.org/content/food-aid-flows-2009-report

Hoar Zahm, S. & Ward, M. H. (1998). Pesticides and childhood cancer. *Environmental Health Perspectives, 106*(3), 893–908.

Kenner, R. (Producer and Director). (2008). *Food Inc.* [Motion Picture]. River Road Entertainment, Participant Media, and Magnolia Pictures.

Kerton, S. & Sinclair, J. (2010). Buying local organic food: a pathway to transformative learning. *Agriculture and Human Values, 27*(4), 401–413.

Kesavan, P. C., & Malarvannan, S. (2010). Green to evergreen revolution: ecological and evolutionary perspectives in pest management. *Current Science, 99(7),* 908–914.

Krupke, C. H., Hunt, G. J., Eitzer, B. D., Andino, G. & Given, K. (2012). Multiple Routes of Pesticide Exposure for Honey Bees Living Near Agricultural Fields. *PLoSONE 7*(1), 1–8.

La Via Campesina. (2012). [Official website]. Retrieved from: http://viacampesina.org/en/

Legun, K. (2011). Cultivating institutions: Organic agriculture and integrative economic choice. *Society and Natural Resources, 24,* 455–468

LifeCycles. (2012). [Official website]. Retrieved from: http://lifecyclesproject.ca/initiatives/

MacNair, E. (2004). *A baseline assessment of food security in British Columbia's Capital Region.* Victoria: Capital Region Food and Agricultural Initiatives Round Table. Retrieved from: http://www.communitycouncil.ca/pdf/CR-FAIR_FS_Assessment_2004.pdf

Manzini, E. (2009). *Small, local, open, connected: An orienting scenario for social innovation and design, in the age of networks.* [Abstract of a public lecture]. Glasgow, Scotland. Retrieved from: http://www.scottishinsight.ac.uk/Portals/50/ias%20documents/Designing/Manzini_Full%20Abstract.pdf

Martínez-Torres, M. E. & Rosset, P. M. (2010). La Vía Campesina: the birth and evolution of a transnational social movement. *The Journal of Peasant Studies 31*(1), 149–175.

McMahon, M. (2001). What to think? Ecofeminism and eco-agriculture in Ireland. *Women and Environments,* pp. 36–37.

McMahon, M. (2002). Resisting globalization: women organic farmers and local food systems. *Canadian Woman Studies, 21*(3), 203–206.

McMahon, M. (2011). Standard fare or fairer standards: Feminist reflections on agri-food governance. *Agriculture and Human Values, 28*(3), 401–412.

Ostry, A., Ogborn, M., Bassil, K. L., Takaro, T. K. & Allen, D. M. (2010). Climate change and health in British Columbia: Projected impacts and a proposed agenda for adaptation research and policy. *International Journal of Environmental Research and Public Health 7,* 1018–1035.

Pilgeram, R. (2011). "The only thing that isn't sustainable ... is the farmer": Social sustainability and the politics of class among Pacific Northwest farmers engaged in sustainable farming. *Rural Sociology 76*(3), 375–393

Pollan, M. (2006). *The omnivore's dilemma: A natural history of four meals.* New York: Penguin Press.

Pollan, M. (2008). *In defense of food: An eater's manifesto.* New York: Penguin Press.

Polyface Farm. (2012). [Official website] Retrieved from: http://www.polyfacefarms.com/

Prügl, E. (2008). Gender and the making of global markets: An exploration of the agricultural sector. In S. Rai & G. Waylen (Eds.), *Global governance: Feminist perspectives* (pp. 43–63). NewYork: Palgrave MacMillan.

Puska, L., Clements, L. & Chandler, K. (2011). *Climate change and food security on Vancouver Island.* Discussion paper produced by the Vancouver Island Community Research Alliance, Local Food Project. Victoria, BC: Office of Community Based Research.

Rainbow Chard Collective. (2012). *Farmer tans.* [Fundraising calendar to support the actions and events of the Rainbow Chard Collective]. Victoria, BC. Restakis, J. (2010). *Humanizing the economy: Co-operatives in the age of capital.* Gabriola Island, BC: New Society Publishers.

Saanich Organics. (2012). [Official website]. Retrieved from: http://www.saanichorganics.com/

Schor, J. B. (2010). *Plenitude: The new economics of true wealth.* New York: Penguin Press.

Shiva, V. (2005). *Earth democracy: Justice, sustainability, and peace.* Cambridge, MA: South End Press.

Schuurman, J. (1995). La Via Campesina at the crossroads. *Development in Practice, 5*(2), 149–154.

Slow Food Canada. (2012). [Official website] Retrieved from: http://www.slowfood.ca/

Smith, A. & MacKinnon, J. B. (2007). *The 100-mile diet: A year of local eating.* Mississauga, ON: Random House Canada.

Spurlock, M. (Producer and Director). (2004). *Supersize me* [Motion Picture]. USA: Roadside Attractions, Samuel Goldwyn Films, and Showtime Independent Films.

Stewards of Irreplaceable Land. (2012). [Official Website]. Retrieved from: http://www.soilapprenticeships.org/

Sumner, Jennifer. (2003). Visions of sustainability: Women organic farmers. *Canadian Woman Studies 23*(1), 146–150.

Sumner, J. (2005a). Small is beautiful: The response of women organic farmers to the crisis in agriculture. *Canadian Woman Studies 24*(4), 78–84.

Sumner, J. (2005b). *Sustainability and the civil commons: Rural communities in the age of globalization.* Toronto, ON: University of Toronto Press.

Sumner, J. (2008). Protecting and promoting indigenous knowledge: Environmental adult education and organic agriculture. *Studies in the Education of Adults 40*(2), 207–223.

Sumner, J. (2009). Sustainable Horticulture and Community Development: More Than Just Organic Production. *Journal of Sustainable Agriculture 33*(4), 461–483.

Torrez, F. (2011). La Via Campesina: Peasant-led agrarian reform and food sovereignty. *Development, 54*(1), 49–54.

Tunnicliffe, R. (2009). *Deconstructing Dinner: So you want to be a farmer?* [Audio-recording]. Kootney Co-op radio, CJLY. http://www.kootenaycoopradio.com/deconstructingdinner/022609.htm

Tunnicliffe, R. (2008). Saanich organics: A model for sustainable agriculture through co-operation. *BCICS occasional paper series, 2,* 1–28. Victoria, BC: New Rochdale Press.

Tunnicliffe, R. (2011). *How do [or can] local farmers make it work?* [Unpublished Masters Thesis]. University of Victoria, Victoria, BC.

World Food Programme. (2012). *Frequently Asked Questions (Section 5).* Retrieved from: http://www.wfp.org/hunger/faqs

World Wide Opportunities on Organic Farms. (2012). [Official website]. Retrieved from: http://www.wwoof.org/

MARK MALONE

12. TWEETING HISTORY: AN INQUIRY INTO ASPECTS OF SOCIAL MEDIA IN THE EGYPTIAN REVOLUTION

What can we learn from the recent Egyptian revolution to help in our struggles for a more egalitarian world? In January 2011 I was, like many activists across the globe, transfixed by what seemed a spontaneous wave of popular uprisings across much of North Africa and the Middle East. In what western commentators dubbed the 'Arab Spring', Tunisia, Egypt, Libya, Syria and Bahrain all witnessed large-scale popular dissent against their authoritarian regimes, all of which continue today. Mainstream media coverage presented these manifestations of popular revolt as the result of technological determinism. Facebook and Twitter were singled out for particular note as being instrumental in the revolutions. That narrative remains a reductive mainstream media/popular discourse that clouds a critical understanding of the human agency at the heart of these uprisings. It is also contradictory, in the sense that the same social platforms lauded – and the culture of sharing information freely they engender are considered disruptive technologies, particularly to the newspapers of those same media corporations. This polarised debate ignores how activists purposefully use social media to create counter-power.

In 2011 I carried out research into aspects of the roles of social media in social transformation as part of a Masters (MA) in Community Education, Equality and Social Activism at the National University of Ireland, Maynooth. I had previously interviewed Egyptians and shared these via my blog and social network platforms. I was able to download my Twitter history and use this as a springboard for further critical thought.

With the exception of telephone interviews with Egyptian activists – who themselves where organised using Twitter and Facebook – and approximately five hardcopy books borrowed from the library, I made use solely of online book and journal depositories e.g. www.library.nu, which has since been shut down for copyright infringement. I used free-to-use open source software as well as using several software programmes that would have cost money to purchase if they had not been 'cracked' versions. 'Cracking' software is a process of creating false verification on the computer, very often by using a stand alone code generator that has been developed and supplied by people who take a political-philosophical stance in favour of the free sharing of computer code, and the free movement and sharing of information. It is relatively easy to find cracked versions of most software applications on the Internet, complete with instructions on how to install

B. L. Hall, D. E. Clover, J. Crowther and E. Scandrett (Eds.), Learning and Education for a Better World: The Role of Social Movements, 169–182.

and use them. These are great tools and resources for activist enquiry and knowledge generation. The low monetary cost (zero) and ease of availability means that some barriers of both individual and collective learning, enquiry and practice are removed.

As part of the process of research and reflection I created four 'how-to' video guides for using social media as radical media tools. They were created to help those who may not be familiar with using social media platforms as radical media tools, to understand how these specific platforms work. The aim is not just to provide useful practical skills, but also to encourage a critical thinking about we how best these tools. These can be found at http://vimeo.com/user1523091.

HISTORY FROM BELOW

Much of the discourse about the Egyptian revolution in early 2011 removed agency as the central foundation of challenging power in struggles for emancipation, and misplace social media in an ahistorical context. It also does a tremendous disservice, both to the commitments, sacrifices and successes of human endeavour of Egyptian activists, but also to the telling of a history that ignores the specific context within which this revolution occurred. Egyptians themselves are using social media tools and the Internet to document the recent revolution.

This can be seen in many online projects such as www.TahrirDocuments.org, dedicated to scanning, and translating from Arabic to English, real world publications, pamphlets, flyers and leaflets produced by activists groups and organisations. This is a project telling history from below, of making visible to the world via its website the demands, critiques and on-going debates as told from the perspective of the revolutionary youth, workers' movement, pro-democracy organisations, Islamic groups, and unaligned individuals. For activists and critically minded researchers there is a treasure trove of information, experiences and stories that will form the basis of further research, which can facilitate a much more nuanced understanding of history from below as opposed to the normative history of winners so prominent in formal education setting. Other similar sites such as http://www.18daysinegypt.com/ and www.18youm.org both focus on creating participatory online libraries of people's own videos, images, writings, opinion and so forth over the 18 days from the uprising on 25th of January, to 11th February. A central premise to these projects is the democratic and participatory process of telling of people own experiences.

SOCIAL MEDIA CONNECTING PRO-DEMOCRACY
AND WORKERS' MOVEMENTS

Pro-democracy activists in Egypt did not have the option of engaging with mainstream state controlled media. Under Article 3 of the Emergency Law, the state could also confiscate and shut down any political publications. The activists that were to become the organisers of the April 6th Movement had been active in the pro-democracy Kifeya movement and they had built links with worker movements from 2004. Workers' struggles in Egypt had been on the increase from the mid 1990s as a result of impacts of neo-liberal policies of privatisation, direct foreign investment etc. Unemployment rates rose to 12 per cent in 2003 according to official figures but many commentators suggest it could have been double that in 2010. There had been a significant rise in worker militancy with over 1.7 million workers engaging in some kind of work place action in the years 2004 to 2008. (Benin, 2010)

It was from a call to support a day of workers' action in Mahalla that the April 6th Movement found its wings. Asking Waleed Rashed, an organiser in the April 6th Movement about their beginnings said:

> We were thinking many times can we make the revolution in Egypt. We don't know exactly how. After we know how to make it, we were thinking it is civil disobedience. But it will take many steps; it will not be in one day, two days or one year. It will take long time. But the point of the April 6th exactly is that we got an invitation and we become as a movement after 6 April 2008. Not before 6th of April 2008. Before the 6th of April it was a normal day. We got an invitation from the Mahalla Coop. [...] there is a lot of workers are working there. They are telling us they are going to make a strike in our city in 6th of April. So we attend, so we ahh, we create an event in Facebook. It was our page and in a few hours only we got a lot of members [...] We start this event in Facebook as any normal event, we did not know that this event would be a big event in the whole all of the country or like that. But we say to people why will the strike only to be in Mahalla coop lets make it as a general strike in whole Egypt. After 6th of April by the end of the day and April 7th the day really is a success and we come to learn and know many things from that day. We told the guys on Facebook in the event page about why we must close the regime, shut down the regime. We say let's go for another meeting and from this meeting we will go for movement.

That a general strike could be organised via a call on Facebook only makes sense in the context of tightly controlled media. This link with workers was significant and was mutually beneficial to both. For the most part the April 6th was made up of mainly educated youth under thirty who kept close connections with the workers' movements across Egypt. But Waleed argued. "If each group of workers has any problem in his company we must go to him. We must go to support him; we must open channels with him because someday of course you will come to ask him "please support me in the revolution." This connection between pro-democracy and workers' movements is important. It was quite probable that without these links, without a common narrative that sought to address both social injustices and economic inequalities, the regime may have been able to hold on.

SOCIAL MEDIA AS A TOOL FOR ACTIVIST JOURNALISM

Case Study 1 Blog Post "Breaking in #Alexandria: People Storm State Security HQ" http://bit.ly/ecjZfe

On the evening of Friday 4th of March 2011, I noticed some people I had been following on Twitter were discussing that that there was a demonstration in the city of Alexandria, outside the building that housed the State Security Headquarters. This tweet in particular caught my attention:

State Security in Alexandria is throwing Molotov cocktails & tear gas on protesters surrounding "Alfara'na" office #Jan25 #amndawla https://twitter .com/#!/NahlaMohamed/statuses/43751238331924481

The State Security had been regularly involved in intelligence gathering, illegal abduction and torture and acted with a vicious impunity – not just in squashing political dissent but also in the intimidation of many citizens. My own knowledge of the State Security was limited to reading about Khaled Said, a young computer programmer who had been working uncovering police corruption. Much like Mohammed Bouazizi who set himself on fire on Dec 17th 2010 in Tunisia, Khaled Said's death at the hands of the State Security became a touch stone which resonated deeply with people living under the regime, and embodied a specific example of state impunity and injustice.

On the 6th June 2010, State Security officers arrived at an Internet café in Alexandria and arrested him. Friends and the family of Khaled say he had video evidence that State Security forces and police where involved in drug dealing and that the suppression of this evidence was the real motivation of his arrest and subsequent beatings and death. The State Security, alleging he was carrying illegal drugs and was very badly beaten up on the street in full view, picked up Khaled. His death at the hands of the police would have just been another in a long list had it not been for the fact that Khaled's brother Ahmed secretly took photographs with his mobile phone and uploaded them to the Internet. The effect was significant. The graphic image of his brutalised face as he lay in a city morgue became a visual meme that represented and resonated with the experience of millions of Egyptians, a rallying point against the State Security forces in particular and the regime in general. Wael Ghomin soon posted these images of Khalid's broken body, alongside photos of Khaled as a healthy young man online on the "We Are All Khaled Said" Facebook page. Alongside the April 6th movement and youth wings of the Muslim Brotherhood, people working together under the "We Are All Khaled Said" banner played a significant role in organising the mass mobilisations and occupation of Tahrir Square that fermented the fall of Mubarak. It was on this Facebook page that the initial call for a "Day of Rage" on the 25th of January 2011 in Cairo was called. The Facebook page also was a significant source of updates and commentary from the perspective of those occupying Tahrir Square during its initial stage in January 2011.

It was in this context that I sensed that a late evening gathering outside the State Security was likely to be both contentious and dangerous. Some people were using Twitter to make brief reports from the ground, others making suggestions about what actions should or should not be done if the building was breached. Using Tweetdeck, I was able to follow hashtags #Alexandria, #Alex and #amndawla and identify specific people tweeting in real time. By observing what tweets were being re-tweeted it was relatively easy to see who was actually there so I began to follow these people including someone using the name @Abalkhair. Through a conscious process of filtering, searching and observing – with the specific aim of finding people who were on the ground – I could get to see information and individual narratives being shared. What was not clear at the time was a larger context. Ahmad Shafiq, the prime minister installed by Mubarak had just resigned and according to Ahdaf Soueif "minutes after the new prime minister had spoken in Tahrir, people noticed plain-clothes men carrying garbage bags out of state security headquarters in Alexandria. They intercepted the men and found the bags contained shredded documents. The people formed a cordon and insisted nothing leave the building."

As people where posting up photos, descriptions and video, it became clear that this was a concerted effort to overrun the police force protecting the building and to gain access to it. Having made a choice to search out people on Twitter taking part in the demonstration it made sense to me at the time that rather than simply satisfying a personal curiosity about what was unfolding – in essence being a passive, if interested voyeur – I could use the position I'd put myself in to collate the fragments into a news report. My decision to create a news blog post came after I sensed that it could be a useful thing to do with the information I had available. I posted this tweet:

"@Abalkhair I'm happy to collect and collate footage, tweets and photos and post via twitter, FB blogs etc" http://twitter.com/soundmigration/statuses/ 43761719901814784

@Abalkhair, who was posting photographs from the ground re-tweeted this tweet to his followers. I downloaded all of the photographs I could come across that had been posted online with the hashtags mentioned above, and collated the descriptive tweets to write up what I felt was as accurate and honest a picture from the information available to me. I embedded a video that had been uploaded from the demonstration as well as the written piece and posted the blog. This took less than about 30 minutes. I linked the URL posted on to several Facebook page groups. I shared the blog report directly with many of the Egyptian activists based in Cairo, as well as other mainstream journalists and activists who has been actively tweeting from around the globe on the uprising:

Ive posted report from tonights situation from Twitter info in #Alexandria #Jan25

#Egypt #alex here http://bit.ly/fN87K

Breaking report of events #alex @marklittlenews @MaryFitzgerldIT @Liberationtech

@jilliancyork @3arabawy @mfatta7 http://bit.ly/fN87Ki

Report from #alexandria tonight at SS HQ #egypt http://bit.ly/fN87Ki @Gsquare86

@guardiannews @anonops @paulmasonnews @kyrah @Sandmonkey

I also posted the report onto several Facebook pages such as the April 6th Facebook page and the 'We' are all Khaled Said page. It was quickly picked up Global Voices, 'an online global network of bloggers and citizen media' and other human rights websites.
http://globalvoicesonline.org/2011/03/05/egypt-protests-and-clashes-at-state-security-building-in-alexandria/

USING SOCIAL MEDIA AS A PUBLIC SPACE FOR CONVERSATION

Case Study 2: Inside Egypt: An Interview with Mohamed Abdelfattah, Alexandria.

My main aim in interviewing Mohamed Abdelfattah was to make a mini audio-documentary that enabled people in my online and real world social network hear about the recent experiences of the Egyptian revolution from the perspective of someone who was involved. He was one of the first people I came across tweeting from within Egypt, when I began to follow the Twitter conversation on the #Jan25 hashtag. Mohamed is a journalist, blogger and, at the time, a student from Alexandria who participated and reported during the uprising. At the time of interviewing Mohamed, I was unaware that he was one of the first journalists to cover the story of Khaled Said's murder by State Security police force in Alexandria in 2010. (On September 21st 2011, Mohamed was awarded the 2011 International Press Freedom Awards from Canadian Journalists for Free Expression (CJFE) for his role in covering the murder of Khaled.) Here I will focus on our discussion about social media.

Social Media as a Spark

We have to understand that the spark of this revolution was organised on Facebook. When the Egyptian youth watched videos of what happened in Tunisia, and the fact that toppling an Arab dictator is possible; Tunisia sent a lot of energy into our blood. And then very famous Facebook page for a young man who was killed by the police called Khaled Said – this fan page is called We Are All Khaled Said. By January 25th, this Facebook page had almost 400,000 members. It had called before for demonstrations against police brutality and other abuses. Immediately after what happened in Tunisia this page started campaigning very heavily for a similar revolution in Egypt. And this is actually what happened on January 25th, against the expectations of many people.

We used to mock actually this event and say how can everything start from Facebook. It's going to be the usual couple of hundred people showing up at the demonstration. The majority of the Egyptian people are not on Facebook and they are not aware of what is going on. (Abdelfattah)

With regards to what role Mohamed felt social media tools had during the 18 days from 25th of January to Mubarak's fall on the 11th of February he goes on to say:

> During the revolution you can say that Twitter and Facebook for the first days broke the information monopoly that the state media and other private media exercised. But we have to understand that for four days [from 27th of January] the Internet was totally cut off and on other days mobile phones where shut down. The organisation of the work has totally been offline on the ground. The people had already been on the streets and the absence of social media didn't hurt the movement. One thing to say also, when Mubarak delivered a divisive speech calling for the people to calm down because he will leave office in six months, that caused a division in the public opinion between the people in the streets – between those who want to leave Mubarak in office until he leaves at the end of his term and those who do not believe Mubarak and say he has to go now. When the Internet got back the people saw brutal videos of the police killing peaceful unarmed civilians in the demonstrations. So what was not seen on state television they saw after the Internet got back and the movements got momentum again more than ever. That is another way in which social media has helped break the information monopoly that the state media and other private media exercised.

What is Different About Social Media?

Given the significant rise in the use of social networking and social media sites, it is useful to examine what the implications such changes may have for building social movements that can reshape our societies. Understanding the relational changes between alternative/radical media and mainstream media entities can assist social movements in developing more coherent and effective strategies in struggles for social justice, equality and direct democracy. To do this we must ask how our current models of thinking about strategies of communicating fit with the actuality of the contemporary existing media landscape.

What I am *not* trying to do is theoretically dissolve away the tensions between mainstream media and radical/alternative media. There will always be contradictions between the aims of media corporations, including those that use social media platforms, and the aims of anti-capitalist movements for social justice. There is a conflict inherent in the relationship and it would be a weakness in critical thinking to seek to dissolve that. This is ultimately a discussion about power, best understood via Gramsci's notion of hegemony and counter-hegemony.

Firstly, however, what I *am* suggesting is that there are:

a) Specific vulnerabilities within the particular business model of corporate media, namely getting people to pay for a product that tends now to be available for free, that for many corporations is an extended existential crisis. This is largely caused by the rise of social media networks of sharing on the Internet, viewed as "disruptive technologies" from the perspective of many media corporations. This itself is shaping mainstream media practice towards engaging non-professional (not paid) contributions through comment sections, discussions etc. Within a context of a global recession, which is seeing advertising revenues plummet, things are fairly gloomy for traditional media corporations. This is a situation that we should seek to exploit.

b) Specific characteristics and dynamics of social media tools and networks facilitate the free movement of counter-hegemonic ideas, meanings, education and practices at both a low cost and high speed. Again, to express this in its most simple form: large numbers of people now often have the ability to relate their own experiences and share those experiences, while learning about others, with a speed and scope not seen before. This is of course a generalisation that does not address issues of social media literacy, unequal access to tools etc. The point is to suggest the architectural framework is there for using such networks and tools to facilitate strong counter-hegemonic narratives that make sense of people's experiences in a time of genuine crisis.

GRAMSCI, POWER AND MEDIA

Radical media (Downing, 2001), also referred to as "alternative media" (Ardizzoni, Cox, et al., 2010), "social movement media" (Atton, 2003) or "citizen media" (Rodriguez, 2001) is about the creation of meaning from below that seeks to challenge power from above (Ardizzoni, Cox, et al., 2010). This relates to Gramsci's concept of counter-hegemony as central to understanding the function of corporate and state media entities. He argues that the subordination of the interests of most members of a society is central to how the interests of a dominant elite continue to be served.

Such structural inequality and injustice is not solely achieved and reproduced by controlling the means of material production. He argues that, at another level, the same elites also have the ability to project their ideas of how societies "should be" from their dominant perspective. In essence, control over the making of common sense is central to maintaining a discourse that says "this is just the way things are". This doesn't just relate to controlling media, but can be extended to other forms of institutions, where the reproduction of meaning is tailored to suit the demands and logic of capitalism and power. Examining this from a critical pedagogical perspective provides much of our understanding of popular education (Freire, 1970; Illich, 1971).

Egyptian activists clear understanding of hegemony played a role in strategising for mobilisations that would lead to toppling the regime. This is rooted in what Gramsci suggests is a relationship between the existing and the desired, between the experiences of oppression and the imagination of other possibilities that acts as the driver of human agency. "If the ruling class has lost its consensus, i.e., is no longer 'leading' but only 'dominant', exercising coercive force alone, this means precisely that the great masses have become detached from their traditional ideologies" (Gramsci 1971, p. 276).

NARRATIVE-MAKING IN THE EGYPTIAN REVOLUTIONARY MOVEMENTS

In a presentation to the Personal Democracy Forum 2011 in June this year, Alaa Abd el Fattah, a prominent activist blogger and participant in the revolution, spoke about narrative making in the Egyptian context in a short discussion about the role of technology in the revolution. He was quite clear that no one knows the full story of the revolution, as it is the work of over 30 years of resistance, most of it unstudied. However, in relation to Gramsci's notion of counter-hegemony, what he said is enlightening:

> The fact that it's a dictatorship doesn't mean that people are, you know, complacent and silent. There has been constant resistance and also constant politics... people are highly opinionated, very ideological, we talk politics all the time... we've managed to win space for speech but it was always contested. It didn't hit the media until the nineties, but there was always spaces where you could do political speech... Factories and universities ... have always been the most important places where politics happened. There wasn't party politics, well there was, but that is not where the real politics was happening. There was politics, in every single institution where people have some sense of agency or some sense of ownership. [...] what technology did, it offered a perfect medium to try and build a single narrative of a revolution. [...] What the Internet offered was that you start a small group somewhere, but you can make noise that is louder than the size of your group online and then connect with others. And also you are no longer dependant on saturating any institution because there's a lot of individuals who do not belong to a union, do not work in a public sector workplace and are no longer in university or have never been to university. But they can access you online or they can access your speech that is online through their own physical social networks, so even if you are 'uneducated' or don't have access to the Internet it might filter through because you have heard people talking about it.(Alaa Abd El Fattah, June 2011) http://www.youtube.com/watch?v= BfVVk2_T9AY

For the Egyptian revolutionaries, engaging with the mainstream/state media simply wasn't an option. Neither was it to be desired; a large part of the population clearly distrusted mainstream media. The youth movements that co-ordinated the original occupation of Tahrir Square, were working within a public sphere where that dissonance between official voices, and people's lived experiences was collectively felt and understood.

THE INTERNET AS A SITE OF STRUGGLE

So far I've made a case that the Internet is a public space, and that social media tools, and cultures of sharing and participation has played some role is organising strategies of social movements, including the pro-democracy movements in Egypt. I've also shown how these same tools can be used for research and radical media production via case studies of my own practice. However, it would be remiss to ignore other co-existing realities. The Internet itself is a site and medium of multiple struggles, involving many actors; national states, formal oppositions, dissidents, corporations and hacker collectives. These struggles for the most part remain hidden and irrelevant to most people's lives.

Murbarak, the Internet and the Hidden Picture

The decision by Mubarak's regime to cut off the Internet on the night of the 27th of January 2011 is recognised as a significant moment, though the nature of the significance is contested. Mohamed Abdelfattah (quoted above) stated that the cutting off of the Internet had a minimal impact, since most of the organising was happening in the streets. Mohamed interestingly suggested that, from the perspective of the revolutionary movements the impact of the net returning four day later was much more significant.

From another perspective, what is important is less the impact on the revolutionary momentum of the Internet being cut off but the fact that the regime thought that cutting off the Internet would be in its benefit. A graph visually representing the response to this decision to cut off the Internet shot around the Internet and was shared by thousands of people.

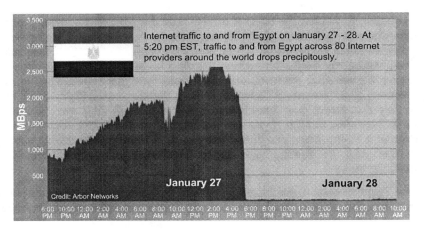

This image is significant both in what it conveys and also in what it unintentionally disguises. It portrays drama, power and panic. The area of blue with an almost vertical drop to zero is visually compelling and contributed to a narrative increasing the significance of the Internet within Egypt at that specific time, from an international perspective looking in. It contributed to the depiction of a dictator hitting a kill switch or sabotaging network hubs in a panic to hold onto power. In one sense the *idea* captured in that picture – a falling dictatorship grasping at straws to retain power and authority – imbues 'the Internet' and social media networks used by the revolutionary youth with a significance it didn't actually have at that time.

Those with access to tools to measure such events e.g. Internet analysts such as the organisation Renesys, understood that was not an automated shut down, or a physical rupture of connections where everything was shut off at once. This point is illustrated by the image below, which displays different information on the same event revealing a very different perspective. All Internet providers switched off connections within several minutes of each other, with the exception of one provider, which ensured the Egyptian Stock Exchange stayed live until the 31st of January. Renesys suggested at the time that it was a coordinated decision between the state and the companies providing Internet connections. The state just phoned each of the providers up one after the other and told then to shut up shop. Recent evidence confirms this initial impression was indeed correct. On the 21st October 2011, the Guardian website published a video by writer and documentary maker Jon Robson. He speaks to activists who stormed State Security Headquarters in Cairo. They found amongst many rooms full of shredded documents, evidence that State Security leaders had met with mobile phone and Internet providers to arrange a protocol for shutting down all internal telecommunication capabilities in the event of a popular uprising or revolution. When Ronson met with Khaled Hegazy, currently Director of External Affair for Vodafone Egypt, he confirmed that such a meeting had happened and that arrangements had been made between all the telecommunications companies and the State Security that in the case of a popular uprising that the Internet would be shut down, on the command of the regime. So instead of a panicking dictatorship, we have the more complex reality of a panicking dictatorship working in tandem with large corporations to enact massive censorship across a whole nation. What is also of note is that developing a decisive 'kill switch' is very difficult, since a structural principle by which the Internet operates is the ability to bypass outages, missing or broken connections within a larger network.

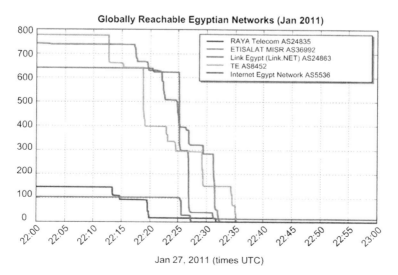

Jan 27, 2011 (times UTC)

Whilst the events discussed above highlight the role of multinational corporations in supporting, or at the very least cooperating with authoritarian regimes. One should be open to the possibility that Egyptian activists, whilst not made public, probably expected this plan. Certainly the level and scope of the international network of activists working to assist and provide technical routes around the state Internet blockage suggests some level of prior planning on their behalf. (It should also be acknowledged that people died as a result of the telecommunications blockade. Several people who were shot bled to dead as no ambulances could be contacted.) At the end of his piece for the *Guardian*, Ronson noted that other information retrieved from the State Security named an English corporation that provided software and hardware technology to the secret police to enable online surveillance of Egyptian population, particularly pro-democracy and revolutionary youth movements.

THE INTERNET AND TECHNOLOGY CORPORATIONS

Evgeny Morozov (2011) has explored this "dark side" of the Internet as it pertains to both to authoritarian regimes and in critiquing broader cyber-utopianism as presented by the main protagonist Clay Shirky and others. The labelling of cyber-utopianists and cyber-pessimists can be a rather clumsy representation that frames a straw-man 'debate' between supposedly coherent and distinct schools of thought. Shirky argues that the Internet and social media are inherently tools for democracy and progress. Such views often originate from people living in neoliberal democracies. A reflective appraisal would be that those who proffer a more optimist vision of social media and cultures of participation also have a lot to say on the use of communication networks as tools for education and citizen journalism. There is, however, a significant absence of critical thinking in Shirky's writing on capitalism and power and how both relate to democracy. Existing forms of 'democracy' under neoliberalism appear to be the suggested resolution to authoritarianism. This is not a particularly high ambition given the systemic nature of inequality and the increasingly repressive nature of state responses to dissent across neoliberal democracies. Exploring emancipatory potentials in technology is incredibly useful work that should be part of activist practise.

Jillian C York, Director of International Freedom of Expression at the EFF, working in the areas of 'free expression, politics, and the Internet, with particular focus on the Arab world, (York 2011) consistently puts human agency at the centre of her description of the dynamics between the Internet and political outcomes. She argues that only by contextualising social media and the Internet used as part of an activist tool kit can we best understand the role of technology is social change. When writing about the Tunisian revolution which preceded and helped precipitate the Egyptian revolution she says "to call this a 'Twitter revolution' or even a 'WikiLeaks revolution' demonstrates that we haven't learned anything from past experiences in Moldova and Iran. Evgeny Morozov's question –'Would this revolution have happened if there were no Facebook and Twitter?'– says it all.

And in this case, yes, I – like most Tunisians to whom I've posed this question – believe that this would have happened without the Internet". (York, 2011 blog)

AUTHORITARIAN REGIMES AND THE INTERNET

Amidst the uprising across North Africa and the Middle East, we are also witnessing an explicitly new online phenomenon – the online army. This is a clear example of social media and Internet not just as tools for struggle, but also a site of public struggle. A recent report by the Information Warfare Monitor focuses on the emergence in Syria of the Syrian Electronic Army (SEA) in May 2011. It states "The Syrian Electronic Army claims on its website that it was founded by a team of young Syrian enthusiasts who did not want to stay passive "towards the fabrication of facts on the events in Syria." Information Warfare Monitor (IWM) research found that the group has a connection with the Syrian Computer Society, which was headed in the 1990s by the current Syrian President Bashar al-Assad before he became president."

The SEA mainly attacks pro-democracy sites within Syria and as well as western sites, though these seem to be sites that are easy to attack and not very high profile such as the Leamington Spa town council website in the UK. Currently it has a private group on Facebook and also posts videos on YouTube of some of its defacements. The report also notes the fact that the Syrian regime lifted a block on Facebook and YouTube in February 2011, which facilitates the SEA's publicity (IWM website). As the above illustrates any attempts to theorise the Internet and its inherent usefulness to social justice movements, or society generally, will be rendered meaningless if they fail to take account the ways it can be used to oppress.

CONCLUSIONS

One of my central aims when I began to formulate a structure from research that, for the most part was very open ended, was to dispel the suggestion that certain technologies were the cause of the revolution by presenting evidence to the contrary. The primary reasons for the revolution lay in a combination of the collective agency of pro-democracy movements in the face of both increasing repression and rising inequality. Certain technologies, however, were important because of the function they served in facilitating mobilisation efforts, and making visible counter narratives that formed the backbone of the strategy of the youth movements.

There was also conscious movement building efforts by April 6th Movement to create strategic links with workers movements, so that when the time came to call on workers to support the call for solidarity, they would be confident of the call being answered in the positive. Nothing was inevitable about the outcomes however.

This is a field worthy of much more research by activists. We are living in times where our own position in rejecting the 'end of history' thesis is more popular than ever. Economic, ecological and political crises are converging with a crisis of capitalism and the emerging responses to the material effects of this on our lives. The battle of ideas is out in the open. Our ability to share and make visible our own counter narratives to the logic of austerity, and our ability collectively to resist the erosion of gains made by those before us can be greatly assisted by exploring how we can think about and utilise communication tools within emerging networked public spheres.

REFERENCES

Abaza, Academic tourists sight-seeing the Arab Spring – Opinion – Ahram Online. [ONLINE] Available at: http://english.ahram.org.eg/News/22373.aspx. [Accessed 28 October 2011].

Beinin (2010). Justice for all: The struggle for worker rights in Egypt. Solidarity Center

Chomsky, N. (2002). Media Control, The Spectacular Achievements of Propaganda. Seven Stories Press ISBN 1-58322-536-6.

Chomsky, N. (2003). Understanding power – the indispensable Chomsky. Vintage.

Cox, L., Mattoni, A., Berdnikovs, A., & Ardizzoni, M. (2010). "Voices of Dissent: Activists' Engagements in the Creation of Alternative, Autonomous, Radical and Independent Media". *Interface: a journal for and about social movements, 2*(2), 1–22.

Freire, (1971). Pedagogy of the Oppressed. Penguin.

Graeber, D. (2004). Fragments of an anarchist anthropology. Prickly Paradigm Press.

Habermas, J. (1984). Theory of Communicative Action, trans. Thomas McCarthy, Boston: Beacon Press.

Illich, I. D. (1971). Celebration of awareness – a call for institutional revolution. Penguin.

Illich, I. D. (1971). Deschooling society. Pelican.

Lievrouw, L. A. (2011). Alternative and activist new media – digital media and society series. Polity.

Evgeny Morozov, (2011). *The Net Delusion: The Dark Side of Internet Freedom.* Edition. PublicAffairs.

Shirky C, (2009). *Here Comes Everybody: The Power of Organizing Without Organizations.* Reprint Edition. Penguin (Non-Classics).

Soueif, A. (2011). 'In Egypt it was silence or shouting. Now it's a great conversation. The Guardian Tuesday 8th March 2011 http://www.guardian.co.uk/world/2011/mar/08/egypt-silence-shouting-great-conversation [Accessed 2/3/12].

AUTHORS BIOGRAPHY

Stephen Brookfield is currently Distinguished University Professor at the University of St. Thomas, Minneapolis-St. Paul. He has taught for over 40 years in adult and higher education in Britain, Canada and the United States. Stephen is interested in how to learn about, and help others fight against, ideological manipulation. His work within and outside the academy focuses on teaching critical thinking, democratising the classroom, and understanding the responsible use of teacher power. Currently he is working on a book entitled *Powerful Techniques for Teaching Adults*. His 2010 book with John Holst entitled *Radicalizing Learning: Adult Education for a Just World,* has been used by study groups in the Occupy Wall Street movement. Stephen facilitates workshops worldwide and gives his exercises and techniques away for free at www.stephenbrookfield.com.

Aziz Choudry is assistant professor in the Department of Integrated Studies in Education, at McGill University, Montreal. He is co-author of *Fight Back: Workplace Justice for Immigrants* (Toronto: Fernwood, 2009) and co-editor of *Learning from the Ground Up: Global Perspectives on Social Movements and Knowledge Production* (Palgrave MacMillan, 2010) and *Organize! Building from the Local for Global Justice* (PM Press/Between The Lines, Toronto, 2012). With over two decades experience as a social and political activist, educator and researcher, Aziz serves on the boards of the Immigrant Workers Centre, Montreal, and the Global Justice Ecology Project. He is also a co-initiator and part of the editorial team of www.bilaterals.org, a website supporting analysis of, and resistance against, bilateral free trade and investment agreements.

Darlene E. Clover is Professor of Leadership Studies, Faculty of Education, University of Victoria, Canada. Her areas of research and teaching include community and cultural leadership, feminist and arts-based adult education and research. Her current study focuses adult education in libraries, art galleries and museums in Canada and the United Kingdom. Darlene has guest-edited five special editions of academic journals on the arts, creativity and/or arts and cultural organisations and published an edited volume in 2007 entitled *The arts and social justice: Re-crafting adult education and community cultural leadership* (Leicester: NAICE). She is currently co-editing a book entitled *Lifelong learning, the arts and community cultural engagement in the contemporary university: International Perspectives* to be published in 2013 by Manchester University Press.

Jim Crowther is Senior Lecturer in Adult and Community Education, University of Edinburgh, Scotland. He has been actively involved in a wide range of social and community organisations for the past twenty-five years. He is a founder member and co-ordinator of the International Popular Education Network, which was started in 1997. His most recent (edited) books include *Popular Education: Engaging the Academy* (2005), *Lifelong Learning: Concepts and Contexts* (2007) and *More Powerful Literacies* (2012). Prior to his current academic post Jim was a tutor and organiser of adult literacy in Edinburgh. He researches and writes on adult literacy, popular education and the politics of policy. Since 2010 he has been the Editor of the international journal entitled *Studies in the Education of Adults*.

Catherine Etmanski is an Assistant Professor in the School of Leadership Studies at Royal Roads University (RRU). She has a passion for integrating the arts into her research and teaching. Her doctoral work employed participatory theatre as a research method with international students. Catherine's primary areas of teaching have included arts-based and environmental leadership, and action-oriented, participatory approaches to research. She was awarded for excellence in her pedagogical approach, which incorporates a range of creative elements and experiential learning strategies. Catherine is currently co-editing a book titled *Learning and teaching community based research: Linking pedagogy to practice* to be published by the University of Toronto Press.

Budd Hall is currently the Co-Director of the UNESCO Chair in Community Based Research and Social Responsibility in Higher Education, based in the School of Public Administration, University of Victoria, British Columbia, Canada. He is formerly Director of the Office of Community Based Research and a former Dean of Education at the University of Victoria. He is best known for his early work in developing the theory and practice of participatory research, for international work in the field of adult education when he was Secretary General of the International Council for Adult Education (ICAE), for his research in community university research and engagement and for his passion for deepening our understanding of the role of learning in social movements. Budd is also a poet.

Anne Harley is a lecturer in the Centre for Adult Education at the University of KwaZulu-Natal in Pietermaritzburg, South Africa. Since joining the university in 1994, Anne has undertaken a number of research and/or materials development projects, most of these commissioned by civil society organisations. She was the Co-coordinator of *The Women's Handbook* project, which produced, printed and distributed thousands of copies to women in the Midlands region of the province in English and isiZulu. She teaches in the field of adult education and participatory development at both postgraduate and undergraduate level. Anne currently heads up the Paulo Freire project, based at the Centre and is interested in issues relating to development; gender the environment and the possibilities for change through genuinely grassroots social movements.

Liam Kane graduated as a linguist, trained as a teacher and lived, worked and travelled in Spain, France, Portugal and Latin America before returning home to live in Glasgow, in 1984. He worked for eight years as a development education worker with Oxfam, learning about 'popular education', from the work Oxfam supported in Latin America. Since 1992 he has been a lecturer in the Department of Adult and Continuing Education in the University of Glasgow, where he teaches modern languages and organises a large programme of language courses for the public. Liam researches on popular education and teaches and post graduate courses in education. He is author of *Popular Education and Social Change in Latin America* (Latin American Bureau) and is an elected *conselheiro* of the Brazilian NGO, Popular Education Forum, for the West of São Paulo Region.

Emilio Lucio-Villegas holds a Ph.D. in Pedagogy and is a Profesor Titular in adult education and participatory research at the University of Seville, Spain. He is author or co-author of more than 100 articles, chapters and books including: *Citizenship as Politics* (Sense Publisher); and *Between Global and Local: Adult Learning and Development* (Peter Lang). Emilio was Head of the *Instituto de Ciencias de la Educación,* from 1992 to 1995 and is currently Head of the *Paulo Freire Chair at the University of Seville,* tasked with implementing relationships between the University and communities. Emilio is a member of the Steering Committee of the European Society for Research on the Education of the Adults (ESREA) and Convened their Network entitled: 'Between Global and Local: Adult Learning for Development'.

Mark Malone is an anarchist and activist based in Dublin, Ireland. He is a founding member of the Seomra Spraoi autonomous social centre project and along side other activists, has helped develop media training workshops for progressive campaigns and projects in Ireland. Mark has also co-produced as part of Radio Solidarity audio documentaries that look at areas of struggle ignored by mainstream media. In early 2011 he undertook a series of interviews with Egyptian activists about their ongoing experiences within the revolution. Mark is particularly interested in how we can use social media technologies and tools as means to assist disruption of hegemonic narratives and develop counter narratives that contextualise our lived experiences under capitalism and patriarchy. His Twitter handle is @soundmigration.

Marjorie Mayo has worked in adult and community education and development, including working with trade unions and communities at Ruskin College Oxford. She has been based at Goldsmiths, University of London where her research has included a focus upon learning for active citizenship, and access to justice in disadvantaged communities.

Her publications include: *Imagining Tomorrow: Adult Education for Transformation*(1997), *Cultures, Communities, Identities: Cultural Strategies for Participation and Empowerment*, (2000), *Global Citizens*, (2005), with Paul Hoggett and Chris Miller, *The Dilemmas of Development Work*, (2008) and with John Annette *Taking Part?: Active Learning for Active Citizenship and beyond,* (2010)

Eurig Scandrett is lecturer in Sociology at Queen Margaret University and programme leader for courses in environmental justice, gender and social justice. After an initial career in scientific research he spent 15 years in adult education, community development and campaigning on environmental, peace and gender issues, including as Head of Community Action at Friends of the Earth Scotland. His academic interests focus on learning and education in support of social movements and community campaigns. He is coordinator of the Bhopal Survivors'

Movement Study and edited *Bhopal Survivors Speak: emergent voices from a People's Movement* (2009), Word Power Books). He is a trustee of Zero Tolerance Trust and the Bhopal Medical Appeal, a Fellow of the Centre for Human Ecology and a member of the Iona Community.

Elisabeth Steinklammer is a Ph.D. candidate in the Political Science Department, University of Vienna. She currently works as a teacher for the political education department of the Austrian White Collar Workers Union as well as other trade union institutes. Elisabeth also worked for several years for different adult education organisations and since 2008, has been actively involved in research projects on work councils, trade unions and political education. She is the author of *Work Council Realities – The Assertiveness of Work Councils and Trade Unions at Company Level in the Context of Globalization* (ÖGB Verlag 2010). She has written several other articles – based on the theories of Antonio Gramsci, Paulo Freire and Klaus Holzkamp – on workers organising and questions of power relations in adult labour education.

Astrid von Kotze has a background in theatre work and creative writing. Until recently she was Professor of Adult Education and Community Development at the University of KwaZulu-Natal, Durban, South Africa. Her research interests include popular education, livelihood studies, community-based risk reduction, women's health and performance arts. She has done extensive work developing participatory teaching/learning materials with a social-justice purpose. Astrid is now a community education and development practitioner associated with The Division of Lifelong Learning at the University of the Western Cape where she oversees a Popular Education Programme in poor communities in / around Cape Town. Past publications focussed on theatre-based popular and the transformative potential of project-based learning in university adult education.

INDEX

CPSIA information can be obtained at www.ICGtesting.com
Printed in the USA
BVOW02s1912091114

374375BV00001B/7/P